Life Writing and Victorian Culture

Life Writing and Victorian Culture

Edited by
DAVID AMIGONI
Keele University, UK

ASHGATE

Published by
Ashgate Publishing Limited
Gower House
Croft Road
Aldershot
Hants GU11 3HR
England

Ashgate Publishing Company
Suite 420
101 Cherry Street
Burlington, VT 05401-4405
USA

Ashgate website: http://www.ashgate.com

British Library Cataloguing in Publication Data

Life writing and Victorian culture.—(The nineteenth
   century series)
   1. English prose literature – 19th century – History and
   criticism 2. Biography as a literary form 3. Autobiography
   4. Great Britain – History – Victoria, 1837-1901 – Biography
   – History and criticism 5. Great Britain–Intellectual life
   – 19th century
   I. Amigoni, David
   828.8'0809492

Library of Congress Cataloging-in-Publication Data
Life writing and Victorian culture / edited by David Amigoni.
      p. cm. – (The nineteenth century series)
      ISBN 0-7546-3531-7 (alk. paper)
   1. English prose literature – 19th century – History and criticism. 2.
Great Britain – History – Victoria, 1837-1901 – Biography – History and
criticism. 3. Great Britain – Intellectual life – 19th century. 4.
Biography as a literary form. 5. Autobiography. I. Amigoni, David. II.
Series: Nineteenth century (Aldershot, England).

   PR788.B56L54 2005
   828'.80809492—dc22

   ISBN-10: 0 7546 3531 7

2005005544

Typeset by Express Typesetters
Printed and bound in Great Britain by TJ International Ltd, Padstow, Cornwall

Contents

List of Figures

List of Contributors

David Amigoni is Professor of Victorian Literature at Keele University; he is the author of *Victorian Biography: Intellectuals and the Ordering of Discourse* (1993) and numerous essays on Victorian life writing. He is editor of the *Journal of Victorian Culture*.

Alison Booth is Professor of English at the University of Virginia. She is author of *How to Make It as a Woman: Collective Biographical History from Victoria to the Present* (2004), and *Greatness Engendered: George Eliot and Virginia Woolf* (1992), and editor of *Famous Last Words: Changes in Gender and Narrative Closure* (1993) as well as co-editor of the *Norton Introduction to Literature* (9th ed. 2005). Her articles have appeared in *Victorian Studies, Narrative, Kenyon Review, American Literary History*, and elsewhere. Her interest in prosopography contributes to her current project on collected memoirs of pilgrimages to authors' houses.

Laurel Brake is Professor of Literature and Print Culture at Birkbeck, University of London. She has published widely on aspects of nineteenth-century literature and culture, the press, and gender. Her books include *Subjugated Knowledges* (1994), *Walter Pater* (1994), and *Print in Transition* (2001). She has co-edited various collections including *Encounters in the Victorian Press*, co-edited with Julie Codell (2004), *Walter Pater: Transparencies of Desire* with Lesley Higgins and Carolyn Williams (2002), and *Nineteenth-Century Media and the Construction of Identities* (2000) with David Finkelstein and Bill Bell. Laurel Brake is Director of the ncse project, an AHRC digital edition of six nineteenth-century journals, and co-editor of a Dictionary of Nineteenth-Century Journalism. She is also writing a biography of Walter Pater.

Trev Lynn Broughton is senior lecturer in English and Women's Studies at the University of York. She is currently editing an anthology of essays on Victorian Fatherhood with Helen Rogers for Palgrave, as well as a four volume collection of major works on Auto/Biography for Routledge.

Julie F. Codell, Professor Art History and English at Arizona State University and Affiliate in Asian Studies, is the author of *The Victorian*

Artist (2003). She has also edited *Film and Identities: Genre, Gender, Race, and World Cinema* (2006) and *Imperial Co-Histories* (Fairleigh Dickinson, 2003); and co-edited (with Laurel Brake) *Encounters in the Victorian Press* (2004) and *Orientalism Transposed* (1998), currently being translated into Japanese (forthcoming). Julie is currently preparing a book on British coronations in Delhi, 1877–1911, a project for which she received fellowships from the American Institute of Indian Studies, National Endowment for the Humanities, and Huntington Library.

Matt Cook is Lecturer in History at Birkbeck College, University of London. He is author of *London and the Culture of Homosexuality, c.1885–1914* (2003) and is currently working on gay diary writing in the twentieth century.

Martin A. Danahay is Professor of English at Brock University, Canada. His publications include *Gender at Work in Victorian Culture* (2005), editions of H. G. Wells' *The War of the Worlds* and Robert Louis Stevenson's *The Strange Case of Dr. Jekyll and Mr. Hyde*, and *A Community of One: Masculine Autobiography and Autonomy in Nineteenth Century Britain* (1993). He has also published numerous scholarly articles on Victorian culture, the theory and practice of autobiography, as well as popular pieces on the *Matrix* films.

Martin Hewitt is Professor of Victorian Studies at Trinity and All Saints, Leeds, Associate Editor of the *Journal of Victorian Culture*, and Hon. Sec of the British Association for Victorian Studies. He has published broadly on the cultural history of the nineteenth century and is currently exploring the period identity of the reign of Victoria.

Donna Loftus is Lecturer in History at the Open University. She worked with Robbie Gray on his project on the autobiography of Victorian middle-class men. She has recently published 'Capital and Community: Limited Liability and attempts to Democratize the Market in Mid-Nineteenth Century England' in *Victorian Studies* (2002). She is currently involved in projects on cultural conceptions of the self, the market and society in nineteenth-century Britain.

Helen Rogers is a Senior Lecturer in Literature and Cultural History at Liverpool John Moores University. She is the author of *Women and the People: Authority, Authorship and the Radical Tradition in Nineteenth-Century England* (2000) and with Trev Broughton is co-editor of *Gender and Paternity in the Nineteenth Century* (forthcoming, 2007). She is pursuing her interest in life writing in a book project on 'Domesticity and the Working-Class Woman'.

Valerie Sanders is Professor of English at the University of Hull. Her most recent publications include *Eve's Renegades: Victorian Anti-Feminist Women Novelists* (1996), *The Brother-Sister Culture in Nineteenth-Century Literature* (2002), and the volume on Elizabeth Gaskell (2005) for Pickering and Chatto's 'Lives of Victorian Literary Figures' series. She is currently planning a monograph on versions of Victorian fatherhood.

The Nineteenth Century Series
General Editors' Preface

The aim of the series is to reflect, develop and extend the great burgeoning of interest in the nineteenth century that has been an inevitable feature of recent years, as that former epoch has come more sharply into focus as a locus for our understanding not only of the past but of the contours of our modernity. It centres primarily upon major authors and subjects within Romantic and Victorian literature. It also includes studies of other British writers and issues, where these are matters of current debate: for example, biography and autobiography, journalism, periodical literature, travel writing, book production, gender, non-canonical writing. We are dedicated principally to publishing original monographs and symposia; our policy is to embrace a broad scope in chronology, approach and range of concern, and both to recognize and cut innovatively across such parameters as those suggested by the designations 'Romantic' and 'Victorian'. We welcome new ideas and theories, while valuing traditional scholarship. It is hoped that the world which predates yet so forcibly predicts and engages our own will emerge in parts, in the wider sweep, and in the lively streams of disputation and change that are so manifest an aspect of its intellectual, artistic and social landscape.

Vincent Newey
Joanne Shattock
University of Leicester

Dedication and Acknowledgments

In July 2001, a number of contributors to this volume presented papers on Victorian life writing at the 'Locating the Victorians' international conference in London. They had been drawn together by Robbie Gray, who was working on a major project on autobiographical writing and the Victorian middle class. Sadly, Robbie Gray was not present to participate in the strand that he had put together; he had died on 19 March 2001. His unique blend of learned authority, intellectual generosity and modesty was much missed.

This volume draws together many more contributors to the field of Victorian life writing than were present at the conference, yet all the contributors to this volume work in ways that Robbie Gray would have recognised: pursuing the complex history of Victorian culture through the analysis of equally complex and diverse modes of life writing. For this reason we dedicate this book to the memory of Robbie Gray.

The editor would like to thank all the contributors for their work and unfailing cooperation, and in particular Matt Cook for helpful conversations and advice; Ann Donahue of Ashgate for her sound editorial advice and patience; Rachel Lynch, Vince Newey and Joanne Shattock for their interest in the project; and the anonymous reader who helped us to improve the book in so many ways.

Victorian Life Writing: Genres, Print, Constituencies

David Amigoni

Life Writing

Harold Nicolson, in *The Development of English Biography* (1928) argued that the 'development' of biography could only be discerned upon understanding 'the proper relation [of the genre] to such cognate modes of expression as journals, diaries, memoirs, imaginary portraits, or mere jottings of conversation'.[1] From Nicolson's perspective in deepest Bloomsbury, the point of acknowledging these 'cognate modes of expression' was a preliminary to sweeping the artistic floor clean. Having recognised the background noise, Nicolson used this to define his sense of 'pure' biography, a generic shape that needed to be rescued from the detritus of formless scribbling.

Later twentieth-century critics have been less inclined to accept claims about the generic purity of either biography or autobiography: as Richard D. Altick observed in 1965, biography in the nineteenth century was 'an unstable compound'.[2] More recently, Linda H. Peterson's study of traditions of women's autobiography in the nineteenth century acknowledges that 'women's auto/biography is often a hybrid genre', and her recognition of 'the diversity of [nineteenth-century life-course] forms' leads her to include the term 'life writing' in her subtitle.[3] *Life Writing and Victorian Culture* takes those insights into generic instability and hybridity as the basis for further exploring the 'diversity of forms' that is signified by the term 'life writing'. Thus, while the volume contains chapters on Victorian biography and autobiography, it also explores hitherto neglected forms: collections of life histories, or 'prosopographies', that include visual representations of and memorials to individuals, diaries, letters and obituaries. It includes, as Donna Loftus reminds us in her chapter on male middle-class autobiography, 'rituals of recognition' such as the after dinner speeches that were printed in memoirs of businessmen, the very form of self-narration into which Mr Deane in George Eliot's *Mill on the Floss* (1860) falls so readily as he rehearses for young Tom Tulliver 'a retrospect of his own career'; a Smilesean narrative of 'self-help' that he had clearly performed for dining audiences 'more than once before', so that he 'was not distinctly aware that he had not his port wine before him'.[4] Eliot's fiction aimed to disclose relationships between inner lives, domesticity and the public world, a model which this volume aims to follow in focusing on acts of life writing by diversely situated nineteenth-century individuals: from Oscar Wilde and Walter Pater to J.A. Symonds; from Mary Russell Mitford to Josephine Butler and Hypatia Bradlaugh; from Thomas Carlyle and Samuel Bamford to Gandhi; from Arthur Munby to A.C. Benson and George Ives.

'Life writing' focuses on practices of inscription, reading and interpretation that invite us to suspend and re-examine the historically received functions of, and hierarchical relations between, genres. Martin Danahay's chapter argues that all texts are spaces for forming identity, and texts such as diaries and letters explicitly articulate some of the more unsettled, displaced and repressed modes of identity that can be glimpsed in both the canonical texts of Victorian culture and its journalistic practices. In this respect, the volume interrogates a key element of Victorian gendered identity that has been the subject of much revisionist work in recent years: masculinity. Danahay's chapter on Thomas Carlyle and Arthur Munby examines letters and diaries as sites of identity formation; it argues that Carlyle's masochistic construction of the labouring subject was a painful way of maintaining masculine conscious-ness while repressing that latter's condition of material embodiment. Danahay indicates that masculinity was a more fraught and fragile mode of embodied identity than ways of writing about Victorian biography and autobiography before the 1990s have acknowledged. Accordingly, many of the chapters in this volume examine life writings that were produced by dutiful, hardworking and publicly aware subjects, but who were also desiring, sexual and emphatically embodied subjects.

Victorian identity is now regularly acknowledged to be a complex compound derived from multiple sources: sexuality and gender, class and status, colonial, ethnic and familial. The challenge for nineteenth-century life writing research is to use its rich textual resources to map the relations between these sources of identity, and this introduction offers a draft of such a map. It begins by using the diary to rethink relations between life writing genres and forms. It goes on to explore life writing in the context of technologies of print, publication, audiences and communities. It finally explores shortcomings in the idea of one-dimensional literary 'tradition' for writing about biography and autobiography in cultural history. It argues positively that Victorian life writing is best seen in terms of complex, overlapping contested constituencies such as class, gender, familial and domestic relations; these contest 'literature' as a source of identification. All three phases of the argument offer an introductory commentary on the chapters that follow, indicating the ways in which they contribute to this map, moving beyond established positions to encourage innovative ways of thinking about relations between life writing and the complex formation of Victorian culture.

Between Elizabeth Fry and the Romance of a Mince Pie: Mapping Genres and Cultural Identities

Kathryn Carter has shown how the mid nineteenth-century diary was a powerful focal point for mapping relations between genres as sites for self-constructions grounded in class and gender; if the diary constituted an important site for defending individual privacy, other genres – theatrical farce is the particular mode that Carter focuses on – could dramatise dangers posed by the unfettered individuality that the diary was in danger of permitting.[5] Martin Hewitt, Martin Danahay and Matt Cook all examine diaries in their chapters for this volume. Martin Hewitt makes the important point that diaries can be 'post-autobiographical': in other words, we ought not to see the diary as an unprocessed autobiography; instead, reversing the usual relations between diary and autobiography, Hewitt shows how the radical Samuel Bamford used a diary to shore up the autobiographical persona that he had constructed earlier in life. Viewed in this light, the diary can be seen as a means of mapping relations between different acts of life writing.

An example of this can be found in the diary of Joseph Romilly, by profession the Registrary for the University of Cambridge. Romilly's diary, which he maintained between 1829 and his death in 1864,[6] is perhaps best known as a major source for the writing of another, more famous life, that of the Cambridge geologist Adam Sedgwick, whom Romilly encountered most days, professionally and socially. But Romilly's diary was not simply a source for tracing the trajectory of Sedgwick's life course; neither was it a slight 'personal' document, undeserving of the status of a 'public' record of university life as Sedgwick's biographers claimed.[7] Romilly's diary may not have recorded the battles in the Senate, but it still establishes grounds for a 'thick descriptive' account of the public and private meanings attached to reading a life in Victorian culture.

On Thursday 17 February 1848, the same day that Romilly records taking a new Cambridge house to rent for him and his sister, Lucy, he also notes that he 'Read loud Mrs Fry' (RCD, p.6). Three days later, Romilly records concluding his reading of the life of Elizabeth Fry, the Quaker and philanthropic prison reformer:

> Sun. 20. ... Tonight I finished the life of Mrs Fry:- her afflictions
> from domestic losses come upon her most severely in her latter days.
> – I am impressed with the deepest admiration of her piety & her
> energy ... I did not know that she had visited Denmark, as well as
> Holland, Belgium, Prussia etc etc. & she had interviews with all the
> Sovereigns. (Romilly, p.6)

Romilly was reading *Memoirs of the Life of Mrs Fry, by two of her daughters*, published in 1847. This biography marked a double feminine entry into the public sphere: the philanthropic life of the mother being recorded by her daughters, a filial act of the kind that Helen Rogers's chapter for this volume traces in its analysis of biographies of political fathers written by their daughters.[8] Romilly's choice of a biographical subject is telling: his interest in the philanthropic prison activist is in keeping with his own broadly Whiggish politics and descent from a family of political and administrative public servants: he was the nephew of the legal reformer Sir Samuel Romilly (1757–1818). Yet what he invested in the identification with Elizabeth Fry is perhaps redolent of the complex play of forces that shaped what subsequent scholarship has come to construct as a typical 'Victorian' subjectivity. Thus the unmarried Romilly was affected by the 'afflictions from domestic losses' that Mrs Fry experienced, a resonant domestic identification perhaps for one who had recently lost his eldest sister and was moving to a new home with his surviving younger sister (Romilly, p.1).

As John Tosh has argued in his important revisionist work on the place of domesticity in the nineteenth-century social and cultural economy, this imaginative space constituted 'one of the most important expressions of the awareness of individual interiority which had developed since the Enlightenment'; it played an important role in shaping Victorian middle-class masculinity precisely because of the manner in which successful 'management' of this interiority could be demonstrably balanced against activity and purpose in the public world.[9] Romilly is thus 'impressed' by the 'piety & ... energy' to which Mrs Fry's life attests: piety and energy displayed in public works were the very engines of reformist power that demanded recognition and indeed emulation from the monarchies of Europe. For traditional aristocratic power structures were vulnerable: just four days later, Romilly would record the 'Great excitement at Paris' as King Louis Philippe was toppled (Romilly, p.6). It is significant that Romilly should 'read aloud' the life of Elizabeth Fry, presumably to his surviving sister Lucy. It identifies him as responsible centre of a household, called upon to perform vicariously the values of a public world through the life of a pious, energetic woman. Romilly's diary productively complicates the dominant literary ideal of autonomous masculinity summed up by Martin Danahay's influential description of the genre of autobiography as 'a community of one'.[10]

But this responsible masculine self-image, poised authoritatively between the public world and the domestic domain, could be fractured in the diary's mapping of distinctly modern social spaces, rhythms and pleasure-seeking experiences; as Martin Danahay's account of Arthur Munby's diary for this volume demonstrates, his journal was less a device for exploring his psyche, and more a means for recording its writer's wanderings in London in voyeuristic (and masochistic) pursuit of working women. Romilly's pursuits were tamer. Yet his diary for 1 February 1848 records his catching the 10.45 mail train from Cambridge to London, and it was precisely railway travel that offered Romilly different kinds of 'seductive' opportunities as a consumer and reader:

> I bought for my amusement 'the Bal Masqué' and 'the Romance of a Mince-pye'. – I lent this last (without looking at it, & seduced by its name) to a little girl of about 8 or 9 (– I think her Father, who was sitting by her, is one of Matthew and Gents establishment). In about an hour the missy complained of being sick, & upon my book being returned to me I found it not at all fitted for a child: much about poisoning, suicide and such horrors: – I must never lend a book again to a child without reading it ... (Romilly, p.3)

In some sense, Romilly here reflects on a masculine identity that is publicly found wanting. 'Seduced' into purchasing sensationalist print which he then lends to a child to amuse her on the journey, Romilly's superior class position is undermined by the outcome: *The Romance of a Mince-Pie*, by Angus B. Reach (a writer for *Punch*) is returned to him as unsuitable, presumably by the little girl's tradesman father ('Matthew and Gents' was a grocery and china shop in Cambridge, Romilly was travelling second class).[11] The diary entry closes with a terse disciplinary memo to the self: 'I must never lend a book again to a child without reading it ...' The point is that life writing in diary form records and negotiates between different kinds of reading experiences: the pious biography celebrating public works read in the home, the sensationalist narrative consumed on the train, it crucially illustrates the way in which the construction of identities, communities and constituencies through life writing and competing forms of inscription was both enabled and complicated by the development of print culture.

Print and the Fluid Boundaries of Life Writing

These identities, communities and constituencies emerged out of, to borrow Raymond Williams's term, a long revolution in communication extending from the mid-eighteenth century to the late nineteenth century, and embracing a great diversity of life-writing forms. At the beginning of the period for instance, the historian Michael Masuch has shown how John Wesley's serially published *Journal*, which appeared between 1740 and 1791, played an important part in establishing and sustaining modes of evangelical sensibility, and it did so precisely as 'part of the expanding newspaper culture of eighteenth-century England'.[12] As Masuch points out, Wesley's inner life as revealed through conversion was only a small fraction of the narrative persona on offer in this 'periodical': the journal freely offered worldly advice, and moral commentary on the art and literature of the moment (Sterne's *Sentimental Journey* was dismissed as being both fashionable and nonsensical).[13] As contributors to this volume indicate, an expanding newspaper and periodical culture continued to have an impact on life writing practices throughout the long nineteenth century. Alison Booth's chapter on collections of life histories points to the function of periodical-based publications such as Hazlitt's *Spirit of the Age* for situating 'living figures in the [emergent] historical canvas'. Martin Hewitt points to the way in which Samuel Bamford incorporated newspaper cuttings into his diary. And, as Matt Cook's chapter on the diaries of George Ives demonstrates, newspaper culture continued to be used into the early twentieth century in the reflective construction of new modes of selfhood. Cook's chapter shows the way in which Ives fashioned a homosexual self in his diaries, using his own complicated 'voices' and a scrapbook of press cuttings that commemorated episodes in the public reception of homosexual identity. Laurel Brake's chapter on press obituaries analyses the coded manner in which this public reception took shape.

The alliance between periodical publications, life writing and emergent communities of readers was being negotiated across regional, national and colonial constituencies in the latter phases of the long nineteenth century. Julie Codell reminds us that Gandhi's autobiography was serialized weekly in Gujarati in *Navajiyan* and in English in Gandhi's *Young India* newspaper before it was issued as a book in 1925. Donna Loftus's chapter points to the way in which late nineteenth-century local newspapers published lives of regional worthies in acts of 'civic remembrance'. Such acts could also be adapted for a British national stage. In 1906, *The Review of Reviews* carried an article entitled 'The Labour Party and the Books that Made it', celebrating the election of fifty-one labour MPs to the House of Commons. Historically the article marked a decisive shift in distributions of class power: a working class that had been partially enfranchised since the late 1860s, and more decisively since the mid-1880s, was finally electing its own representatives to an aristocratic and middle-class institution. In marking this moment, the article focused on the relationship between reading and the inscription of exemplary lives.

The MPs had been approached by the editor of the *Review*, W.T. Stead, and asked to write accounts of 'the books which you found by experience most useful to you when your battle was beginning'. In reporting the results, Stead's editorial 'Notice' speaks through the voice of a biographer who now has access to the cultivated inner life, virtues and motivations of a collective biographical subject or, as Alison Booth describes it in her chapter for this volume, a 'prosopographical' subject: 'if we may judge men by the companions they keep, we may form a shrewd conception of the kind of men they really are by knowing the silent companions of their leisure hours'.[14] The reader of the *Review* would come to share this understanding by reading the autobiographical discourses of the MPs. Stead's commentary emphasised the disseminating powers of his journal; he contended:

> Nothing has been printed for many a long day so calculated to stimulate and inspire the minds of the young men of to-day than these authentic records of the early struggles of those now making history in the Commons House of Parliament. ... In order to facilitate this I shall reprint this article at the end of the month, and shall supply copies at 6s. per 100, post free, to any who may desire to circulate it.[15]

The power of print that Stead presumed may have been overstated, but his commentary sought to connect with earlier legitimating discourses of self-improvement that were so important to the idea of being a 'self-helping' notable, as Donna Loftus's chapter on male middle-class autobiography for this volume shows. The imagined link between the recorded battle for life as source of inspiration, and circulated print, was a powerful one.

The 'authentic records' that Stead undertook to circulate were fragments of autobiographical discourse recording the formative reading habits of the workingmen who had been elected Labour MPs. If the *Review*'s readers were invited to peer into these collective inner lives, the inscribed relationship between reading and life experience was not always grounded in inspirational homilies; instead, reading could be recalled as an opaque experience. Keir Hardie's account provides a striking example of this:

> About that age [16], or perhaps a year later, a friend sent me *Sartor Resartus*, and one of the most abiding remembrances of those days is the attic in which I used to read by the light only of my collier's lamp whilst going through Carlyle's most impressive book. I felt I was in the presence of some great power, the meaning of which I

> could only dimly guess at. I mark the reading of *Sartor*, however, as a real turning point, and went through the book three times in succession until the spirit of it somewhat entered into me. Since then I have learned much of the human failings and weaknesses of Carlyle, but I still remain a worshipper at his shrine.[16]

Hardie's acknowledgment of Carlyle's 'failings and weaknesses' is an allusion to the great controversy of the 1880s that followed Froude's revealing biography of Carlyle and his posthumous publication of Carlyle's own *Reminiscences*. This was a controversy that diminished Carlyle's public reputation, as conflicting accounts of his marriage and domestic life were published and scrutinised, at the same time as it occupied a central place in late nineteenth-century debates about life writing.[17] This, however, is only one of the Carlyle-inspired discourses of Victorian life writing at work in Hardie's account of his reading of the 'sage'. Another is the prevalent discourse of 'hero worship' (Hardie worships at Carlyle's 'shrine'). Yet another is a romantic discourse of revelation. Hardie, in an implicit move beyond the 'imitative' model of reading life writing that Stead had claimed was his purpose in publishing these accounts of reading, aligns himself with what M.H. Abrams was later to define as the romantic turn to illumination: reading *Sartor*, symbolically with the workman's collier's lamp, promises – even if it cannot transparently deliver – luminous truth. Hardie as a young autodidact perceived himself to be in the presence of some 'great power, the meaning of which I could only dimly guess at'.

Hardie was responding to the complex invitation offered in *Sartor*, for Carlyle's work dramatises in its very form the challenge of reading and understanding a written life. Its 'editor' is a reluctant biographer who seeks to understand a body of writings by a German professor, Teufelsdröckh, consisting of a philosophy of clothing, but also autobiographical fragments which narrate a turning point, a conversion away from the sceptical 'Everlasting No' to the 'Everlasting Yea'. *Sartor* employs some of the central narrative conventions of autobiography, such as the conversion experience, while ironically refusing their capacity to transcend an unsettled, sceptical frame. Carlyle thus remains a pivotal figure in Victorian life writing, this in part because of his idea of 'heroic' biography, which as Laurel Brake's and Matt Cook's chapters demonstrate, could be appropriated by homosexual writers who sought to fashion new versions of the 'heroic' life to bond homosexual writers and readers into what was described as 'the new culture'. But in marked tension with the unique object of hero worship, yet in anticipation of the concept's appropriation, Carlyle's writing was also preoccupied with the democratic effects of technologies of printing, or, as he puts it in *Sartor*, '"*Moveable Types*"', for the invention of 'the Art of Printing' 'was disbanding hired Armies, and cashiering most Kings and Senates, and creating a whole new Democratic world'.[18]

Consequently Carlyle continues to merit a surprisingly important place in the study of Victorian life writing. This is in part because, as Martin Danahay's essay shows, his own writing articulated some of the central tensions with which Victorian masculinity wrestled. In addition, it was because Carlyle himself became a subject cast and re-cast in 'movable type'. This had important consequences for what I have elsewhere described as the 'portable' nature of Carlyle's legacy, which was indeed open to multiple cultural appropriations.[19] Thus, some while after Keir Hardie had been reading *Sartor* in a Scottish attic with the aid of a miner's lamp, a young Indian lawyer from South Africa, resident in London, probably read the same text. Gandhi, as Julie Codell's chapter demonstrates, was affected by Carlyle's critique of social relations under the regime of political economy in ways that Keir Hardie would have recognised. But, in addition, Codell's argument shows how Carlyle's life writing, especially *Sartor Resartus*, offered Gandhi the scope to construct an autobiographical self that constructed an 'excursive–discursive' identity from metaphors of clothes and diasporic wanderings. Codell's approach to the concept of the self has far-reaching consequences: she argues that this self enabled Gandhi to fashion an extended Indian national self as a transnational identity, one that offered the prospect of a globalised, rather than a localised India, and which thus continues to generate important cross-cultural implications in the post-colonial present.[20]

In other words, this volume's approach to life writing provides possibilities for radically redrawing the boundaries of the Victorian 'life and letters' format and its associated constituencies, for these could oscillate between 'home' and 'colonial' contexts to produce quite complex patterns of meaning and power relations. Donna Loftus's chapter on male middle-class autobiography looks at the way in which masculine identity was bolstered by narratives of travel in the empire. Loftus points to the way in which the Liverpool cotton broker Samuel Smith suffered a nervous breakdown, but 'reaffirmed his useful masculine agency by taking a trip to India'. Loftus argues that the colony 'became the landscape for his contemplation on the nature of progress, a move that perhaps suggests that travel to more "exotic" locations was often undertaken after an illness, a breakdown or in retirement ... as a way of reaffirming masculine identities that had been challenged'. Extending the implications of one of Martin Danahay's lines of argument in his chapter, this reaffirmation perhaps found the source of its legitimacy in Carlyle's emblematic construction of himself as a manly labouring subject, in contrast to the feminised body of the Caribbean plantation hand. However, as Julie Codell argues, colonial subjects such as Gandhi would go on both to incorporate and to critique Carlylean discourses of heroic masculinity.

Trev Lynn Broughton's chapter provides another perspective on colonial governance and the masculine self at work; it explores Philip Meadows Taylor's *The Story of My Life*, a neglected work of autobiography that recorded the life of an administrator in colonial India. As Broughton illustrates, Meadows Taylor's life story was interpreted nostalgically, through reviews in British-based periodicals, as an exemplary life of masculine independence and energy, a life that was no longer possible under the new conditions of patronage and 'time serving' that marked the reformed civil service in India. Yet, as Broughton argues by situating *The Story of My Life* in the context of a 'life-writing industry' (that is, the broader contexts of publication, editorial promotion and reviewing that framed and mediated this autobiography) its celebration of colonial manly independence was carefully designed to forge new forms of obligation to protect the financial interests of Meadows Taylor's daughters. Thus Broughton's chapter reaches two important conclusions: first, that 'we need to move beyond exclusive concentration on "the text", and to a study of life writing as a complex and multifarious cultural field'; secondly, that Victorian life writing 'both revealed and mitigated the fragility of masculinity as a construction' when viewed in familial and domestic contexts.

Beyond 'Tradition' in Life Writing

As early as 1916, Waldo H. Dunn's *English Biography* constructed a literary tradition of biography as 'the record of the best thought of a race expressed in such artistic form as to inspire and elevate the soul', a formulation clearly derived from Matthew Arnold.[21] In 1974, A.O.J. Cockshut's study of Victorian biography imposed a stronger 'masculine' gloss upon this. *Truth to Life: the Art of Biography in the Nineteenth Century* presented itself as an account of 'our great biographical tradition'. According to Cockshut, a biographical tradition extending from Boswell's *Johnson* of 1791 to Maitland's *Stephen* of 1906 manifests 'variations ... within a common frame of reference'. It is a tradition that 'describes men who did what they intended to do, men who either were not tempted by strong impulses, or who were successful in rigidly suppressing them'.[22] For Cockshut this was backed up by an approved style of 'disinterested' depiction and 'detached' judgment. Reticence and reserve were dispositions of which Cockshut approved; in a comment on one of Macaulay's letters, which reveals feelings for his sister not appropriate to a brother, a letter published without comment by his nephew–biographer G.E. Trevelyan, Cockshut opines that, in tactfully side-stepping the matter, 'we can be grateful for the solid, documented, unemphatic biographical tradition to which Trevelyan belongs' (Cockshut, p.133). Traditions actively discourage certain reading strategies and yet the discursive contours of the tradition reveal, simultaneously, the basis of its own strategies of containment and eventual undoing. Even Cockshut seems to glimpse the latter when he wonders aloud 'whether any group of men, taken collectively, was ever so strong and inflexible in purpose as a reading of nineteenth-century biography would suggest' (Cockshut, p.18). Whether a group of men really was so strong and inflexible does depend how one reads, and in the contexts that one situates, that reading.

Donna Loftus's chapter indicates the way in which the 'men of letters' canon has narrowed the range of Victorian biographies and autobiographies singled out for scholarly attention. Indeed Cockshut's idea of a literary tradition of biography honouring men of indomitable will, written in the disinterested voice of tradition, continues to exert an influence on understandings of Victorian life writing. Clinton Machann's recent work on autobiography, for instance, emphasises 'tradition' as a kind of principle of generic containment, even when his focus is the sexually subversive subject matter of J.A. Symonds's memoirs. Machann examines Symonds's unique impulse to 'confess' his 'inverted' sexual identity.[23] In doing this, Machann's analysis of Symonds's autobiography valuably identifies characteristics that Matt Cook's chapter for this volume points to in his account of the 'voices' of the homosexual diarist George Ives (one 'dialect' of which was the discourse of sexology); in particular, Symonds's attempt 'to reach out to an as yet undefined audience of the future'.[24] However Machann's preoccupation with 'tradition' leads him to conclude that ultimately Symonds had written 'a very conventional work' which was 'constrained by tradition'. [25]

Linda H. Peterson's recent emphasis on plural traditions in nineteenth-century life writing by women is a helpful move forward, not least for the way in which it draws attention to the processes of nineteenth-century canon formation and textual selection that have helped to shape traditions, a point that Machann tends to overlook.[26] And yet there may still be a need for a different critical language that enables more complex ways of exploring the relation between life writing and Victorian culture. Thus, instead of looking at Symonds's memoirs as 'tradition'-bound, it may be more helpful to shift focus towards their embeddedness in multiple, overlapping contexts: scholars of Victorian life writing are thus urged to attempt, in the words of Trev Lynn Broughton, 'the patient reconstruction of shifting and mutually activating constituencies' signified in its complicated repertoire of genres: shifting, because categories of identity were in flux, evinced in Symonds's and Ives's struggle to identify themselves and their sexuality; mutually activating because constituencies such as 'domesticity', 'the family' and 'literature' were contested sites of discourse, and impinged on one another as they adapted to the pressures that new modes of identity exerted.

Viewed from this angle, a singular notion of 'tradition' has always been less than adequate for appreciating the subtle contexts of conflict and contestation that connect acts of life writing. Even Cockshut had to recognise the inadequacies when he came to account for Victorian men who were, contrary to the terms of the 'tradition' by which he would measure them, found to be tempted by strong impulses that they were unable to suppress, and who went against intended courses of action. This was the case with Charles John Vaughan, headmaster of Harrow (1844–59), former pupil of Dr Thomas Arnold and friend of his biographer, the churchman Arthur Stanley (Vaughan also married Stanley's sister). Cockshut mentions in passing, and as a kind of cautionary tale, Vaughan's 'uncontrollable tendency to paederasty, which led to his sudden departure from Harrow' (Cockshut, p.28). But Vaughan's story merits more than a cautionary mention. Indeed Vaughan and Symonds are interesting test cases for exploring alternative approaches to reading life writing 'between men'; their lives intersected at Harrow over the issue of 'paederasty': Vaughan was headmaster at the time that Symonds was a pupil. Symonds played an important role in Vaughan's departure; as a consequence, both had complicated relationships to the various writings that recorded their lives.

Vaughan, the former headmaster, who died in 1897, had his life written for the DNB (vol. 20, published 1899), a repository of the 'tradition' of Victorian manliness that Cockshut celebrated. The biographical entry was composed by Charles Edwyn Vaughan, Vaughan's nephew (1854–1922), and at the time of writing Professor of English Literature at Armstrong College, Newcastle upon Tyne. The life that the nephew wrote of the uncle is remarkable, first for its disarming final sentence: 'He left a strict injunction that no life of him should be published' (p.160); an instruction violated, in part, by the context in which it appeared; and, second, for the narrative evasions that can be glimpsed through the codes of 'manliness' in which, nonetheless, the prohibited biography is couched:

> At the end of 1859 Vaughan resigned his headmastership of Harrow. A few months later Lord Palmertston, who as chairman of the governing body, had formed the highest opinion of his capacity, offered him the bishopric of Rochester. He accepted without

hesitation. A day or two later, probably after a severe struggle with his ambition, the acceptance was withdrawn. It is commonly believed that offers of a like sort were renewed more than once; but even to his closest friends he never spoke of them; his determination had been taken once and for all. In the latter part of 1860 he was appointed to the important vicarage of Doncaster, and threw himself heart and soul into the ordinary work of a town parish. (p.160)

The paragraph ends by asserting the values of selfless, disinterested, yet heart-felt public service, confirmed in C.J. Vaughan's 'determination' to remain true to a humble station, despite the renewed offers of high ecclesiastical office from men in the highest positions of state. Vaughan is portrayed as independent of mind (he speaks not even to close friends of his decision), yet his unbending determination to do ordinary work in a town parish is contradicted by his prior acceptance 'without hesitation' of the bishopric of Rochester, which he subsequently withdraws. And what did it mean for Vaughan to have 'probably' entered into a 'severe struggle with his ambition' as a prelude to his withdrawal?

The complicated answer emerges from Phyllis Grosskurth's 1964 biography of Symonds, and her 1984 edition of his unedited memoirs (begun in 1889) that includes an account of his school days at Harrow.[27] Symonds recalls discovering that his headmaster had exchanged love letters with one of his friends and fellow sixth formers. After leaving the school and going up to Oxford, Symonds could no longer keep the secret to himself. He informed an Oxford tutor and, on the advice of the tutor, his father. As Machann points out, Symonds 'was profoundly ambivalent about his actions, for although he sympathised with Vaughan's homosexuality, he condemned the man's hypocrisy and misuse of power'.[28] Vaughan's resignation from Harrow followed swiftly, along with a stipulation that he should not accept high office subsequently. Symonds's father threatened to expose Vaughan on learning that his ambition had got the better of him and he had accepted the bishopric of Rochester. Vaughan headed for Doncaster. The fact that this story could not emerge until 1964 is substantially due to Horatio F. Brown, Symonds's literary executor. Brown, along with Edmund Gosse, carefully edited Symond's memoir before publishing a highly selective life of their friend in 1895, though one that drew from a wide variety of life writing genres, including letters, diaries and autobiographical narrative. This power to select enabled Brown to claim that 'the autobiography of the Harrow period is not copious', a claim which displays a reticence to match C.E. Vaughan's in the biographical account of his uncle.[29]

Significantly Laurel Brake's chapter for this volume is framed by a quotation from Arthur Symons's review of Brown's life of Symonds; Symons's review was remarkably alert to the 'artful' reticence and concealment that was produced by Brown's suppression of materials and use of selective biographical commentary. Laurel Brake's chapter goes on to examine press obituaries and *DNB* entries to explore the role of the ephemeral life writing which constitutes the sources of biographies of the future; her chapter enables us to appreciate the importance of 'the messy scramble at the point of death to control the media and avert scandal, fix representation, and to suppress, repress and displace available meanings'. Indeed Brake's chapter demonstrates a very complex relationship between press obituaries, Brown's life of Symonds, and the life of Symonds that appears in the *DNB*. There are two points here: first, the codes of reticence and reserve that mark Cockshut's 'great biographical tradition' were the product of complex cultural pressures; secondly, the very exertions of those complex cultural pressures suggest the difficulty of locating Symonds's memoir in one 'linear' literary tradition.

The chapters in this volume demonstrate that literary culture was a source of belonging and identification that was actively contested by a variety of constituencies. Fin de siècle homosexuality was one, as the chapters by Laurel Brake and Matt Cook show. But, focusing on an earlier period, Alison Booth argues that mid-nineteenth-century prosopographical writings celebrated domestic partnerships in literary and cultural work that reacted against the Regency excesses of men without women, or of women among men. Booth argues that 'the weird Lambs might be the forerunners of the Victorian working couple, but the Gaskells, the Brownings, the Carlyles, and the "Leweses", for all their different tempers and circumstances, suggest the domestic literary mission of the age'. Booth shows how the 'family' and the 'home' became categories for organising appreciative responses to literary lives, topographies and works. However such a domestic literary 'mission' was never beyond contestation; Booth's argument points to the formation of the circle that clustered around *Fraser's Magazine*, which was depicted visually as an exclusively 'manly' formation and, as such, the forerunner of the academic homosociality that defined late nineteenth-century 'prosopographies' such as the *DNB* and 'English Men of Letters'.[30]

Above all, the discourse of domestic relations, the family, and the bonds of loyalty that it created remained a powerful multivalent force in Victorian life writing. On the one hand, it was a source of aversion. The call for biographical writing in the late nineteenth century to become disinterested and professionalised was couched negatively in the language of familial relations, given that the biographer who was taken to be partial, keen to suppress material, distorted of sight and judgment and therefore unreliable, was characterised by Edmund Gosse in 1901 as 'the widow'.[31] On the other hand, a familial bond between biographer and biographee could result in acts of life writing that subtly revised dominant power relations. Helen Rogers's chapter focuses on biographies about fathers by daughters. Her argument challenges the two dominant paradigms of western Feminism: 'the Freudian myth of the daughter's seduction by the father, and feminism's understanding of patriarchy as the institutionalised power of the father'. This in turn leads Rogers to revise the feminist narrative of anxiety of autobiographical female authorship as set out by Gilbert and Gubar in the late 1970s, arguing that 'biographies [of fathers by daughters] throw some light ... not only on the much-neglected history of father–daughter relationships but also on the politics of paternity and political ancestry for feminists in the present'. For Rogers, constructions of masculinity were central to Victorian feminisms, inflected as they were by opposed Evangelical and secularist traditions of life writing. As Rogers points out, Josephine Butler's biography of her father involves a subtle revision of what it meant to be a public man: John Grey had not stood for Parliament or written a book, so in some sense was excluded from that definition; but other Evangelically inspired meanings, for example managing a hospital estate, were being deployed by Butler's biography. Indeed Rogers argues that discourses of domesticity were important for asserting political legitimacy for embattled secularism in the public world: her account of Hypatia Bradlaugh's narrative of her father's domestic life was an important means of demonstrating the political legitimacy of secularist politics.

In the end, literary professionalism and the family need to be seen as overlapping constituencies rather than opposed sources of identification. The overlap is demonstrated by the fact that professional homosocial biography's suspicion of the family biographer was a legitimating discourse rather than a necessary expression of disinterestedness; as a discourse, it could encourage the misrecognition of actual relationships. This can be demonstrated in the previously cited example of Charles Edwyn Vaughan's *DNB* biography of Charles John Vaughan, the headmaster of Harrow. Charles Edwyn Vaughan, educated at Bailliol, was a notable academic figure in the emergent field of English literary studies. Between 1889 and 1898, Vaughan held the chair of English literature at University College, Cardiff. At the time he published the *DNB* entry on Charles John Vaughan he was taking up the chair of English at Armstrong College, Newcastle upon Tyne; before his retirement in 1913, he would hold the chair of English at the University of Leeds.[32] A specialist on Edmund Burke, Vaughan's biographical prose exemplified the values of academic, homosocial manliness. And yet, in applying this prose to the *DNB* life of his uncle and its concealed secret, it is clear that the nephew was writing from the position of 'the widow', protecting his family's name and reputation.

Laurel Brake has demonstrated elsewhere the way in which A.C. Benson's role as biographer of Walter Pater for the 'English Men of Letters' series effectively blurred the boundaries between the 'professional' and 'widow'. If Benson secured the role because he had not been a friend of Pater and was therefore deemed to be the 'professional', this has to be balanced against the fact that Benson was so embedded in Oxford academic and homosocial networks that he came to conceal the truth about Pater's sexuality rather in the manner of a 'widow'.[33] Valerie Sanders's concluding chapter focuses on the Benson family's complicated relationship to what she describes as 'the life-writing industry' in the late nineteenth and early twentieth centuries. As Sanders notes, the Bensons have become an increasingly important family unit for historians of masculinity; John Tosh's work, for instance, takes as its starting point the career and domestic life of E.W. Benson, Headmaster of Wellington College, Archbishop of Canterbury and father to A.C. and E.F. Benson.

Sanders looks in detail at the Bensons from the perspective of their almost obsessive impulse towards the production of auto/biographical materials; her chapter complements Martin Hewitt's account of A.C. Benson as a diarist (around four million words in 180 volumes). Sanders accounts for the Bensons' experiments in life writing as exercises in 'domestic accountability', or attempts to come to terms, in writing, with the father's impact on the life of other family member through the reconstruction of the lives of the '"silent"' members of the family who were on the margins of the life-writing industry – their mother, their sisters, and even their father'. These experiments culminated in A.C. Benson's *House of Quiet* (1904), a complex play on fiction, real life and identity. For Valerie Sanders, this genre-crossing bespeaks a much more profound sense of merging, in which identities blur into one another; in Sanders's chapter, collective literary identity has shifted from the domestic prosopographical exemplarity of the kind analysed by Alison Booth to a kind of self-consciously contagious haunting, initiated by the life of the father and spreading between sibling lives and the modes of inscription that that they leave behind.

Valerie Sanders's chapter also acts as a conclusion to the volume: as she suggests, cultural historians are familiar with a narrative about the late Victorian avant-garde, increasingly aware of psychoanalysis, and poised on the cusp of Modernism. In this respect, it is normally Bloomsbury that is cited as the critical terminus for Victorian life writing, in the form either of Strachey's *Eminent Victorians* (1918) or of Virginia Woolf's experiments with genres of life writing and fiction (for instance, *Jacob's Room*, *Flush*, *Orlando*). Valerie Sanders points to parallels between the family pedigrees of the Bensons and the Stephens:

while the Benson children spent their lives trying to account for their reaction to the tremulous domestic intensity of the great public man in their midst, Virginia Woolf was, as is well known, continually seeking to exorcise the ghost of Sir Leslie Stephen, the father figure who was also the nation's custodian of biographical propriety. However, as Sanders also points out, the Bensons' experiments in life writing were launched some twenty years prior to those of the Woolf circle. This is not simply a revision of origins, or an argument about anticipation. Instead it is an important reminder of the fact that the Bensons could embark on their own explorations by drawing seamlessly on experiments in life writing that had been practised throughout the Victorian period, and in the multiplicity of spaces on which that 'period' impinged. As Julie Codell's chapter reminds us, Gandhi's *Autobiography* was fashioned out of numerous 'high' Victorian sources, and it was subtitled an *Experiment with Truth*. Thus Victorian life writing was always already premised on experiments that played restlessly upon the boundaries between public print and private inscription, masculine and feminine, notability and obscurity, the centre and the margin, conformity and dissidence, the collective and the individual, the formally polished and the chaotically inchoate.

Notes

1. Harold Nicolson, *The Development of English Biography* (London: The Hogarth Press, 1928), p.8
2. Richard D. Altick, *Lives and Letters: A History of Literary Biography in England and America* (New York: Alfred A. Knopf, 1965), p.181.
3. Linda H. Peterson, *Traditions of Victorian Women's Autobiography: The Poetics and Politics of Life Writing* (Charlottesville and London: University Press of Virginia, 1999), p.x.
4. George Eliot, *The Mill on the Floss*, ed. A.S. Byatt (London: Penguin, 2003), pp.241–2.
5. Kathryn Carter, 'The Cultural Work of Diaries in Mid-century Victorian Britain', *Victorian Review*, 23:2 (Winter 1997), 251–67; Carter focuses on the popular farce by Mark Lemon and Charles Dickens, *Mr Nightingale's Diary* (1851), pp.256–7. Martin Hewitt's chapter discusses this farce.
6. Selections from Joseph Romilly's diary have been published by Cambridgeshire Records Society; the first volume covers the period 1842–47, the second, from which my discussion is drawn, covers the period 1848–64; *Romilly's Cambridge Diary 1848–1864*, edited by M.E. Bury and J.D. Pickles (Cambridge: Cambridgeshire Records Society, 2000); references to this text will be given in the main discussion.
7. See J.W. Clark and T.M. Hughes, *The Life and Letters of the Reverend Adam Sedgwick*, 2 volumes (Cambridge: Cambridge University Press, 1890), I, pp.ix–x; the entry on Joseph Romilly for the *DNB* cites his diary as a major source for Sedgwick's life.

8. An earlier volume by another daughter, *Memoirs of Mrs Fry, by her daughter, R.E. Cresswell*, was published in 1845.

9. John Tosh, *A Man's Place: Masculinity and the Middle-Class Home in Victorian England* (New Haven and London: Yale University Press, 1999), p.4. For a perspective on 'domestic authority' in Victorian life writing, see Julie F. Codell, 'Victorian Artists' Family Biographies: Domestic Authority, the Marketplace, and the Artist's Body', in *Biographical Passages: Essays on Victorian and Modernist Biography*, ed. Joe Law and Linda K. Hughes (Columbia and London: University of Missouri Press, 2000), pp.65–108.

10. See Martin Danahay, *A Community of One: Masculine Autobiography and Autonomy in Nineteenth-Century Britain* (Albany: State University of New York Press, 1993).

11. I am indebted here to the scholarly apparatus to Romilly's diary, supplied by Bury and Pickles.

12. Michael Masuch, 'John Wesley, Superstar: Periodicity, celebrity and the sensibility of Methodist society in Wesley's *Journal* (1740-1791), in *Egodocuments and History: Autobiographical Writing in its Social Context since the Middle Ages*, ed. Rudolf Dekker (Hilversum: Verloren, 2002), p.146.

13. Masuch, 'John Wesley, Superstar', pp.140, 150.

14. W.T. Stead, 'The Labour Party and the Books that Helped to Make it', *The Review of Reviews*, 33 (June 1906), 568–82, p.568.

15. Stead, 'The Labour Party and Books', p.568.

16. Keir Hardie, 'The Labour Party and Books', pp.570–71.

17. See Trev Broughton, *Men of Letters, Writing Lives* (London: Routledge, 1999).

18. Thomas Carlyle, *Sartor Resartus* (1831),Works, Centenary Edition, ed. H.D. Traill (London: Chapman and Hall, 1904), p.31.

19. David Amigoni, *Victorian Biography: Intellectuals and the Ordering of Discourse* (Hemel Hempstead: Harvester Wheatsheaf, 1993), ch.2.

20. Not that these always move in a positive, progressive direction: following the Congress Party's success in the Indian elections (2004), Sonia Gandhi (widow of the assassinated Rajiv Gandhi) renounced the premiership despite leading her party to victory. This was in part due to criticism of her Italian (or un-Indian) ethnic origins. Arguably the language of life writing figured in the controversy: Sonia Gandhi reached the decision to renounce after listening to her 'inner voice'.

21. Waldo H. Dunn, *English Biography*, The Channels of English Literature (London: J.M. Dent, 1916), p.264.

22. A.O.J. Cockshut, *Truth to Life: the Art of Biography in the Nineteenth Century* (London: Collins, 1974), p.16, p.18, p.143; future references will be given in the main discussion.

23. Clinton Machann, 'The Memoirs of John Addington Symonds and Victorian Autobiography', *A/B: Auto/Biography Studies*, 9: 2 (1994), 202–11, p.202.

24. Machann, 'The Memoirs of John Addington Symonds', p.207.

25. Machann, 'The Memoirs of John Addington Symonds', p.209.

26. See Peterson, *Traditions of Victorian Women's Autobiography*, esp. ch. 1.

27. See Phyllis Grosskurth, *John Addington Symonds: A Biography* (London: Longmans, 1964), pp.27–41; see also John Addington Symonds, *The Memoirs of John Addington Symonds*, ed. Phyllis Grosskurth (New York: Random House, 1984).

28. Machann, 'The Memoirs of John Addington Symonds', p.205.
29. Horatio F. Brown, *John Addington Symonds: A Biography Compiled from his papers and correspondence*, 2 volumes, 2nd edn (London: Macmillan, 1903), I, p.62.
30. For homosociality and the *DNB*, see Broughton, *Men of Letters, Writing Lives*; for 'English Men of Letters', see David Amigoni, *Victorian Biography*, and 'Sincerity in Every Department: Masks, Masculinity and Market Forces in Eighteenth-century English Men of Letters', in Francis O' Gorman and Katherine Turner (eds), *The Victorians and the Eighteenth Century: Reassessing the Tradition* (Aldershot: Ashgate, 2004), pp.182–202.
31. See Laurel Brake, *Subjugated Knowledges: Journalism, Gender and Literature in the Nineteenth Century* (London: Macmillan, 1994), pp.188–9.
32. For the details of Charles Edwyn Vaughan's career, see *Who Was Who 1916–28*, 1929.
33. See Brake, *Subjugated Knowledges*, ch.10.

CHAPTER ONE

Diary, Autobiography and the Practice of Life History

Martin Hewitt

What is the relationship between diary and autobiography? The traditional answer has been that the diary is subautobiographical, raw material for, perhaps aspiring to, but always falling short of, the complexity and richness of autobiography.[1] Recently this hierarchy has been challenged by work from within women's studies which has suggested that, given the ways in which Victorian protocols effectively denied the validity of women's lives as fit subjects for autobiographical construction, for women at least, the diary, along with the letter and other more ephemeral or episodic texts, needs to be approached as a potentially complex form of life writing on its own terms.[2] By challenging the marginalisation of the diary as life writing, and by pointing to the richness of its capacities and forms, this scholarship offers hitherto underexploited ways of reconsidering the diaries of those figures, both women and men, who were active in the nineteenth-century public sphere, not least in raising neglected questions about the way the diary might relate to as well as substitute for the autobiography. Addressing these questions demands the reconsideration of a number of persistent but not always helpful assumptions about the distinctions between diary and autobiography: the contrast between the simple compositional structure of the diary, rooted in its dailiness, and the complex strategies of self-representation available to the autobiography; between the diary as 'natural' and the autobiography as 'artful'; between the diary as open and plotless and the autobiography as predicated on emplotment and a search for closure; between the diary as introspection and the autobiography as projection; between the diary as a private mode and the autobiography as a public mode.

The purpose of this chapter is to explore some of the potentialities and operations of the diary as a mode of life writing, and to consider the nature of its exchanges with other forms of writing of the self. It seeks, in Regenia Gagnier's formulation, to look at diaries as 'rhetorical projects embedded in concrete material situations',[3] as text, artefact and practice. It uses some of the questions posed by the case of Samuel Bamford to interrogate both the broad field of nineteenth-century diary writing and – in more detail – the specific cases of the history painter

Benjamin Robert Haydon, the Fabian Socialist and reformer Beatrice Webb, and Arthur Christopher Benson, the turn-of-the-century biographer and man of letters.[4] No attempt is made to claim these diarist–autobiographers as 'characteristic', or as emblematic of a particular chronological development of diary writing. Rather they are deployed as exemplary of the possible interactions between diary and life writing, of the abilities of the diary to transcend the apparent limits of its form, and in the process to colonise spaces often seen as specifically autobiographical.

Until very recently Samuel Bamford was known primarily as one of the most compelling of the nineteenth-century autodidact auto-biographers. His two autobiographical volumes, *Passages in the Life of a Radical* (1839–42, 1844) and *Early Days* (1847–48, 1848) have been exploited and analysed both by historians and by literary scholars.[5] But although Bamford has been invoked above all as an autobiographer, the precise nature of his autobiographical practice – the peculiar nature of his autobiographies, the extensive deployment of autobiographical materials in the rest of his published writings, and in particular the extent to which his public career increasingly came to be dominated by an attempt, recorded in detail in his diary, to propagate a specific life history – has attracted little attention.

Bamford was an autobiographer who did not write an autobiography. *Passages* and *Early Days* together did not take his life story beyond 1821, when he was 32, produced an interrupted narrative even when juxtaposed, provided a surprisingly sketchy portrait of his personality, and rarely placed his life story at centre stage. *Passages* offered no attempt to plot the incidents and events it recorded into a pattern which related to Bamford's own biography.[6] *Early Days* offered a more conventional account of Bamford's growth to manhood, but side-stepped any attempt to trace his personal development as a radical, and failed even to take the story up to the commencement of *Passages*. Both books were less interested in Bamford's individual history than in presenting his life as embodying lessons which could speak to the contemporary exigencies of his class, a narrative which combined the personal history of the wronged radical (the peaceful proponent of legitimate reforms victimised by a cruel state and then unjustly spurned by the radical movement) and a collective lesson of the primacy of gradualist reform and self-improvement over revolutionary posturings. Although at the end of *Early Days* Bamford promised to resume his autobiography in future published writings, such a continuation was never made.

As a result, when during the 1840s and again in the later 1850s Bamford threw himself into the propagation of his life, *Passages* and

Early Days needed to be supplemented by the briefer but more complete autobiographies provided in the introductions to the volumes of poetry he published in 1834 and 1843, and sustained by assiduous attention to the management of his reputation in the press and on the platform. Elements of the process can be seen in the additions which Bamford made to the 1844 and 1858 editions of *Passages*, as well as in various materials reprinted in his *Walks in South Lancashire* (1844), in the series of autobiographical circulars he issued in 1859 and 1860,[7] and in a number of his other pamphlets. Above all, however, the attempt is encapsulated in the pages of his diary, which survives for a four year period during which Bamford returned to Manchester after a number of years living in London, a period marked by a sustained if largely unsuccessful attempt first to mobilise his life story on the political and educational platform and subsequently to seek a civil list pension as 'just compensation' for his imprisonment both before and after Peterloo. Bamford's diary is a hybrid text, incorporating a great deal of ancillary material with which the regular and often detailed daily entries engaged in a sustained dialogue, including a large number of letters (both to and from Bamford), newspaper cuttings reporting Bamford's public activities, or concerning other people or events on which Bamford felt drawn to comment, copies of his circular and other items of printed ephemera.

It would be possible to read the diary merely as a 'record' of Bamford's management of his public persona. At one point the text suggests that he sees it as a dossier of his claims for compensation and the manner in which they are treated, leaving his correspondents, 'to the judgement of posterity' (3 August 1859) and, towards the end of the diary, at the urging of friends, Bamford did begin to consider the preservation and publication of his manuscripts after his death, eventually leaving them to a local scientific figure as his literary executor. It is unlikely, however, that this recording function alone brought Bamford to diary writing. The habit did not come easily to him. At the end of the 1840s he confessed to Elizabeth Gaskell that he would 'rather walk 20 miles than write a letter any day'.[8] The diary's combination of materials and persistent internal dialogue makes sense only when considered as an active intervention in the management of his autobiographical project, in the constant negotiation and renegotiation between Bamford the activist, Bamford the historical figure, newspaper editors and journalists, and other contributors to the press. The diary records an intense and intensifying letter writing to the press, involving careful modulations of voice and authority, as he intervenes under his own status as the longest surviving radical prisoner of 1817 and 1819, as well as various anonymous guises. It demonstrates his constant vigilance over the nature and extent of press coverage of his platform performances to ensure that, as he put it in discussing a speech in Bury in November 1859, his activities 'had a circulation wide enough' (7 November 1859), including regular personal contacts with newspapers in Manchester and the surrounding towns, direct interventions to revise copy concerning his speeches or to urge the publication of a letter or poem, and the annotation of cuttings of reports both of his own interventions and those of others which he saw as inadequate or inaccurate. At times his observations may seem carping and egotistical, but the thrust of the whole diary is a sustained and systematic concern with the management of his public face, and in particular his autobiographical narrative.

Bamford's commitment to this narrative constantly forces its way through the notional contemporaneity of the diary form, and in this sense the diary, far from laying down the raw materials for later processing into an autobiography, plays out and amplifies an already fully formed life story. It is not just that the briefest of acquaintances with the diary leaves no doubt of the extent to which Bamford's pysche is dominated by his sense of the past, his recollection of key events, his elephantine consciousness of old slights, grievances and feuds, typified in the resolution the diary records 'to unmask [his enemies] and to gibbet them to infamy' (31 May 1859). It is the extent to which the diary embodies his autobiographical project, its opening sentence 'This day I complete my 70th year of age' echoing the openings of other contemporary journals and autobiographies. It was a retrospectively crafted document; in the Spring of 1861 Bamford recorded in it that he had spent several days sorting his papers and destroying much unwanted material (18 April 1861). Nevertheless, far from being proto-autobiographical, it rested on a fully formulated and consistent sense of the shape and meanings of his life story. The diary was not the foundation of an autobiography: an autobiography was the foundation of the diary.

Bamford's case thus challenges conventional understandings of the nineteenth-century diary and its relationships with autobiography. His diary is not private in the sense traditionally understood; it represents no impetus towards self-improvement, self-awareness or self-valorisation. In preoccupation and material focus it is public. While it has the shifting perspective and the lack of narrative structure often taken as typical of the diary, satisfactory reading requires attention to its complex textual form, and also to its relationship to Bamford's other writings. Nor, although the precise nature of its influences remains unclear, can we treat it as if it operated in a generic vacuum, unaffected by available examples of diary and life writing. This much is clear from the extraordinary parallels it displays with the diary of Benjamin Robert Haydon.

Haydon's diary writing extended over a much longer period than that of Bamford, from July 1808 until a few moments before he committed suicide in June 1846, and in its early years was much more conventionally involved in attempts to define a set of life purposes. Nevertheless there is a remarkable degree of congruence between both diarists and diaries: in the shape of their careers as constructed and recorded in the diaries, including the periods of imprisonment, persistent struggles with poverty and the attempt to make a living by trading on their public reputation by giving lectures, or by selling odd copies of their books on commission; in their campaigns for government assistance which blurred the lines between public and private interest and threatened their strenuously guarded independence; in their powerful self-image as liminal reformers battling against the injustices of the system, abandoned by friends and persecuted by enemies; in the way in which Haydon like Bamford presented himself as a 'man who has suffered for a principle and would lose his life for its success', 'who has been oppressed without ever giving the slightest grounds for oppression';[9] but above all in their shared determination to vindicate their position and provide useful lessons to others, and their deployment of their diary as journal, letterbook and scrapbook, both to record and to manage the propagation of this autobiographical narrative.

There is no indication that Bamford was influenced consciously by Haydon, although he would have known of Haydon from the latter's involvement in the establishment of the Manchester School of Design in the 1840s, and would have found it difficult to avoid discussion of Haydon's life in the aftermath of the publication of Tom Taylor's *Life of Haydon from his autobiography and journals* (1853) when he was living in London. Both might have drawn independently on other models, such as the diaries of Thomas Holcraft, published in Holcraft's *Autobiography* in 1816 and reissued in 1852, which in its account of Holcraft's literary career, indictment for high treason in 1794 and subsequent discharge after emphasising his longstanding commitment to peaceful reform, contained a number of parallels, more especially with Bamford's life; or on the life of Robbie Burns who in his poverty and lack of recognition provided the archetypical story of 'humble men with great talent'; 'Just the tragedy of Burns over again,' Bamford remarked of his life in one of the copy-letters preserved in his diary.[10]

Although diary keeping had a long history,[11] there is no doubt that its emergence in the early nineteenth century as a widely practised and even more widely consumed literary genre meant that by the 1830s it was impossible for a diarist to write without a degree of self-conscious positioning within a published tradition, and without being fully aware of the ambiguous status of the diary's claim to privacy. The publication of the first Letts diaries in 1812 symbolises the rapid expansion of the scope, popularity and visibility of the form.[12] The industrialisation of time created wide demand for desk and pocket diaries to record meetings arranged and transactions conducted. The rise of bureaucracy brought the spread of the diary as a tool of management; in the emerging town missions, for example, regular journals played a key role in surveillance and control. By mid-century the diary operated increasingly in public spaces, in the periodical press, lecture stands and the court room, where it was used both by witnesses attempting to establish their version of events, and also by the police as a source of evidence to incriminate the accused (a presence reflected in the anxieties of George Ives, discussed in Matt Cook's chapter in this volume).

Simultaneously the popularity of the early versions of the diaries of John Evelyn and Samuel Pepys which first appeared in the 1810s and 1820s prompted a flood of diary publications which peaked in the 1860s but ebbed thereafter only slowly; even the Queen herself was moved to join in, publishing *Leaves from a Journal of Our Life in the Highlands* in 1868.[13] Diaries became commodities, not merely in their own right, but as components of popular fiction (including that of the Brontës and Wilkie Collins), periodical journalism, popular drama and, most fecundly, in the copious extracts at the heart of many of the weighty 'Life and Letters' biographies so characteristic of Victorian letters.

With the exception of Burns, Bamford had little to say about his models or inspirations as diarist, but in this he was unusual because even if few diarists began like Edwin Waugh, the Lancashire dialect writer, by pasting into his diary a number of cuttings discussing the appropriate forms and purposes of the diary,[14] it is nonetheless clear, from the frequency with which nineteenth-century diarists acknowledged the influence of particular diaries or quoted others, that they wrote conscious of a rich tradition of diary writing. Haydon had the model, not only of his father's own diary, but of a number of published diaries, of Byron, whose journals he read on more than one occasion, of Fanny Kemble, of Sir Walter Scott and of David Wilkie, the account of whose journals and memoir, when they appeared in Allan Cunningham's *Life*, spurred him on to the further organisation of his own papers and journals, not least because of his sense of Cunningham's distortion of Wilkie's life.[15] A.C. Benson was explicitly inspired by the publication of the *Letters and Journals of William Cory*, a book which his diary records him reading and rereading constantly, which 'stir[red] the deepest founds within' him, while Beatrice Webb rediscovered her sense of the significance of her diary through reading Harriet Martineau's *Autobiography*.[16]

It is easy to lose sight of this significance of the diary as public writing, not least because of the tenacity with which the Victorians clung to the ideal of the private diary. 'Use your diary with the utmost familiarity and confidence; conceal nothing from its pages nor suffer any other eye than your own to scan them' counselled an essay by John Letts in the 1820s.[17] Reviews of published diaries again and again emphasised the authenticity and frankness which diaries drew from the putative confidentiality of their utterances. Some Victorian diarists did practise what others preached. Beatrix Potter, for example, not only kept her journal in her own private code, but did not mention it even to her closest friends, admitting to its existence only once, five weeks before she died.[18] Many, like Edward Herford, the early Victorian Manchester coroner, employed some form of shorthand for their more sensitive entries although, as discussions of Pepys shorthand have noted, this provided more of a guard against casual perusal than a robust defence against the inquisitive. But in most cases privacy was an issue of relatives not absolutes, often literally, given the way the diary frequently functioned as family document, shared within the domestic circle. Circulation around the family was so much a feature of the 1820s diary of Thomas Giordani Wright, a Newcastle doctor, that he took to referring to himself as its 'editor' as though he was conducting a magazine.[19] Haydon moved in circles saturated with diaries, from the diaries of his father, to the manuscripts of Joshua Reynolds's journals, to the extracts of his diary which the phrenologist George Combe sent to him in 1844.[20] As Rebecca Steinitz has remarked, we should not read too much into the locks adorning many diaries. They decorated the diaries of Sir Edward Hamilton, even though Hamilton let his fellow private secretaries read them, made extracts for Gladstone and Rosebery, and allowed John Morley borrow several volumes for his biography of Gladstone.[21]

The manifold publicities of the Victorian diary and the extent to which it came to be conceived as integral to the authentic presentation of a Victorian life are powerfully illuminated by the case of Arthur Christopher Benson, who between 1897 and 1925 composed about four million words of diary stretching over 180 volumes.[22] In her concluding chapter in this volume, Valerie Sanders notes the extraordinary extent to which this popular late-Victorian and early-Edwardian writer and critic seemed compelled to write and rewrite familial biography. Tangential to Sanders' concerns, but nevertheless a central aspect of Benson's public performance of the private, was his character as diarist and diary purveyor. Benson's diary emerged from and operated in a number of ever-extending circles. He not only shared his diary with his siblings, especially his sister Maggie, with whom for a while he exchanged diaries,[23] he also kept it as a visible presence in his drawing room and study; it was read aloud to house guests and parties of visitors, and even sent to friends for their amusement.[24] And although, unlike some of his contemporaries, Benson did not attempt to publish the diary during his life, he traded constantly in diaries. A number of extracts appeared in or formed the basis of chapters in his collections of essays, in his tribute to his brother, Hugh, and in semi-fictional form in his *Memoirs of Arthur Hamilton B.A.* (1886). Invented diaries appeared in other works, including *The House of Quiet* (1904), *The Altar Fire* (1907), *The Gate of Death. A Diary* (1909) and a novel, *Chris Gascoyne. An Experiment in Solitude, from the diaries of John Trevor* (1924). Almost inevitably, his most substantial works of scholarship also involved the presentation of diaries, those of Queen Victoria herself, and those of his father, and his father's contemporaries in his two-volume *Life of Edward White Benson, Archbishop of Canterbury* (1900), the second volume of which presents long passages of extended extracts from the diary with a bare minimum of editorial contextualisation.

The frequency with which diaries were published in the traditional Life and Letters volume as extracts, as one of a range of personal testimonies, and even when published in their own right were seldom presented in their entirety, encouraged an enduring indifference to any integrity they had as discrete texts. Victorian critics acknowledged that 'diary' or 'journal' covered a range of styles and subject matter, from the dissenting diary of conscience through the travel journal to the collection of anecdotal observations, but, rather than exploring the particularities of these different modes, they ignored them, as they ignored the distinctions between diaries and other forms of 'intimate' writing, including letters and memoirs, and between these and more formally composed life writing. The diary was conceived of as a collection of fragments, as a series of photographs or pictures, rather than a narrative, free from deliberate composition.[25] Virginia Woolf's description of the diary as a 'capacious hold-all in which one flings a mass of odds and ends' thus inscribed a long-established denial of the significance of the shape and structure of the diary.[26]

In fact, however, closer examination of the practice of Victorian diarising and the complexity of the documents produced suggests the need for a much greater attention to the forms which diaries took, and to what we might describe as their intratextualities, the exchanges which took place between the different elements of the text. This is not to argue that together the published diaries established a firm and focused set of generic expectations. Nevertheless the commonness of multiple journalising, where several diaries were kept in parallel, implies some sense of distinct function and form. The artist David Wilkie began his journal in 1808; over the next decade or so he was also using a general memorandum book, a 'journal of occurrences', as well as a separate journal of a visit to Paris in 1814.[27] At the same time, individual diaries had a tendency to move backwards and forwards between different modes, from the record of reading to the summary of daily transactions, to the travel journal, and back, just as in the course of 1880 Beatrice Webb's diary shifted from being primarily a record of reading, to a travel journal of a visit to Italy.

The sequence of dated entries was in any case often only one plane of a layered textuality. Of course the edited and published versions of diaries often produced a sustained dialogue between diarist and editor, of the kind which characterised Taylor's *Life* of Haydon. But this sort of exchange was not merely a feature of publication, because even manuscript diaries were often layered texts, with original entries glossed by additions from friends, from family members or others to whom the diary came after the death of the diarist, as well as by the diarist themselves. David Wilkie's journal of his visit to Italy in 1825 as published in Allan Cunningham's *Life* contained marginal annotations from his friend Thomas Phillips, who accompanied Wilkie on the trip (interestingly the Brotherton Library at the University of Leeds contains the copy which John Murray presented to Phillips, with further manuscript annotations). As Matt Cook's chapter on George Ives in this volume demonstrates, such glosses provided another way in which the diary was able to produce narrative perspective.

Multiple perspectives were also produced by the practice that was so central to Bamford's diary of inserting correspondence, newspaper cuttings and other ephemera. The frequency with which such material was accumulated in diaries is obscured by the way in which it was ignored or treated as separate by biographers and editors who used manuscript diaries, and by the tendency of such material to become detached and lost. It was difficult for contemporaries to reconstruct the diary's precise nature from the published materials, however full these seemed to be. Yet the surviving letters often formed part of a carefully managed and selected archive, in Haydon's case what remained after he had looked through them all and weeded and 'burnt hundreds' (28 April 1844). Those letters, especially those from the later 1830s and early 1840s eventually published by his son, rehearsed, indeed developed, key aspects of his life story. Beginning in letters to friends such as Seymour Kirkup, and eventually transferring into his more public correspondence with patrons and politicians, Haydon articulated his sense of the life of struggle, the ultimate vindication of his principles, but his own failure to obtain just reward.[28] Similarly he used his diary volumes to compose lectures and essays, as well as, at times, for exercises. In a similar vein Ruskin inserted all manner of material in his (sketches, notes on reading, accounts) in chaotic fashion. In many such instances the diary was merely providing convenient blank paper; but often the lists of reading or summaries of arguments were as much a part of the record of living as the chronicle of activities.

Moreover those diarists who had a more conscious sense of their diary as a book of life, were inclined to supplement the regular entries with material encompassing those parts of their life not covered by the diary: sometimes little more than the key dates provided by John Henry Newman at the beginning of his journal, or the brief summaries with which Thomas Moore attempted in his last years to compensate for abandoning the habit of keeping up-to-date with his diary, sometimes, though, a substantial introductory memoir sketching the life story up to the time of the commencement of the diary of the sort provided by Laurence Banville, the Norfolk gamekeeper whose manuscript diary began in typically autobiographic fashion, 'It was in a town of the name of Cullenstown in the County of Wexford I was born', or the extended (72-manuscript page) autobiographical preface added by John Wodehouse, Earl of Kimberley, eight days after beginning his diary in 1862.[29]

Segments such as this of course challenge conventional preoccupation with the dailiness of the diary and point to its narrative potentialities. If in Victorian theory, dailiness was central to the benefits of diary keeping as a process, guaranteeing the immediacy, freshness and authenticity of the writing, in reality it was less a discipline than a device, a compositional stratagem amenable to a variety of usages. A proper understanding of the diary requires a close attention to its deployment. A number of examples of complex processes of compilation, such as the staged composition of Arthur Munby, making short notes in a Letts diary, which he later expanded into red, leather-bound volumes, from which in turn he often made summaries, are well known. What is perhaps insufficiently acknowledged is how few diarists – perhaps only Benson of those considered in detail here – were able in reality to sustain the discipline of daily entries. In most cases dailiness was a matter not of writing daily as of writing dailiness in.[30] In fact, the overwhelming majority of diarists deliberately rejected the rhythm of daily entries on the basis that this structure did not best serve their purpose. In her *Diary of a Lady in Waiting*, Lady Charlotte Bury remarked that she had 'so often determined to write a consecutive journal, and ha[d] so often failed, not from idleness, ... but from the danger of telling all I think – all I know – that I have ... thought it better, ... to forget entirely the passing events of the day, than to record them'.[31] A considerable number of diaries were marked by extreme irregularity, with bursts of activity interrupted by periods of suspension, or were, as in the case of Edward Lee Hicks, eventually Bishop of Lincoln, deliberately constructed as occasional.[32] In this sense it is more helpful to think of the diary as signified by the dated rather than the daily entry.

Beatrice Webb's diary epitomises the impotence of the daily form to constrain the perspective of the individual entry. Webb kept a diary or journal intermittently from early childhood, and more consistently from 1873 when she was fifteen until eleven days before her death in 1943. In its early years the diary was preoccupied with her search for a mission in life, and a number of Webb's pronouncements about the purposes of her diary emphasise its confessional role, as well as its function as a 'safety valve' for her emotions (25 November 1882). During this period Webb shifted repeatedly between almost daily entries and others which summarised weeks, and at times months, during which no entries had been made. Just as Haydon had come increasingly to use his annual stocktakings to rehearse and reaffirm a personal narrative of sacrifice and betrayal,[33] Webb was assiduous in her use of the completion of her diary booklets and the ends of the years to cast her eyes over the previous period and pass judgment on that phase of her life, a widespread practice which intruded even into many diaries which were otherwise confined to the incidental details of daily life.[34] One of the most striking examples is Webb's entry for 1 January 1901, which begins with the conventional annual stocktaking, but broadens out into nearly 2000 words responding to the fundamental autobiographical question, 'looking back on my life as a whole how does it read?'

However Webb's diary also operates in a number of more directly autobiographical ways, in establishing and reinforcing her sense of the shape of her life as an entity: performing exegesis as well as mimesis. One way in which this exegetic function is manifest is the preoccupation of the diary with the shape of her life. Where other diarists worried about wasted days, Webb was preoccupied with the wasting of a life, and the idea of her 'life' is invoked repeatedly in the diary, along with a fundamentally autobiographical concern with its velocity, with her 'work' or her 'mission', which was as much prospective as retrospective, 'thought and feeling [which] drifted far out into the future' (5 May 1890). Another is the way Webb's entries focused textually as much on the past and future as on the present, and operated as a technology of memorialising, their notice of key anniversaries structuring her life as it progressed. Indeed much effort was invested in partitioning one 'portion of our life' from another 'period', and in identifying turning points or watershed moments, the 'turning point from middle to old age' of Webb's partial nervous breakdown in late 1916 or the 'sort of watershed in our career' provided by the long holiday over Christmas 1925. For Webb ultimately the ability of the diary to construct the meaning and shape of the 'life' led to exactly that sense of closure which diaries are traditionally considered to lack, 'the consciousness of a sort of end of our life' as she put it (3 January 1917), a supposition which is common in her diaries of the early 1920s, and which appears to be reflected in the apparently declining impulse to make annual accounts at the year end visible from 1918, and in moves from 1917 onwards towards 'writing up' her life in the volumes that were to become *My Apprenticeship* and *Our Partnership*.

To this extent Webb's later diaries echo the sense of closure, of being somehow post-autobiographical, visible in Bamford's diaries. Yet Webb went, as had Haydon before her, someway further, seeking to use her diary as the core of an autobiography. From 1917 she was selecting and preparing diary material for the publication of what became *My Apprenticeship* (1926) and *Our Partnership* (1946). In both cases, but particularly for *Our Partnership*, these volumes relied heavily on the presentation of extracts from the diary, with linking and contextualising editorial material. In 1839, Haydon had already begun the task of composing an autobiography out of his diary and other papers. By the time of his death he had produced two volumes of a manuscript 'Life and Correspondence', but these only took the story up to 1820. At times during the preparation of her autobiographies, Webb wondered whether she might not just transcribe and prepare her diaries, and leave them as the account of her life, and in the will which he composed just before his suicide in 1846 Haydon placed himself in pretty much this position; leaving his manuscripts and memoirs in the possession of Elizabeth Barrett, he indicated that he wanted them published, remarking that in addition to the 'Life' up to 1820, 'my journals will supply the rest'.[35]

How far could a diary act in such a way in lieu of an autobiography? Nineteenth-century diarists seem to have envisaged a number of different ways in which it might do so. For some it was simply their physical form which enabled diaries to embody autobiography, as in the 26 nearly uniform vellum-bound volumes (8″ by 13″) along with three smaller notebooks which made up Haydon's diary, or the 54 handsome black morocco bound leather volumes in which Sir Edward W. Hamilton preserved and displayed his.[36] Even Arthur Benson's diary, although written in a large number of unprepossessing notebooks, was given some element of the status of imposing material object by its preservation in a specially constructed great black wooden chest echoing the cabinets on stands in which Joseph Farington preserved his diary, or the chest in which Lady Arbuthnot's diary was preserved after her death.

For others the diary, although itself lacking the form necessary to ape a published autobiography, was nevertheless conceived along with related papers as comprising a personal 'archive' which could be bequeathed to family members or to a literary executor for publication as a testament, even if those to whom the job was entrusted often proved unreliable instruments. Michael Millgate's study of a number of nineteenth-century 'testamentary practices' has alerted us to the extent to which the tradition of the Victorian 'life and letters' biography was associated with the careful management of personal archives, and this practice was widespread among nineteenth century diarists, prominent or obscure, many of whom followed Haydon's use of a will to provide for the posthumous publication of their diaries.[37] Significantly, many diarists who had assumed for most of the period of their writing that their diaries would be destroyed on or at their death, ultimately chose, even if selectively, to have them preserved.

The preparation of one's diaries for posterity was widely practised. Sometimes this involved little more than the writing up of a fair copy of the diary, of the sort that John Allen Giles produced in 1878 out of his volumes of diary letterbooks, in effect creating a set of memoirs.[38] Gathorne Hardy, the politician who kept a diary from the time he left Oxford in 1837 to his death in 1906, commenced in 1872 a summary of the diary, intended as an abridged version for this children, after which he planned to destroy the originals. Ultimately the summary only reached 1885 and the whole of the original text survived. Even for those unable to resist the temptation to make good errors and polish the prose, the intention exemplified by the diaries of Charles Greville, one of the most widely read of the nineteenth century diarists, remained publication in its original diary form. It was quite normal for diarists to censor their texts, sometimes engaging in wholesale mutilation and destruction of the manuscript, as in the case of Olive Garnett, most of whose diary from its inception in 1890 to its conclusion just before her death in 1956 was carefully preserved, although eight of the 15 booklets for the period June 1890 to October 1892 were entirely destroyed, and pages were ripped from the rest. Although such activity was clearly designed to produce a more defined and controlled record, it could also serve to generate an ever more complex set of autobiographical practices. Hence John Wodehouse, Earl of Kimberley, not only added an autobiographical preface, but also later engaged in a systematic process of editing and excision, while at the same time compiling a journal of events and a thousand-page manuscript memoir based largely on his diary but with supplementary material (which was subsequently destroyed, although the diary survived).[39]

Often, however, as the cases of both Haydon and Webb demonstrate, diaries were exploited for the purposes of producing a memoir or autobiography that transcended the diary text, although it drew extensively on it in ways which mimicked the life and letters tradition. There are signs that both Haydon and Webb considered the process of constructing an account of their lives out of the record of their own diary and the parallel material available in the autobiographies and biographies of their contemporaries as straightforward exercises; 'have I not got the diaries and bits out of other people's autobiographies to play with?' remarked Webb; Webb also saw the exercise as one of 'piecing it together into a connected whole' which the diary itself lacked. Yet both instances also suggest a certain ambivalence, and the possibility that this process involved a degree of deference to the diary sufficient (at the very least) to constrain the autobiographical impulse, and perhaps even impede it. Like many diarists who sought to write an autobiography, Haydon's writing of his life allotted the diary a much more significant role than that of source. For the years after 1808, indeed, verbatim transcriptions of the diary, with occasional intrusions of new material, particular for those periods when the diary was sparse, provided the bulk of his text. Likewise Webb's two volumes are marked by a progressively greater reliance on wholesale transcription of the diary text, framed by editorial commentaries which were largely confined to making good gaps in the diary record or providing the contextual material necessary for the reader to understand the diaries fully. In effect, what both Haydon and Webb produced was more a self-edited edition of their diaries than an autobiography.

It was common for Victorian and early twentieth-century biographers to regret not having a diary on which to draw when writing their memoirs. Yet the record suggests that the richer and more comprehensive the diary record, the more inhibiting it could be to the preparation of an independent autobiography. Take John Epps, nineteenth-century phrenologist and radical, who had a longstanding desire to prepare his autobiography, composed a number of autobiographical fragments, dictated some accounts of his life to his wife, but never managed to proceed further, so that on his death his life had to be compiled by his wife in the traditional manner out of his diary and surviving corres-pondence.[40] Diaries challenged autobiographers with an authenticity which magnified the treacheries of hindsight.[41] They undercut those processes of mapping a coherent narrative and constructing a unified subject which were at the heart of the autobiographical project. They could create a powerful sense of alienation and lack of comprehension between the autobiographer and their former selves. Composing his autobiography in 1877, the artist William Bell Scott remarked that old letters and memoirs he had been rereading had 'affected me as if I must have had *a double*: a creature personating me, whose writing these documents were – so much do we change with the changing years'.[42] In composing his *Memoirs*, Mark Pattison, the Oxford don, engaged with his diary as if it were that of a stranger; instead of using it to jog his memory and prompt recollection, Pattison confessed having 'great difficulty' with the diary, and was forced to treat it as a text which required analysis, ultimately conceding, as had many before him, that '[p]erhaps the best way of exhibiting my state of mind in this period is to give some extracts from the Diary', the combined capitalisation and capitulation itself indicating the status he accorded the manuscript as a record of his life.[43]

It is notable how few Victorian autobiographers were long-term diarists, and those that were either produced the sort of impersonal memoirs which focused attention, not on the author, but on character sketches and anecdotes of those with whom they had been acquainted, or were those who had maintained the sort of brief chronicle which Charles Darwin kept, which did not trench unduly on the exercise of reconstruction involved in his extended autobiographical chapter.[44] The most successful Victorian diarist–autobiographers were those who deliberately repudiated an intent to produce a comprehensive narrative of their lives, and concentrated instead on the representation of a particular strand. Ruskin's comment in *Praeterita*, that 'How I learned the things I taught is the major, and properly, only question regarded in this history',[45] or Newman's acknowledgment that the account of the development of his religious ideas he presented in his *Apologia pro Vita Sua* did not represent an 'adequate account' of his life, even for the limited years it covered, both demonstrate this strategy at work.

Newman was one of many diarists, including Webb, whose continuation of their diaries after the publishing of an autobiography, or whose confession of a sense of having completed their 'life's work' marked their diary as an element in a continual struggle to maintain control over that life story.[46] Not content with the common weeding and burning through which most diarists sought to establish control, Newman wrote two further autobiographical manuscripts in the 1870s, and also kept a further journal whose scattered entries were especially preoccupied with his life and its meanings.[47] These writings demonstrate that Bamford was not alone in deploying the diary less to make sense of his life than to manage its circulation and reception, and they also show the way that, as for both Bamford and Haydon, the diary operated as the unifying nexus of an autobiographical presence which came to be embodied in a number of disparate texts operating interdependently with the diary.

At the moment at which Victorian Britain came of age, its diarists and their diaries were already a matter both of ridicule and of concern. That at least was one of the messages of *Mr Nightingale's Diary*, Dickens' and Lemon's farce, performed on behalf of the Guild of Literature and Art at the Theatre Royal, Haymarket, in May 1851, and in the following months and years at a number of provincial towns and cities. Mr

Nightingale's diary invited audiences to question much of the conventional wisdom of diary keeping. Although harbouring the 'terrible secret' that he had been regularly paying off his wife while pretending that she was dead, the notional privacy of the diary was constantly challenged by its visibility, its physical intrusiveness and indeed by Mr Nightingale's tendency to leave it lying around where it could be read by all and sundry. Far from providing a mode of self-discipline and self-help, the diary served as a corrosive psychological crutch, and sign of his weakness of character. Begun as an aide-mémoire, the diary had become Nightingale's only memory, producing not only an unconquerable compulsion to enter information and observations of events as they happened, but an inability to conceive of his life outside its pages, indeed a conflation of life and journal. 'Really,' Nightingale remarks at the height of the play's action, 'this will be the most eventful day in my Diary, except one, – that day which consigned me to Mrs Nightingale and twenty years of misery'.[48] The time has perhaps come when we can take up the challenge *Mr Nightingale's Diary* offers to the ways in which we conceive of the relationship between the diary and autobiography, to recognise the complex cultural, symbolic and textual operations of the diary, and to place it at the heart of discussions of life writing, with respect not just to the feminine or domestic life, but also to the masculine and the public life.

Notes

1. This is perhaps to oversimplify the conclusions of the most significant study of diary writing before the 1990s, Robert Fothergill's *Private Chronicles. A Study of English Diaries* (London: Oxford UP, 1974), which does explore the ability of some diaries to operate as a 'book of life'; but Fothergill's approach is that these diaries are exceptions which transcend the limits of the genre (p.34 and *passim*), in contrast to the argument advanced here that the autobiographical function of the diary is inherent in and integral to the genre.
2. For some of the most important recent texts of this considerable literature, see Suzanne Bunkers and Cynthia A Huff, *Inscribing the Daily: Essays on Women's Diaries* (Amherst: University of Massachusetts Press, 1997); Rachel Langford and Russell West (eds), *Marginal Voices, Marginal Forms: Diaries in European Literature and History* (Amsterdam: Rodopi, 1999).
3. Regenia Gagnier, *Subjectivities; a history of self-representation in Britain, 1832–1920* (London: Oxford UP, 1991), p.31.
4. For texts of these diaries see Martin Hewitt and Robert Poole (eds), *The Diaries of Samuel Bamford* (Aldershot: Ashgate, 2000), manuscript held in the Manchester Central Libraries, Archive Department; W.B. Pope (ed.), *The Diary of Benjamin Robert Haydon* (Cambridge, MA: Harvard UP, 5 vols, 1963), manuscript in the Haydon Papers (MS Eng 1331), Houghton Library,

Harvard University; Norman and Jeanne MacKenzie (eds), *The Diary of Beatrice Webb* (London: Virago, 4 vols, 1982–85), manuscript British Library of Political and Economic Science, Archives Division, available in typescript and holograph on microfiche, Chadwyck-Healey, 1978. Only small fragments of Benson's diary have been published, first in Percy Lubbock (ed.), *Diary of A.C. Benson* (London: Hutchinson and Co, 1926) and then in David Newsome, *Edwardian Excursions* (London: Murray, 1981); manuscript, Magdalene College, Cambridge. In all cases reference to these diaries will be parenthetically by date of entry wherever appropriate.

5. Philip Davis, *Memory and Writing. From Wordsworth to Lawrence* (Liverpool: Liverpool University Press, 1983); Brian Maidment, *The Poorhouse Fugitives: self-taught poets and poetry in Victorian Britain* (Manchester: Carcanet, 1987); Gagnier, *Subjectivities*.

6. In its basic structure, *Passages*, with its highly fragmented presentation of particular episodes, roughly stitched together, might be said to be written as much as journal or travel diary as autobiography.

7. See Bamford *Diary*, pp.358–66.

8. J.A.V. Chapple and A. Pollard, *The Letters of Mrs Gaskell* (Manchester: Manchester UP, 1966), Letter 59.

9. Tom Taylor (ed.), *The Autobiography and Memoirs of B.R. Haydon* (London: Peter Davis, 1926; or.1853), p.1.

10. Bamford to Charles Potter, 20 February 1859, Bamford, *Diary*, p.70.

11. Stuart Sherman, *Telling Time: Clocks, Diaries and the English Diurnal Form 1660–1785* (Chicago: University of Chicago Press, 1996), Felicity Nussbaum, *The Autobiographical Subject. Gender and Ideology in Eighteenth Century England* (Baltimore: Johns Hopkins UP, 1989); *Letts Keep a Diary* (London: Letts, 1988).

12. Rebecca Steinitz, 'Shared Secrets and Torn Pages: Diaries and Journals in Nineteenth Century British Society and Literature', PhD dissertation, University of California, Berkeley (1997). Professor Steinitz's thesis provided an important point of departure for this essay, as well as some key ideas. I am grateful also for copies of a number of items of work in progress which she provided.

13. Kathryn Carter, 'The cultural work of diaries in mid-century Victorian Britain', *Victorian Review*, 23:2 (Winter 1997), 252–67, esp. 254–5. For *Leaves* see Steinitz, 'Shared Secrets', 174–94.

14. For the very interesting case of Waugh, see P. Joyce, *Democratic Subjects. The Self and the Social in Nineteenth Century England* (Cambridge: Cambridge UP, 1994), pp.23–82.

15. Haydon, *Diary*, 13 April 1838, 25 January 1838, 31 January 1838, 16 April 1843, 3 June 1843.

16. David Newsome, *On the Edge of Paradise. A.C Benson: the Diarist* (London: John Murray, 1980), p.80; Lubbock, *Diary of A.C. Benson*, pp.41, 59, 61, 80, 123, 150, 214; Webb, *Diary*, 31 March 1877.

17. 'The Use of a Diary', cited in Charles Letts, *Notes on Some Celebrated Diarists and Their Diaries* (London: Letts & Co. [1888]), p.14.

18. Judy Taylor (ed.), *The Journal of Beatrix Potter, 1881–1897* (London: Frederick Warne, 1989).

19. A. Johnson, *The Diary of Thomas Giordani Wright. Newcastle Doctor, 1826–29* (Woodbridge: Boydell Press, 2001).

20. F. Haydon, *B.R. Haydon. Correspondence and Table Talk* (London: Chatto and Windus, 1876), p.456.
21. Dudley W.R. Bahlman, *The Diary of Sir Edward Walter Hamilton, 1880–1885* (Oxford, Clarendon Press,1972).
22. See Newsome, *On the Edge of Paradise.*
23. A.C. Benson, *Life and Letters of Maggie Benson* (London: John Murray, 1917), pp.260–410.
24. Evan Charteris, *The Life and Letters of Sir Edmund Gosse* (London: William Heinemann, 1931), p.375; E.H. Ryle, *Arthur Christopher Benson as seen by some friends* (London: Bell, 1925), p.16.
25. For examples of these attitudes, see 'Diarists of the Last Century', *Quarterly Review*, 197 (1903), 186–207; Letts, *Celebrated Diarists* [1888]. There is a useful discussion of the nineteenth-century reviews of Pepys in Steinitz, 'Shared Secrets', 142–74.
26. Diary of Virginia Woolf, 20 April 1919, cited in Harriet Blodgett, *Centuries of Female Days: English Women's Private Diaries* (Rutgers, NJ: Rutgers UP, 1988), p.21.
27. Allan Cunningham, *Life of David Wilkie* (London: John Murray, 1843); other examples include John Wodehouse: see Angus Hawkins and John Powell (eds), *The Journal of John Wodehouse, First Earl of Kimberley for 1862–1902* (London: RHS, Camden, 5th series, 1997).
28. Haydon, *Table Talk*, II, p.247.
29. Norma Virgoe and Susan Yaxley (eds), *The Banville Diaries. Journals of a Norfolk Gamekeeper, 1822–44* (London: Collins, 1986), p.19.
30. For this point, and discussion which has very much influenced the argument of this and the following paragraphs, see Steinitz, 'Shared Secrets', 37–50, 166–9.
31. Lady Charlotte Bury, *Diary of a Lady in Waiting* (London: John Lane, 1838, 1908), p.49. Compare with the comments of Lady Arbuthnot, Francis Bamford and Duke of Wellington (eds), *The Journal of Mrs Arbuthnot, 1820-1823* (London: Macmillan, 1950), I, p.122.
32. See J.H. Fowler, *The Life and Letters of Edward Lee Hicks (Bishop of Lincoln, 1910–1919)* (London: Christophers, 1922).
33. See, for example, entries for 30 December 1841, 19 September 1843.
34. See, for example, Mary Brigg (ed.), *The Journals of a Lancashire Weaver, 1856–60, 1860–64, 1872–75* (Manchester: Record Society of Lancashire and Cheshire, 1982).
35. Haydon, *Diary*, V, p.556.
36. James Greig (ed.), *The Farington Diary* (London: Hutchinson, 1923), Bahlman, *Diary of Sir E.W. Hamilton.*
37. Michael Millgate, *Testamentary Acts. Browning, Tennyson, James, Hardy* (Oxford: Clarendon Press, 1992).
38. David Bromwich (ed.), *The diary and memoirs of John Allen Giles* (Taunton: Somerset Record Society, 2000).
39. *Journal of John Wodehouse.*
40. Ellen Epps (ed.), *Diary of the Late John Epps, M.D.* (London: John Kent and Co., 1875).
41. See, for example, the comments in A.J.C. Hare, *The Story of My Life,* vol. I (London: George Allen, 1896), p.ix.
42. W. Minto (ed.), *Autobiographical Notes of the Life of William Bell Scott,* 2 vols (New York: AMS Press, 1892; 1970), p.4.

43. Mark Pattison, *Memoirs* (Fontwell: Centaur Press, 1969), p.189.
44. Gavin de Beer, *Charles Darwin, Thomas Henry Huxley. Autobiographies* (Oxford: Oxford UP, 1974); Gavin de Beer, 'Diaries of Charles Darwin', *Bulletin of the Natural History Museum* (Historical Series), (1959).
45. John Ruskin, *Praeterita* (Orpington: George Allen, 1889, 1899), p.337.
46. For an example of the latter, see Lord Ronald Sutherland Gower, *Old Diaries, 1881–1901* (London: John Murray, 1902).
47. See Henry Tristram (ed.), *John Henry Newman. Autobiographical Writings* (London and New York: Sheed and Ward, 1956).
48. Leona Weaver Fisher, *Lemon, Dickens, and* Mr Nightingale's Diary: *a Victorian Farce* (Victoria, BC: University of Victoria, 1988), p.171; see also Carter, 'Cultural work'.

CHAPTER TWO

Men and Women of the Time
Victorian Prosopographies

Alison Booth

It is obviously a distortion to personify the 'spirit' of any 'age' through a set of biographies of contemporaries. Yet nineteenth-century Britain could fairly be described as a period that sped up production of collective portraiture of 'men of the time.' Richard Altick in the mid-twentieth century characterised a Victorian 'age of biography' jumbled with biographical collections or prosopographies: series of 'Eminent Women, English Men of Action ... English Worthies'; 'capsule lives' in magazines; 'biographical encyclopedias'; 'specialized compilations' of 'painters, architects ... Irishmen,'; a 'low-brow Protestant *Acta Sanctorum*' of religious and social missionaries.[1] Altick, like most successors of the Victorians, assumes that the generic *type* of biography is the full-length prose work analogous to the novel, representing an eminent individual in their imperfections: in short, Boswell's *Life of Johnson*. Yet Altick's own study of the Victorians, like so many contributions to cultural history, resembles a series of parallel subjects, as in Plutarch or Johnson's *Lives of the Poets*, more than a monument to one great man. The vast majority of 'lives' in any period have been published in groups rather than singly. The British in the nineteenth century proliferated collections of memorial tributes to enhance a national heritage.[2] From William Hazlitt's *The Spirit of the Age: Or, Contemporary Portraits* (1825) to Leslie Stephen's *Dictionary of National Biography* (1885 onward)[3] – and through many symposia of the living or dead, men or women, separately or intermingled – the Victorian age was prosopographical.

Studies of biography have been dominated by an individualist model of identity and development, and have privileged the verbal over the visual text, to the neglect of longstanding conventions of collective representation.[4] Every literate society has generated multibiographies or prosopographies with more or less overt aims of propagating civility. 'Prosopography', literally, the writing of masks, has been a term for positivist methods of composing the history of elite groups through comparative life narratives.[5] In classical or medieval studies, 'prosopography' suggests methods of interpreting patterns in clustered remains: coins, military or religious annals, funerary fragments.[6] I revive the term because of its etymological association with the rhetoric of prosopopoeia: according to the *OED*, 'a rhetorical figure by which an imaginary or absent person is represented as speaking or acting', or 'by which an inanimate or abstract thing is represented as a person'.[7] At the same time, the word signals the importance of the portrait, the representation (*prosopon* or mask) of the embodied person. Far from establishing a representative biographical history, prosopography always reveals the incoherence and exclusivity in what Raymond Williams calls 'selective traditions',[8] or what Benedict Anderson conceives as 'imagined communities'.[9] Victorian prosopographies, like those of today, may take varied forms, ranging from printed books to monuments, plaques, pageants and calendars, as means of registering the interrelated names, narratives and visual representations of personae.

Rather than mount a great exhibition of Victorian prosopography in a brief essay, I shall draw some interconnections among men and women of letters in biographical collections published in London, specifically those that portrayed literary homes. These books incorporate representations in media in several dimensions and diverse locales, including portraits, gravesites, the plaques and signs marking buildings and sites, as well as house museums. I wish to characterise such prosopographical practice, its bricolage of texts, images and sites, as memorials of the changing literary profession and gender ideology across the century. Predictably the recognition of women of various professions burgeons in the Victorian period, both in successful infiltration of women into such reference works as *Men of the Time* (1852–99) and in the explosion of all-female collective biographies, which produced as many as forty books (not counting reference works) in a single year, 1893. But the inter-mixture of renowned women and men follows no simple pattern of progress – or decline. On the one hand, early nineteenth-century literary circles were stratified by gender, and yet some contemporary prosopographies show surprising inclusiveness within a British (often Irish) class of those who wrote for a living. On the other hand, the recollections published en masse in the last third of the century give women a great deal of 'play' as more than hostesses or helpmeets, although at the same time the professionalisation of authorship and criticism tended to deflect attention from women writers. Meanwhile, at mid-century, a model developed for domestic partnerships in literary and cultural work that reacted against the Regency excesses of men without women or of women among men. The weird Lambs might be the forerunners of the Victorian working couple, but the Gaskells, the Brownings, the Carlyles and the 'Leweses', for all their different tempers and circumstances, suggest the domestic literary mission of the age.[10]

To characterize such shifting collective representations, I will exhibit William Hazlitt's and R.H. Horne's different contributions to the *Spirit of the Age*; William Bates's edition of *The Maclise Portrait Gallery of Illustrious Literary Characters*, originally published as a series of portraits by Maclise and prose sketches by Maginn in *Fraser's Magazine* from 1830–38 (1874, rev. edn 1883); and *A Book of Memories of Great Men and Women of the Age, from Personal Acquaintance* (1871) by 'S.C. Hall', that is, Samuel Carter Hall and Anna Maria Hall.[11] I limit my focus to a few contributors to the growing field of literary prosopography who early recognised the desire for a literature *at home* in many senses. This literature was associated with 'at homes' of respectable writers; with representations of the homes and haunts of writers; with nostalgia or home-sickness for the origins of writers as sources of inspiration; and with an effort to reconcile genius and immortality in the English literary canon and domestic ideology. Mary Russell Mitford early perfected the topographical essay and helped her readers to feel welcome in the literary landscape in a way emulated by two literary couples, Mr and Mrs S.C. Hall and William and Mary Howitt. I will concentrate on the Halls, with some consideration of the Howitts and of William Bates, the later custodian of the Fraserian *Gallery* and interpreter of the Halls' *Memories*. Their stories begin to account for the increasing demand for paraliterary material, from signed portraits to short lives to charted and labelled houses. Why, after all, does it matter where and how the poet lived?

The Halls serve as well as any of their contemporaries to illustrate the apportionment of recognition among living or dead men and women, as well as the customs of prosopography of writers, particularly the desire to locate a literary home. They lived in the thick of English and Irish literature and art from about 1820 to 1880, but they are now rather elusive. Both were born in Ireland and transplanted in London. Mrs Hall gained the greater recognition, as an 'Irish' novelist, though she left Ireland at age fifteen. William Bates claims that Mrs Hall 'has become ... naturalized' as an Englishwoman, but is gifted in depicting 'the people among whom her earliest and most impressionable days were passed' (*Gallery*, p.367); for this gift she was featured by Maclise and Maginn as part of the notable literati of the early 1830s.[12] Mr Hall called himself an Englishman, and some sources give him English birth, though he remained in Ireland until his early twenties (longer than his wife ['Keane', p.135]). Perhaps all the more urgently, he insists that 'the native country of a man is not determined by the accident of birth' (*Memories*, p.82).[13] Now dimly identified with the history of English art through his long editorship of *The Art Journal* and its *Illustrated Catalogue of the Great Exhibition, London 1851*,[14] Hall was very much the editor, collector and collaborator in the shadows of writers and artists. The

Halls co-authored an exquisite pioneering guide to Ireland, and they emulated Mitford's and William Howitt's topographical and biographical sketches of 'homes and haunts' in England. Though they put up historic plaques before the 'Blue Plaque Scheme' officially began in 1867, they seem never to have become objects of pilgrimage themselves.[15] The Halls are both well treated (by George Clement Boase) in the *DNB* (8: pp.969–70; 971–3), yet neither appears in that august prosopography, the National Portrait Gallery.[16]

The Halls were professional hunters of birthplaces, though evidently waiving environmental determinism in Samuel Carter Hall's case at least. They regarded it as a duty 'to place memorials of gratitude on the graves of those "who rule/ Our spirits from their urns"' (*Memories*, p.487) and they set great store by such relics as Coleridge's inkstand and favourite tree.[17] Their own role in paying tribute to a collective memory of literary Britain had been dedicated, if insufficiently prescient: 'we have never kept notes, not having foreseen a time when our Recollections of "Great People" ... might become interesting and instructive. Moreover, we have preserved but few of the many letters. ... We have given freely to collectors of Autographs; while with a carelessness we deplore, we have destroyed manuscripts and communication we would now give much to have kept' (*Memories*, p.ix). Nevertheless the Halls might be considered early prophets of a religion of literature that developed new rites in their lifetimes. The value of documents and relics of literary lives clearly rose by the 1870s, and it soars with collectors and scholars today, just as the pilgrimage persists in literary walking tours or house museums. Of course the origins of these practices predate the new literary marketplace associated with early nineteenth-century magazines and annuals in which the Halls and many others were concerned.

Witnesses of the literary movements associated with those publications never quite got over the experience; later scholars, similarly awed but unhindered by personal memory, called the period Romantic and shortened the prosopography to six major male poets. Those who 'knew Wordsworth', in the words of the feckless Mr Brooke in *Middlemarch*, nevertheless knew also that it was a crowded social calendar in those exhilarating days. The memories of those who touched the hem of the sacred garments become more precious as they fade. S.C. Hall recalls, '"There were giants on earth" when I was young'; of late there were many more writers and readers, but of ordinary stature (*Memories*, p.487). William Bates, B.A.,[18] seems awestruck by S.C. Hall as a witness of giants, quoting his 'charming *Book of Memories*' in a new edition of the portraits by Maclise and Maginn (p.xi). Bates testifies that the Maclise images increase in value with the demise of those capable of comparing them with the originals: 'Mr. S.C. Hall, a most competent authority, speaks of them as "admirable as likenesses, and capital as specimens of art"' (pp.vi–vii).

The theme of a golden age and decline is familiar enough. At the same time, the Halls, Bates and others affirm the moral and social progress since the day of those giants. The Victorians' orthodox worship of a great tradition, a tradition much more diverse than the twentieth-century canon made it, takes place in a time of retreat from cavalier male bonding, in an era in which the Halls' domestic collaboration and promotion of cultural knowledge and taste, temperance and Christian faith were considered exemplary. Ironically the ethos that gave Mary Russell Mitford, Anna Maria Hall and Mary Howitt considerable power as literary arbiters as well as models of middle-class femininity contributed to the more segregated literary profession by the end of the century. As the professional guilds and academic disciplines formed, they reproduced the homosocial structure of the 'Fraserians' and other coteries associated with magazines and clubs. Meanwhile later nineteenth-century associations of male writers repudiated the spirit of Evangelical reform and the sentimental literature of the annuals (in which women flourished as poets and essayists) and enforced the separation of spheres that had for a time been a source of women's authority. In due course, critics such as Edmund Gosse and Harold Nicolson sought to purify biography as an art form that represents eminent individuals without veneration. Victorian prosopographies of women and men, designed as clustered eulogies, could not measure up by modernist standards, and are largely forgotten now. From a later vantage, however, it is remarkable that the biographical collections were so durable, preserving unexpectedly diverse images and narratives of both the domestic-minded reformers and their unregenerate predecessors, of women among the men. Mrs S.C. Hall and a set of women writers of the 1830s stand among the 'giants.' Prosopographies of *Literary Characters*, sustained throughout the century, sought glimpses of the homes and origins of both male and female writers.

Men (and Women) of the Time

On the face of it, the adjustments in one forerunner of *Who's Who* reflect the changing climate for prosopography, though the volumes are arid pages of close print without illustrations. As the periodical press expanded from the 1820s onward, writers and readers needed reference works for a key to the living figures in the historical canvas, which attempted to be both national and international. *The Men of the Time* was published in London in 1852, with an ostensibly independent,

Americanised counterpart in New York in that same year.[19] Alphabetised
only by first letter of the surname (with an index), it appears to be an
entirely male catalogue, with the notable exception of Queen Victoria,
whose 'rapidly increasing family' is 'a rather expensive blessing for the
English people' (p.518). Yet there are occasional signs of the existence of
a second sex within the narratives concerning men. Thus Robert
Browning's short entry notes that he is the 'husband of a gifted poetess,
formerly Miss Barrett' (p.66). Carlyle's longer entry notes simply that he
married an unnamed person 'in 1825 or 1826' and then quotes at length
from a letter to Goethe that speaks for both Carlyles, describing their
home in Craigenputtoch as a '"green oasis"' in a '"wilderness"' (p.116).
Several prosopographers of women join the list – Rufus Griswold,
Samuel Goodrich, Charles Sainte-Beuve – but for other reasons. William
Howitt receives significant recognition (longer than that of Ralph Waldo
Emerson) with some notice of Mary Howitt, 'now familiar to the public'
(p.268). Mr Hall claims a brief entry of little weight: he 'was born about
1800. His most successful volumes have been those in which his talented
wife has been also engaged' (p.250). In such a volume, the 'bios' are
truncated narratives: birth, marriage, works, perhaps travels or honours.
Death by definition is extratextual.

   Men of the Time notwithstanding, the year 1852 faced no shortage of
celebrations of women; at least twenty-seven collections of female
biography appeared. Mrs S.C. Hall joined Queen Victoria, Hannah
More, Felicia Hemans and other queens, philanthropists and writers in
Lives of Illustrious Women of England (1853).[20] In 1851, Mary Howitt
had edited a prosopography of English queens.[21] Neither hardworking
writer–wife, Hall or Howitt, reached as high levels of popularity in
biographies as did, in later decades, Elizabeth Barrett Browning and, to
a lesser extent, Jane Welsh Carlyle.[22] Alongside such separate and not-
quite-equal figuration, the mainstream prosopographies seem to respond
to pressure to integrate a more complete picture of the cultural enterprise
of the period. Under the editorship of Alaric Alexander Watts, close
friend of the Howitts who introduced them to the Halls,[23] the British
Men of the Time in 1856 added subtitles: *Biographical Sketches of
Eminent Living Characters; Also Biographical Sketches of Women of the
Time*. These became 'Celebrated Women' in editions of 1857 and 1859.

   The Preface in the 1859 edition gives some indication of the plan and
the need for such a prosopography: it is to be a 'special record' of 'the
Aristocracy of Genius' to complement available lists of the peerage, the
military, and various professions; in being 'limited to no particular class,
[it] addresses itself to all' (pp.iii–iv). The Preface distinguishes the special
requirements of an impartial reference to the living: whereas 'necrologies
of eminent persons' are readily produced and available, records of living

contemporaries are elusive, 'highly coloured by party or professional prejudice' (p.iv) or arbitrarily selected or apportioned (p.v). Following Addenda concerning men inadvertently omitted, the editor Watts assigns women to their own annex (pp.773–895); like the recently dead or missing persons, women supplement Men of the Time.[24] Among more or less prominent women of letters, the appendix includes such perennially famous figures as Florence Nightingale and Queen Victoria (now grouped with the women). Mrs Hall receives an entry almost twice as long as her husband's in this edition. It notes her 'series of pleasant illustrated sketches of the homes and haunts of genius and virtue in our own little island ... "Pilgrimages to English Shrines"', a counterpart to the Halls' study of Ireland (p.831). For the Howitts, the husband's entry extends further than the wife's; it notes somewhat inaccurately William's 1847 work, *Homes and Haunts*,[25] commenting: 'All gossip about poets, and things and places associated with their genius, is full of interest. Mr. Howitt has been on terms of personal friendship with most of his poetical contemporaries, and has really visited all the localities he has described' (p.384). Howitt indeed proved the appeal of a blend of prose pastoral, literary prosopography and travel guide as well as the increasing value of authenticated, on-site reminiscences. He assumed that signs of female genius should likewise be preserved: Mrs Tighe, Mrs Hemans, L.E.L., and Joanna Baillie accompany thirty-seven men in Howitt's two illustrated volumes.

In the 1860s–80s, a succession of editors updated *Men of the Time* with varying subtitles to bridge a gender gap: *Eminent Living Characters (Including Women)*, or *Eminent Characters of Both Sexes*.[26] The twelfth edition, edited by Thomas Humphry Ward in 1887, at last integrates the sexes alphabetically in a thick volume printed in columns. Samuel Carter Hall appears (birthdate wrongly given as 1801) in a somewhat expanded entry. Whereas it claims that a list of the 340 publications of 'Mr. and Mrs. Hall would occupy more space than can be spared in this work' (p.479), it devotes most of Mary Howitt's simplified entry to the much shorter list of the works she wrote 'after becoming the wife of the late Mr. William Howitt' (pp.553–4). Anna Maria Hall has been demoted to a mere listing in the 'Necrology', having died on 30 January 1881 (p.1096), not far from William Howitt (d. 3 March 1879; p.1099). In their death Hall and Howitt couples *were* divided, at least for the purposes of living prosopography. The living/dead difference is, we must agree, less negotiable than the male/female, which this series had overcome at last (though men remained the majority).[27] The longtime publisher of *Men of the Time*, Routledge, finally relinquished the popular title, yielding *Men and Women of the Time: A Dictionary of Contemporaries* (ed. Victor Plarr) from 1889 to 1899.

The Spirit of the Age

Men of the Time is the sort of just-the-facts compilation of half-lives that has become common in the succeeding century and more, from print to digital. Some assemblies of the 'living', however, are more interpretative selections, recording more than birth and deeds. Hazlitt's anonymous *Spirit of the Age*, first published in *The New Monthly Magazine* in 1824, is exclusively male, unlike comparable works before it.[28] Hazlitt's homosocial group portrait was also out of step with the ensuing age in sustaining the concept of 'portrait' as metaphor only, instead of producing illustrations of faces, houses or gravesites. Though *ad hominem* enough to be provoking, Hazlitt's studies lack the biographical or topographical concreteness expected by the 1840s. Hazlitt neither visits a poet's homes nor consults letters or laundry lists, but rather supplies comparative impressions of living writers or political figures and their works.[29]

Richard Henry Horne, with the help of 'several hands', issued a sequel in 1844, *A New Spirit of the Age*,[30] because 'a new set of men, several of them animated by a new spirit, have obtained eminent positions in the public mind' (Preface, p.iv). Lengthy 'Introductory Comments', added to a second edition within the first year, admit: 'I was upon dangerous ground at every step, and I knew it' (pp.vi–vii). *Men of the Time* was likewise a collection of anonymous entries edited by a named individual, but it avoided controversy by eschewing detail or criticism. Horne, accused of running a 'clique and coterie', finds his origins, his works, even 'his place of residence' (p.xviii) are held against him, as they were held against Hazlitt, but Horne counters that he is even better qualified as a gentleman of letters than Hazlitt. If they accuse Horne of being an untravelled provincial, they should note that Hazlitt wrote *The Spirit of the Age* in London at a time when Horne was a junior officer in Mexico and Florida (p.xix). That is, Horne aspires to present a cosmopolitan panorama of the literary world, yet the credentials he presents as an insider in the spirit of the age show rather that his career and identity have been in flux.

Horne's 'new set of men' includes women. Eight out of the thirty-nine names in Horne's table of contents register women such as Harriet Martineau, Mary Shelley and Elizabeth Barrett Browning; the latter was one of his female collaborators.[31] An image of Martineau appears among the printed portraits, another aspect of the greater biographical immediacy of Horne's collection than of Hazlitt's. In harmony with Hazlitt, however, the method is 'synthetic', evoking the spirit of the genius in relation to the times without close reading or scholarly argument.[32] The *New Spirit of the Age* finds no place for S.C. Hall, though his editorial activities overlapped with Horne's project in several ways.[33] Instead, Mrs S.C. Hall surfaces in a paragraph in a chapter on Irish novelists (*New Spirit*, pp.275–6), confirming the name she had made for herself.[34] In 1844, Mr S.C. Hall was her male counterpart, comparatively anonymous as an itinerant editor.

The spirit of the Halls is nevertheless present in Horne's collection. Mary Gillies, probably the anonymous contributor of the biography of William and Mary Howitt, portrays a happy couple much like the Halls. The Howitts profited on new demand for descriptive volumes animating the British Isles and other lands, and they proved 'how much literature may contribute to the happiness of life' without detracting from the wife's domestic duties (*New Spirit*, p.119). The biographer places the Howitts in 'a new class of writing ... the unaffected prose pastoral' (p.113). 'Miss Mitford [with *Our Village*] is undoubtedly the head of this delightful, and at present "small family"' (p.114).[35] This family included the Halls as friends and literary collaborators of the Howitts.[36] Horne himself joined in a series of domestic encounters: he frequently dined with the Howitts (and in 1852 went to Australia with Howitt father and sons ['Woodring', p.160]); like William Howitt and the Halls, Horne wrote a description of Mitford at home. Both Mitford and William Howitt emulated Washington Irving's popular *Sketch-Book of Geoffrey Crayon, Gent.* ('Woodring', p.9),[37] and Anna Maria Hall sought to match Mitford's *Our Village* when she began her writings on Irish life (*Memories*, p.438). Many reviewers drew the comparison between Mrs Hall's rough Ireland and Miss Mitford's temperate Berkshire ('Keane', pp.61–3), according to the customary characterization of writers through their 'haunts' or native landscapes.

The new spirit of the age, it seems, was plural, embodied and down to earth though it told of a long past. A favoured writer would reanimate the *genius loci*, within a collection or 'family' of personified historic places. Both the Halls and the Howitts offered topographical cures for nostalgia or homesickness through tales of a homeland or of the homes of other writers, as they exemplified literary domesticity. The Irish Halls and later the Quaker Howitts had come from different outsider status to gain standing in literary London. Similarly engaged in spiritualism ('Woodring', pp.190, 197), they espoused different politics – Anna Maria Hall opposed women's suffrage (*Memories*, pp.132–4), Mary Howitt was a feminist ('Woodring', p.180) – and different target populations: the Halls promoted the status of English art and the professionalization of governesses and nurses, while the Howitts disseminated knowledge to self-improving workers and children.

The interlocking stories of this 'family' of writers filled literary memoirs toward the end of the century as examples of the compatibility of literary and household work, of the arts and the domestic virtues. There had been a time, and would come a time again, when giants engaged in entertainments unfit for ladies. William Bates, whose belated edition of *The Maclise Portrait Gallery* draws upon the Halls' *Book of Memories*, worships the household gods of the Halls, yet he is nostalgic for the conviviality of the Fraserians. Bates treats the women in the *Gallery* with sentimental favour, but he retains some of Maginn's original misogynist caricature, and he plays Mary Russell Mitford and Mrs S.C. Hall off against each other. The customs of associating woman, the body and home prevail in these prosopographies, as does the interdependence of the narrative and the portrait.

Memories of the Gallery of Men and Women

When the Halls recorded their *Book of Memories*, it was a sort of sequel like Horne's *New Spirit*: an effort to follow up the success of Howitt's *Homes and Haunts*, Mitford's *Recollections of Literary Life* (*Memories*, p.441), and their own anthologies and 'pilgrimage' (*The Book of Gems of Poets and Artists* [1838]; *Pilgrimages to English Shrines* [1850]), among others. The narrator of the *Memories* is a self-styled 'hero-worshipper' (p.2) who had 'peculiar' 'opportunities' to know nearly all 'the distinguished men and women' of the day. The memoirist is the homodiegetic narrator of a kind of 'necrology', a 'series of WRITTEN PORTRAITS', without himself joining the series as he remains alive at the time of utterance. He has been a go-between for the century, an 'on-looker at a banquet', 'below the salt' at 'the Feast of Poets' (pp.vii–viii). Nor is Hall quite himself; the narrator becomes plural as he acknowledges 'the aid I receive from my wife. We have worked together for more than forty years: with very few exceptions my acquaintances were hers'. Much of the text is verbatim from her own publications or her own memories, though they 'have avoided reference to ourselves' (p.viii). The collaboration extends to the unspecified reasons for the sequencing of lives, shaped by the subjects' friendships, similar experiences, or association in the Halls' recollections. Each chapter in *Memories* is headed by an engraved portrait, followed by a sequence of views, usually of the birthplace, later residence, and sites of death and burial, at times embellished with favourite haunts.[38] The chapters are typographical anthologies or bouquets: literary extracts, letters in smaller font, often an enlarged holograph inserted at right angles, epitaphs, footnotes correcting or corroborating the memories, passages in Latin, abrupt shifts between Hall's first-person and 'the "Memories" of Mrs. Hall' (for example, pp.437–41). It is a commonplace book, but it is also a printed Poet's Corner, with a much wider range of women than that monumental miscellany.

In his turn, Bates saw that copies of *Fraser's Magazine* had been plundered for the Maclise–Maginn 'Characters', and that the public demanded ever more paraliterary treasure. Bates (c.1824–84), of course alive at the time of writing, seems to read himself into the carnivalesque mausoleum of the 1830s through the Halls' *Book of Memories*. Born about the time Samuel Hall arrived in London, Bates remains outside the Fraserian coterie, yet he places himself between the reader who was 'born in a later day, and remote, perchance, from lettered haunts' and the greats who inhabit his imagination (pp.x–xi). He testifies to a sort of spiritualist reanimation of the dead: 'there has been the echo of mighty voices in my ears, and a rustle beneath my feet as of dry and withered leaves in Vall'ombrosa'. With 'a deep and increasing personal curiosity' about the 'grand masterful spirits', he loves to 'trace and identify the fugitive piece, ... to snatch the "trivial fond record" from the limbo of oblivion' (p.xi). Happy in the role of mourner, Bates assembles an album similar to *A Book of Memories* in style and structure.

Bates's version of the Maclise *Gallery* and Maginn text at first might appear to be a prosopography of men's literary clubs in early nineteenth-century London, though it features women. Bates further diminishes the biographical autonomy of the women as he adds material from the decades after Maginn wrote. Bates's memoir of Mrs S.C. Hall tilts toward her husband as it approaches the present, signalled by such references as recent editions of *Men of the Time*, *A Book of Memories* (1871), the fact of Mrs Hall's death in 1881 and the forthcoming *Recollections of a Long Life* by S.C. Hall (to be published in 1883). It may have been bliss to be alive and heaven to be young among the giants of the 1830s, but Bates in his prescriptive gendering of writers stands closer to the belated reader in 1883. Unconsciously he serves the male-centred canon of later literary studies.

There was a fiction of presence and synchronicity from the very first articulation of the 'Gallery'. The famous frontispiece, 'The Fraserians', personifies another 'Noctes Ambrosianae' set of literary gentlemen drinking at a roundtable (Figure 2.1).[39] It includes some good friends of the Halls (for example, Jerdan, Lockhart), some figures who remained in the twentieth-century canon (Coleridge, Thackeray, Carlyle) and others who stood in Hall's place (Theodore Hook).[40] Yet the circle of Fraserians was imaginary: major contributors to the journal do not appear, and some at the table hardly or only later wrote for it. It was a powerful collective face or mask for the spirits, not to say dissipation, at the time.[41] The conviviality of the table even then was undermining the hopes for immortality of some of those raising the glass to *Fraser's*. Though

Figure 2.1   The Fraserians
Reproduced from William Bates, ed., *The Maclise Portrait Gallery of Illustrious Literary Characters* (London: Chatto & Windus, 1898)

the Halls and Bates seem awestruck by the giants, in the separate narratives on these heroes they apply the standards of temperance and domesticity.

Bates writes, 'After the *Newgate Calendar*, there are no sadder pages in the history of man than those afforded by the Biographies of authors': that is, of male authors (p.x).[42] The Halls in 1871, and Bates in 1883, dwell for example on Hook's and Maginn's self-destruction; Hall writes that Hook's 'career "points a moral"' about the intemperance of literary men, who make 'for themselves ... useless or pernicious lives, and unhonoured or dishonourable graves' (*Memories*, pp.160, 166; *Gallery*, p.234; and *Gallery*, quoting *Memories* on Maginn, pp.40–41). Quite apart from S.C. Hall's moderate reputation as an editor of competing journals, his absence from the Fraserian circle was consistent with the Christian and temperance teachings of most of his and Mrs Hall's publications and with their own conscientious respectability.[43] In the later context, men of letters were held to standards of propriety similar to those for women of letters (regardless of the harsher penalties for a 'suspect' such as Laetitia Landon than for her counterpart, Maginn).

I have said that women had a place in *The Gallery* of the 1830s, as in Bates's later edition, but it is in a gallery of their own, like specimens of a protected species. One entry in the original series was a prosopography itself, an ecphrasis of a group portrait, 'Regina's Maids of Honour' (that is, the ladies in waiting upon *Fraser's* nickname, 'Regina'), on the occasion of the New Year of 1836 (Figure 2.2). It is a pale, coffee-drinking answer to the male homosocial symposium.[44] The individualized caricatures of clearly named literary men in the frontispiece contrast with the set of generic females, in the inner pages, who need to be indexed. In slapdash verse printed as prose, Maginn patronizes each figure around the circle, beginning with the servant, 'Caesar or Pompey, careful black, one of Afric's injured line, standing behind a lady's back, offers, not the cups of wine, but the cups, as Cowper sings, which cheer and not inebriate' (p.353; possibly alluding to Barbauld's 'injured Afric'). Nothing illicit here:

> What are they doing? What they should; with volant tongue and chatty cheer, welcoming in, by prattle good, or witty phrase, or comment shrewd, the opening of the gay new year. MRS. HALL, so fair and fine, bids her brilliant eyes to glow, – eyes the brightest of the nine, would be but too proud to show. *Outlaw* he, and *Buccaneer*, who'd refuse to worship here. (p.355)

After Mrs Hall, and a footnote explaining the reference to titles of novels by this tenth muse, come L.E.L., Lady Morgan, Caroline Norton, the Countess of Blessington, Jane Porter, Harriet Martineau,

Figure 2.2 Regina's Maids of Honour
Reproduced from William Bates, ed., *The Maclise Portrait Gallery of Illustrious Literary Characters* (London: Chatto & Windus, 1898)

and last, the jolliest of them all, soft-seated on a well-filled bustle, her coffee sips, by Mrs. Hall – dear, darling MITFORD (MARY RUSSELL). Long may she live with graphic touch ... our English scenes in pencillings Dutch ... in all their easy, quiet beauty – their modest forms, or grave, or gay, – their homely cares, their honest duty, with heart all English to display. (p.358)[45]

Of the group, Mitford is praised most in terms of a collective English gratitude rather than as an object of the gaze or as a satiric figure of personal and literary excess.

Each of the 'Maids of Honour' earns her own separate portrait and entry in the *Gallery*. Anna Maria Hall and Mary Russell Mitford, both members of the 'family' of prose pastoralists in Horne's new spirit of the age, receive different 'characters' here. The ambitious playwright of the bluestocking generation (Mitford was born in 1787 and died in 1855) more readily disappears into caricature, whereas Bates writes as a friend of Mrs Hall, who lived till 1881. Mrs Hall may be worshipped as a beauty, but Miss Mitford is jolly, plump, overly animated. Throughout the nineteenth century, Mitford remained the more renowned writer, yet Bates allows Mrs Hall to shape the reception of her predecessor. The two Maclise portraits appear equally complimentary images of celebrity, but with differences that hint at the diverging prose treatments.

Each image shows a woman seated in a domestic scene with a dog at her feet. The 'Author of "The Buccaneer"' appears as a modern Saint Cecilia with one hand on the keys of a piano, Irish sheet music before her (the music's left page appears to bear the title, 'As Down on Bannow', over a harp surrounded by shamrocks, alluding to Mrs Hall's home in childhood) (Figure 2.3). A beautiful married woman, she is drawn in serious rather than playful lines, more closely corresponding with the style of the portraits of men of letters surrounding her. 'The Author of "Our Village"' is floral and charming, perhaps too girlish for her certain age; a cupid-like boy leans to take her letter, and her pen and notebook seem ready to work (Figure 2.4). Our village may be seen through her window. This anticipates the tradition of illustrations of *Our Village*, in print through the mid-twentieth century, illustrations that elaborate only the sweetness, not the gothic or melancholy touches, in the evocative prose.

Although Maginn's original text on Mrs Hall might have been harmless enough,[46] Bates replaces it with praise of his living friend, or rather of the husband-and-wife '"dual unit"' (p.370), no doubt with much loss of satiric verve. Anna Maria Hall's exemplary domestic life, her success through 'independent genius' and her sociable and charitable activities offer, 'fortunately for herself, few points of salient interest to a biographer' (p.367). Her work needs little attention, Bates presumes: the

Figure 2.3   Author of 'The Buccaneer'
Reproduced from William Bates, ed., *The Maclise Portrait Gallery of Illustrious Literary Characters* (London: Chatto & Windus, 1898)

details of publications may be found in 'Men (and Women) of the Time, and such like publications' (p.367; see also p.369).[47] Bates found the Book of Memories 'difficult to lay down' and 'charming throughout' and proudly owns a copy 'with the autograph inscriptions of author and authoress, and their signed photograph portraits to boot'. Bates is privileged to transcribe a poem by Samuel to Anna Maria, 'After Forty Years, January 6th, 1864', 'for distribution among private friends only' (pp.370–71). On their golden wedding anniversary ten years later, they received 'more than fifteen hundred pounds' raised by public subscription (p.371) and Mrs Hall rather superfluously was given a marble 'copy of a bust of her husband, modeled from life', as well as two portraits of Queen Victoria later sent with a signed letter from the monarch herself (p.372). In 1881, the possessor of these likenesses of husband and queen 'left earth life', as Bates puts it, and 'the husband so completely identified with the wife, in actual life and work, as in the preceding sketch, is left ... to finish his journey alone' (p.372). There is yet another gift, one that Bates does not mention. In London in 1872 was printed for private circulation (S.C. Hall is listed as the publisher) a seven-page biography, Mrs. S.C. Hall, said to be from Maclise's Portrait Gallery.[48] This is dual hagiography, encouraged by their shared career names and collective pronoun, as well as by their promotion of domestic cultural work.

In contrast, Bates transmits unflattering portraiture of the long-deceased single woman writer, once lionized in London and consulted internationally as a judge of literary taste. Maginn's text caricatures Mitford in what Bates deems to be a good imitation of Mitford's style:

> our Mary is a good-humoured spinster of a certain age, inclined ... to embonpoint, and the very reverse of picturesqueness. There are, however, very few girls in our village, or twenty villages beyond it, that can dress up so pretty a basket of good-looking and sweet-smelling natural flowers, all of the true English soil, not foreign and flaunting like the flaring dahlias ... nor smelling of turf and whiskey like the strong-scented bog-lilies which are offered to us by the basket-women of the provinces; nor yet at all resembling the faded imitation roses picked up in second-hand saloons. (Gallery, p.63; Watson, Mary Russell Mitford, p.196)

Mitford might be the model for a nation of shopkeepers, purveying a natural English product the reverse of what the Fraserians illicitly consume, and distinct from the excesses of other women writers among the 'Maids of Honour'. The patronising praise hints at the risks of fame for women. Mitford was protected by the scandal of her father's having squandered two fortunes; to immure herself in a country cottage to write to pay his debts was sufficiently feminine domestic sacrifice.

Figure 2.4   The Author of 'Our Village'
Reproduced from William Bates, ed., *The Maclise Portrait
Gallery of Illustrious Literary Characters* (London: Chatto
& Windus, 1898)

Bates not only parrots Maginn but offers his own emulation of Mitfordian pastoral, filtered through the memories of the Halls. As usual, the work is personified in the image of the woman's body: 'These simple and natural delineations of English country life ... charm one in youth, and, like a blind man's bride, retain all their freshness and beauty for us in "hoary eld"'(p.64).[49] Yet for Bates, as for the Halls, nostalgic yearning for a feminine nature and restorative past is arrested by Mitford's comical corporeality, as by the sight of the actual mundane village that she adorned. Bates vicariously describes Mrs Hall's remembered disappointment:

> Miss Mitford was ... 'more fat than bard beseems'. She was described by Jerdan, with truly British lack of gallantry, as 'short, rotund, and unshapely'. My friend, Mrs. S.C. Hall, from whom better things might have been expected, talks of her as a 'stout little lady, tightened up in a shawl', and alludes to her 'roly-poly figure, most vexatiously dumpy'. ... So kindly and refined a person as 'L.E.L.' ... [exclaimed] 'Good heavens! a Sancho Panza in petticoats!' (*Gallery*, pp.65–6).

A Book of Memories indicates that Laetitia Landon made this comment when introduced to Mitford at the Halls' house. Bates indeed is borrowing heavily from Mrs Hall's memory of first meeting Mitford in London in 1828. The occasion, the opening of Mitford's tragedy, *Rienzi*, perhaps suggested to the younger, newly published writer the perils of self-promotion for a woman. The mortification takes concrete form in Anna Maria Hall's memory that the playwright was wearing a massive turban with the price tag still attached (Mrs Hall recalls tactfully removing it).

Mitford the grotesque is not the only Mitford passed down by the Halls, however. Bates pretends to deplore the insults about Mitford's figure, but he omits Mrs. Hall's qualification: 'when Miss Mitford spoke, the awkward effect vanished, – her pleasant voice, her beaming eyes and smiles, made you forget' (*Memories*, pp.438–9). More importantly, Mrs and Mr Hall were lifelong devotees of Mary Mitford at home, where she literally fits in. In this prosopography, the women writers belong in domestic scenes drinking tea; as personifications of nostalgia, they recover *themselves* when at home. *A Book of Memories* celebrates Mitford 'at her humble dwelling', 'a very Flora among her flowers', who could recite 'gems' of 'the old poets' to visitors (pp.440–41). Mrs Hall describes the couple's visit around 1861 to Three Mile Cross and Swallowfield to reconstruct the sites after Mitford's death, finding the garden decayed, the house 'a body without a soul'; and sketching the large cross that marks her grave (*Memories*, pp.442–3).

Memorials to women writers may be insistently domestic, but even of male writers these recollections ask, 'Who's he when he's at home?' I will close with glimpses of the *Gallery* and *Book of Memories* as prosopographies of men of the time: as collections of both representative images and inscribed ancestral monuments. In his piece on Edmund Lodge in the *Gallery*, Bates surveys standard opinions on painted portraiture, which is said to be the only kind of art cherished by the English, a vain nation (p.404). Yet Bates points out that other countries collected biographical portraits a hundred years before anyone did so in England (p.406). Portraits may join biographies as 'valuable incentives to rivalry and imitation' (p.404), while they prolong existence: we wish to 'continue to live, if only *ad simulacrum*, amongst that ever renewed minority which we have quitted' (p.405). 'A good portrait' may 'bring the absent and beloved original before us' (p.407). Here 'we' shift from a lone dying self to a living cohort remembering such an originating self. As civic models, technologies of immortality and prosopoetic devices to give face to the dead, portraits serve well.

The Halls likewise commend spatial or graphic means of preserving a British literary heritage, with their theme of homes sacred to memory. As always, there is rivalry for control of the remains, and concern that the record will be fragmentary and ephemeral. In the first portrait in *Memories*, of Thomas Moore, for example, survivors have a last word: Moore's widow disagrees with S.C. Hall's statements that Moore's father was a common man and his sister was deformed (p.2 n). The Halls unhesitatingly alter the literary landscape, as they follow the poet's own lead in revisiting his homes. They record a visit in 1864 to the childhood home of Moore's mother: 'We are gratified to record that, at our suggestion, a tablet has been placed over the entrance door, stating in few words the fact that there the mother was born and lived', and that Moore paid homage to her there 'in the zenith of his fame' in 1835 (p.3 n). The note then comments upon itself: '(I have used the words "at our suggestion," but, in fact, it was at our sole cost. ... We had thought it in better taste to erect it by subscription; but the attempt to raise money for the purpose was a failure)' (p.3 n). The poet's own birthplace also requires a visit by both the poet (again in 1835) and the biographers (again in 1864). There is an abortive attempt to make this house, also a grocer's, into a national shrine: 'a bust of the poet is placed over the door ... and the fact that he was born there is recorded on a marble tablet. May no modern "improvement" ever touch it!' Again, a note reveals that it was Hall or the Halls who put up the marker. But on a return visit in 1869, the 'white marble slab' had been removed by a new owner who refused either to put it back up or to 'give me back the slab'. 'I trust this note will draw ... some more powerful "intercessor" to the discreditable fact, and that an Irishman will do what I, as an Englishman, failed to do' (p.6 n). Though Hall appears to have forgotten that he once *was* Irish, he appeals to the call of national pride to preserve the landmarks on the literary map.

Much as William Howitt had done in 1847, the Halls portray themselves as unassisted collectors and inscribers of sites ravaged by time and demolition, yet they are hardly alone. Others collaborate: Llewellyn Jewitt supplies Hall with a written description of Moore's humble cottage, Mayfield, where grand works of 'Orientalism' were written (p.11). Jewitt himself 'placed a portrait of Moore over the chimney-piece' in the bedroom (p.12). An author's house, with maternal or nurturing associations, with a tablet announcing who was born, lived or died there, containing the portrait of the person who wrote within, becomes a fitting model for the biographies that are collected in the name of British literature during the nineteenth century. In prose and image they enshrine, inviting mental and actual pilgrimages. These prosopographies include a remarkable contingent of women. Indeed the purpose of these gatherings of literary personalities in part is to represent a spirit of the age in which women would feel at home, as helpmeets if not rivals of their male counterparts.

Historically there is a conjunction among Anglophone canon-building, the rise of the academic discipline of English literature, and the narratives and practices of 'homes and haunts', a conjunction that would entail – and that I hope will reward elsewhere – a full investigation. There is no question, in any case, that the mid-twentieth-century canon of 'English' had become inhospitable to women, even to those women who had served as hostesses in the venerable tradition tracing back at least to Hester Thrale. Yet I have suggested that the Victorians began a kind of self-reflexive ethnographical movement to preserve the reverse of the exotic, the commonplace middle-class interiors of men and women of letters. Even as literary *studies* moved out of the home, back to clubs and into classrooms, written pilgrimages and biographical visits continued to be published.[50] The literary preservation movement bloomed again after each world war, in disregard of New-Critical and poststructuralist efforts to uproot literature from is biographical and domestic groundings. The spirit of the age (circa 1980) could imagine it had nothing to do with what Mitford looked like, or how the Halls arranged their home, yet 'homes and haunts' publications appealed to a public appetite.

Even now the critics and the public are at odds. The return of materialist and biographical concerns in literary studies, through feminist, Marxist and other ideological critiques, has little time for the respectable, middlebrow habitus of literature according to Horne, Bates,

Howitts and Halls. Yet today there is a booming commerce in literary personalities and sites. Whatever else may be said of the current state of literacy, there is no mistaking the widely shared yearning to emulate the writer's lifestyle, envisioned as a stress-free, tastefully arranged cottage industry for equal partners. As if in search of glimpses of genius where it really lives, former English majors and members of reading groups tour literary regions or take literary-ghost walks, visit house museums or celebrity 'galleries' in various media, or consume the relics and auto/biographical narratives of coteries. In many ways our age remains dedicated to literary prosopography.

Notes

1. Altick, *Lives and Letters* (New York: Knopf, 1966), pp.77–8, 87–8.
2. In my study of collective female biography, *How to Make It as a Woman* (Chicago: University of Chicago Press, 2004), I estimate that there are four or five times as many biographical collections of men – or of a minority of women among men – than strictly female groups. My counts include narrative prosopographies (three or more subjects) published in English 1830–1940, setting aside reference works such as *Men of the Time*.
3. Hazlitt, *The Spirit of the Age* (London: Colburn, 1825). Parenthetical citations will refer to Hazlitt, *Lectures on the English Poets and The Spirit of the Age*, ed. Catherine MacDonald MacLean (London: Everyman, 1967); *The Dictionary of National Biography*, 20 vols (London: Smith, 1885–1901). The editorial and publishing history of the *DNB* have been widely discussed. I cite parenthetically as '*DNB*' the reprint of the original 20 volumes, Oxford University Press, 1950.
4. Paul Sturges affirms, 'the oldest established version' of biography is 'collective' and notes 'national biographical collections' from the seventeenth century onward: see 'Collective Biography in the 1980s', *Biography*, 6:4 (1983): 316–17. Comparatively little criticism has been devoted to collective biography. Examples include Donald C. Yelton, *Brief American Lives* (Metuchen, NJ: Scarecrow, 1978); Margot Peters, 'Group Biography: Challenges and Models', in *New Directions in Biography*, ed. Anthony M. Friedson (Honolulu: Biographical Research Center, 1981), pp.41–51; Reed Whittemore, *Pure Lives* (Baltimore: Johns Hopkins UP, 1988).
5. Lawrence Stone defined prosopography in 1971 as 'the investigation of the common background characteristics of a group of actors in history by means of a collective study of their lives'. See 'Prosopography,' *Daedalus* (Winter, 1971), 46–9.
6. See the Prosopography Centre of the Modern History Research Unit at Oxford University, with its newsletter, *Prosopon* (http://users.ox.ac.uk/~prosop/).
7. As Paul de Man influentially notes, prosopopoeia – 'to *give* a face', mask or voice to an absence – is the trope not only of lyric but of autobiography. See 'Hypogram and Inscription: Michael Riffaterre's Poetics of Reading', *Diacritics*, 11 (1981) 17–35, rpt. in *Resistance to Theory* (Minneapolis,

University of Minnesota Press, 1986), pp.44, 47; 'Autobiography as De-facement', p.926, *MLN*, 94 (December 1979) 919–30.

8.   Raymond Williams, *The Long Revolution* (New York: Harper & Row, 1961), p.49, quoted in Robert Lanning, *The National Album: Collective Biography and the Formation of the Canadian Middle Class*, Carleton Library Series 186 (Ottawa: Carleton UP, 1996), p.20.

9.   In Anderson's vision, modern nationhood aligns with 'the inner premises and conventions of modern biography and autobiography'. 'The nation's biography' forms itself upon memorialized 'deaths'. See *Imagined Communities*, rev. edn (London: Verso, 1991), pp. xiv, 194–206.

10. Phyllis Rose, *Parallel Lives* (New York: Vintage, 1984), offers a prosopography of this sort of partnership.

11. R.H. Horne (ed.), *A New Spirit of the Age* (New York: Harper, 1845). Citations will appear parenthetically in the text. See *Men of the Time* (London: Bogue; New York: Redfield, 1852); *Men and Women of the Time* (London: Routledge, 1899); see also variants in this publishing history, mentioned in the text; William Bates (ed.), *The Maclise Portrait Gallery of Illustrious Literary Characters* (London: Chatto & Windus, 1898). Parenthetical citations to '*Gallery*' refer to the 1898 edition, apparently a reprint of the 1883 version; S.C. Hall, *A Book of Memories of Great Men and Women of the Age, From Personal Acquaintance* (London: Virtue, 1871); parenthetically cited as '*Memories*'.

12. With increasing studies of Irish literature, 'Mrs. S.C. Hall' receives a few entries in the MLA Bibliography. Maureen Keane, in *Mrs. S.C. Hall: A Literary Biography*, Irish Literary Studies, 50 (Gerrards Cross, England: Colin Smythe, 1997), considers the threat to Mr Hall of Mrs Hall's much greater renown and achievement, during a period in which women writers and Irish themes were fashionable (pp.1–21). Further citations of 'Keane' will appear parenthetically.

13. Mr Hall's memories of first encounters with many writers and artists locate him in Ireland through his early twenties (e.g. *Memories*, pp.1, 239). *Men of the Time* (1859: 346) claims Samuel Carter Hall was born in Devon, whereas the *DNB* notes that his English parents, both associated with Devon, were in Ireland at the time of Samuel's birth, and that his mother ran a shop in Cork to sustain her twelve children after the father's failure in copper mining (8: 971–2).

14. [S.C. Hall, ed.], *The Art-Journal Illustrated Catalogue, The Great Exhibition of The Industry of All Nations, 1851* (London: Virtue, 1851; rpt. New York: Bounty, 1970). See Debra N. Mancoff, 'Samuel Carter Hall: Publisher as Promoter of the High Arts', *Victorian Periodicals Review*, 24 (1991) 11–21.

15. In 1829, the Halls lived at 59 Upper Charlotte Street, Fitzroy Square ('Keane', p.33). This square enjoys plaques for Woolf and Shaw, but nothing registers the Halls' former residence. In the 1840s, the Halls lived in Chelsea, according to Keane (p.27), but elsewhere she records, 'they moved around London quite a lot. ... The only address for which we have a definite time span is that of The Rosery in Old Brompton, Kensington – 1839 to 1849' (p.199); then they held court in Bannow Lodge, The Boltons, Brompton (p.200). No traces of the Halls appear in Roger Tagholm, *Walking Literary London* (Chicago: Passport Books, 2001), p.66.

16. The National Portrait Gallery does include their now 'minor' contemporaries, Mary Russell Mitford and R.H. Horne. K.K. Yung (comp.), *Complete Illustrated Catalogue 1856–1979* (New York: St Martin's, 1981), lists *Mary Russell Mitford* by John Lucas (1852 or 1853), acquired in 1875, and a later acquisition, Lucas's chalk portrait of her; and *R.H. Horne* by Margaret Gillies (c.1840) and a plaster cast of a medallion of Horne, both donated in 1934. *Anna Maria Hall* by G. de Latre (1851) hangs in the National Gallery in Dublin ('Keane', p.200).

17. These items were transplanted from Highgate to S.C. Hall's desk and garden (*Memories*, p.40). Similarly, the collection of *Memories* features Maria Edgeworth's desk and the pen Walter Scott gave to her (*Memories*, p.116) and many other treasures.

18. Bates, 'professor in Queens College, Birmingham', published a biography of George Cruikshank, a guide to Birmingham and edited the *Literary Remains* of Samuel William L. Parker. See Miriam M. H. Thrall, *Rebellious Fraser's* (New York: Columbia UP, 1934), p.21.

19. Some promotion of national history underlies most biographical compilations. The popular phrase 'men of the time' served also for a prosopography of generals, and later became part of the titles of several national biographical dictionaries in Canada, Australia and Ireland as well as the USA. The American *Men of the Time* of 1852 boasts that it is 'an Index of the World's Active Talent' and a 'companion' to 'the universal newspapers', yet it repeats an endorsement by the President of the United States as an aid to 'every public and intelligent man' in the country (p.5).

20. John Tillotson, *Lives of Illustrious Women of England* (London: Holmes, 1853).

21. Mary Howitt, *Biographical Sketches of the Queens of England, from the Norman Conquest to the Reign of Victoria; or Royal Book of Beauty*, London: Bohn, 1851.

22. In a statistical sample of non-specialized biographical collections, 1880–1900, Barrett Browning appears eight times, Jane Carlyle five (see my Pop Chart in *How to Make It as a Woman*).

23. Carl Ray Woodring, *Victorian Samplers: William and Mary Howitt* (Lawrence, Kansas: University of Kansas Press, 1952), pp.25–8. Further citations to 'Woodring' appear parenthetically in the text.

24. The female appendix includes a number of notable women also portrayed in Maclise's *Gallery* or in the Halls' own *Memories* (for example, Anna Jameson, Harriet Martineau, Caroline Norton, Lady Morgan). Eight of the women subjects had compiled all-female prosopographies or would later do so: Lydia Maria Child, Mary Cowden Clarke, Mrs Newton Crosland, Mary Howitt, Anna Jameson, Julia Kavanagh, Harriet Beecher Stowe and Agnes Strickland.

25. Howitt, *Homes and Haunts of the Most Eminent British Poets*, 2 vols (London: Bentley, 1847).

26. Edward Walford (1862), George H. Townsend (1865), Thompson Cooper up to 1884.

27. This edition announces a companion work edited by Ward, with the explanatory title, *Men of the Reign: A Biographical Dictionary of Eminent Persons of British and Colonial Birth Who Have Died During the Reign of Queen Victoria*, thus providing more than a list of epitaphs for the dead of both sexes.

28. Seventeenth-century prosopographies by Aubrey, Fuller or Clark had included a few women, as did Theophilus Cibber's *Lives of the Poets of Great Britain and Ireland* (1753). See also Margaret J.M. Ezell, *Writing Women's Literary History* (Baltimore: Johns Hopkins UP, 1993), p.89.

29. Only Tooke and Byron were deceased. 'We had written thus far when news came of the death of Lord Byron, and put an end at once to a strain of somewhat peevish invective, which was intended to meet his eye, not to insult his memory. Had we known that we were writing his epitaph, we must have done it with a different feeling' (pp.243–4).

30. Elizabeth Barrett apparently wrote the pieces on Tennyson, Landor, Wordsworth, Carlyle and Monckton Milnes; Mary Gillies wrote on Martineau, Southwood Smith and the Howitts; Robert Bell on 'the novelists' and Macready; Thomas Powell also possibly contributed (Ann Blainey, *The Farthing Poet* [London: Longmans, 1968], pp.142–3). Wordsworth and Leigh Hunt are the two subjects from Hazlitt's work also present in Horne's.

31. David Parroissien, in 'Mrs. Browning's Influence on and Contribution to *a New Spirit of the Age* (1844)', *English Language Notes*, 1971, 274–81, claims that much of the original text was supplied by Barrett Browning, in correspondence.

32. The Victorians' impressionist approach irks David Paroissien (1971), (276–7).

33. Hall had been the editor of a journal, *The Spirit and Manner of the Age*, in 1826 (*DNB*, 8, p.972); sub-editor or editor of *The New Monthly Magazine* from 1830 to 1836, after Hazlitt's series had appeared there; and editor from 1826 to 1837 of an annual, *The Amulet*, that published work by Clare, Hood, Edgeworth, Coleridge and, of interest here, Mary Russell Mitford and Mary and William Howitt ('Keane', p.25; *DNB*, 8: pp.969, 972).

34. What was said to be Anna Maria Hall's first Irish story, 'Master Ben', was published in January 1829, along with Mary Mitford's 'A November Walk', in *The Spirit and Manners of the Age*, by then a monthly featuring descriptions of foreign cultures. According to Keane, however, Mrs Hall's first publications appeared in her husband's *Amulet* in 1826–27 (pp.20, 26).

35. Deidre Lynch, in 'Homes and Haunts: Austen's and Mitford's English Idylls', *PMLA*, 115.5 (2000), 1103–8, observes that Mitford's writings and her home at Three Mile Cross, like other 'literary landscapes', staged 'rituals of homesickness' (pp.1104, 1106).

36. Mr Hall praised Mr Howitt in *Retrospect of a Long Life* (1883, 2, p.128); 'Woodring', pp.150, 220.

37. Vera Watson, *Mary Russell Mitford* (London: Evans, n.d.), p.161. In 1838, Mary Russell Mitford replaced Anna Maria Hall as editor of *Finden's Tableaux* and encouraged Mary Howitt as contributor ('Woodring', p.37).

38. See the chapter on Leigh Hunt, *Memories*, pp.241–54, for example, or the waterfall and a church frequented by Southey (*Memories*, pp.206–7).

39. On the representation of authorship in Maclise's 'Gallery', see Carol A. Bock, 'Authorship, the Brontës, and *Fraser's Magazine*: "Coming Forward" as an Author in Early Victorian England', *Victorian Literature and Culture*, 29 (2001), 241–66.

40. Hook replaced Hall as editor of *The New Monthly Magazine* in 1836 (*DNB*, 8, p.972; *Memories*, p.155).

41. Patrick Leary, 'Fraser's Magazine and the Literary Life, 1830–1847', *Victorian Periodicals Review*, 1994, 105–26. At least six of the twenty-seven revellers never contributed to the journal. S.C. Hall confirmed the 'legend' of *Fraser's* 'band of literary free-lances' giving it the 'name of terror' (*Memories*, pp.111–12).

42. Hall writes, 'How few great men are heroes in their daily communion!' In biographies, poets show 'the loftiest precepts humiliated by the meanest examples' of vice and drunkenness. 'The poet Moore is one of the very few of whom we make think and speak without a blush' (*Memories*, p.15). Southey similarly exalts the vocation of the professional poet, as a true Christian family man (pp.185–208).

43. Keane notes that the Halls had scruples about visiting the Countess of Blessington because of scandals associated with her, and that their long friendship with the Dickens family met an obstacle when they chose to side with Catherine Dickens at the separation (p.201).

44. It appeared in *Fraser's*, 13 (January 1836), 80. Nothing in Bates's edition suggests that this picture is not by Maclise, but its style contrasts with the other 'Croquis' portraits. Patrick Leary notes the proportion of contributors to *Fraser's* (96 men to 17 women) and the fact that the portrait of women writers included only one actual contributor, Landon (p.118).

45. Eileen M. Curran, in a message posted to VICTORIA-L on 30 June 2001, 'Images of Literary Women', calls attention to this illustration, but understandably reads the oblique text as rotating round the table the other way, and claims Lady Morgan is sipping the cup.

46. Keane believes Maginn wrote *Fraser's* sneering review of Mrs Hall's *Sketches of Irish Character, Second Series*, as well as 'a most flattering profile' in the 'Portrait Gallery' (p.8). As her bibliography lists Bates's 1883 edition, I think it is likely that she mistakes the text for Maginn's.

47. Bates writes, 'her first work, I think, was entitled *Sketches of Irish Character*, and appeared so far back as 1829' (p.367), but the first publication appeared in 1826. See my note 34.

48. Examination of the one located copy, as of the editions of the *Gallery* leading up to Bates, awaits further research. No doubt the Halls printed this equivalent to Samuel's bust as a positive memorial; it necessarily omits the remaining nine years of Anna Maria's life (pp.v–vi).

49. Bates's conceit for an unchanging inner vision, 'blind man's bride', echoes a concluding sentence of the Halls' portrait of Mitford, describing Mitford's own homesickness for Three Mile Cross when she moved to Swallowfield nearby: 'the PAST is with the old, ever fresh and young as a blind man's bride' (*Memories*, p.444).

50. The National Trust in Britain, founded in 1895 primarily to preserve landscapes such as the Lake District at the same time that modern house museums began to be established (Dove Cottage opened to the public in 1891, Carlyle's House in 1895), turned only in the 1930s to acquiring the architecturally mediocre homes of authors and artists. See John Gaze, *Figures in a Landscape: A History of the National Trust* (Frome, Somerset: Barrie & Jenkins/National Trust, 1988).

CHAPTER THREE

The Self in Society
Middle-class Men and Autobiography

Donna Loftus

Recent work on self-representation has done much to explore the links between writing and gender and class identities.[1] Little attention, however, has been given to the body of autobiographical writing produced by less celebrated professional and businessmen.[2] Instead the focus of scholarly attention has either been on critical rereadings of famous 'men of letters' or the life writing of marginalised groups such as women, workers and the colonised.[3] Although often of little literary merit, as with other forms of life writing in the nineteenth century, the contributions of many middle-class men can be seen as distinct interventions in contemporary debates about the nature of self and society which sought to represent the present and future in relation to the past.[4] I want to argue here that the life writing of middle-class men was characterised by a particular narrative of improvement that was employed to articulate claims to success and public recognition. As Lejeune has noticed in his studies of French autobiography, life writing by the middling sort was often concerned to stake a claim to notability through the construction of the 'exemplar life' that justified its presence by its potentially instructive nature.[5] As I hope to demonstrate here, this was not necessarily presented in the simple narrative of rags to riches; the narrative of self-help was interwoven with the symbolic spaces of public and private and used to contemplate the conundrum of dependence and independence, self-reliance and relying on others and concerns with the nature and value of success. This fluid employment of self-help can offer insight into the formation of 'middle-class' male identity in the period.

This study is based on a reading of 50 autobiographies written by businessmen, clergymen, lawyers, doctors and civil servants in the period between 1850 and 1914. The majority were composed in the last two decades of the nineteenth century and the first decade of the twentieth century. The increased production of autobiographical writing corresponded with the growth of print culture and a general interest in life stories and retrospection at the turn of the century.[6] Most were written when the individuals concerned had retired from their work or profession but not necessarily from public life. They were either published or printed for private circulation but, interestingly, this had little impact on the narrative composition: increasingly, towards the end of the nineteenth century and into the twentieth, they became more formulaic with a strong emphasis on the 'exemplary' life of the author. The narrative usually began with an account of ancestral heritage, followed by accounts of birth, childhood, education and introduction to profession or occupation. Overwhelmingly, female relations were silenced and masculinity was defined through relations with other men. These often clichéd accounts nevertheless demonstrated an ontology that saw the self emerging out of childhood struggles, to face the challenges and battles that defined early manhood, and the security that rewarded success. This emergent self, however, was plotted through the narrated significance of relationships with family, friends, colleagues and a network of like-minded men. It was a self that was constituted by social narratives.

The problem in reading theses texts as representations of a distinctly middle-class identity is that many of these 'discursive consistencies' are found in the autobiographical writing of working-class men, such as the recounting of ancestry, the focus on childhood, an avoidance of detail about domestic life or work and an emphasis on what Joyce has called the 'romance of improvement'.[7] Whilst this undoubtedly reflected the broad basis of social masculinity in the nineteenth century, certain aspects of these conventions can also be seen in female autobiography. Valerie Sanders's work on anti-feminist autobiographers has similarly noted the marginalisation of female relations and an emphasis on male heroism.[8] The existence of such consistencies across such a range of texts suggests that class and gender do not create clearly defined and demarcated identities. It perhaps also may suggest that the languages available for the expression of self were themselves limited. As recent work by Somers and Gibson has argued, individuals are rarely free to cultivate narratives about themselves, instead they must 'choose from the repertoire of available representations and stories'.[9] But, while the repetition of certain narratives across a range of texts about, for example, childhood innocence or the struggle to establish independence, reflected and created an inclusive discourse of self and society, other strategies worked to define boundaries. I want to argue that the life writing of middle-class men was concerned to demonstrate a sense of self that was informed less through interiority and more through a range of social relations. These social relations were realised through self-help, the development of separate spheres, and a sense of belonging established through a network of like-minded men. As such, life writing bounded the narrated community of the middle-class man.

In these stories individual success was narrated with reference to the progress of wider society. 'Self-culture' or self making was reflected in the narrative movement across boundaries and through time and space in which the author, along with other like-minded men, was presented as an agent of change.[10] The echoes of Smiles are clear in many of these texts in the significance given to the importance of individual good example and the ability of ordinary men of honesty and industry to facilitate progress:

> Even the humblest person, who sets before his fellows an example of industry, sobriety and upright honesty of purpose in life, has a present as well as a future influence upon the well-being of his country; for his life and character pass unconsciously into the lives of others, and propagate a good example for all time to come.[11]

Exemplary masculinity needed to distinguish selfishness from self making. In his preface to the 1886 edition of *Self-Help*, Smiles regretted his choice of title as it had led some to 'suppose that it consists of a eulogy of selfishness'. Instead Smiles argued that 'the duty of helping one's self in the highest sense involves the helping of ones neighbours'.[12] This was clarity of position that most of the autobiographers considered here were keen to establish. Many writers did so by invoking a shared narrative code in which individual success was seen to benefit one's family and one's community, an achievement symbolised in the recognition of notable men. As the anonymous preface to Henry Bessemer's life story, *An Autobiography* (1905), expressed, his life told the 'story of the struggles through which he passed, and the battles he had to fight before the world became enriched by his inventive genius'.[13]

To demonstrate the social benefits of individual achievement, the life writing of many middle-class men employed narratives of self-help in which symbolic spaces were used to demonstrate the progress of self, family and community. As Tosh has argued, the ability to accommodate the often conflicting demands of home, work and all-male association was a key marker of success for the middle-class man.[14] Many of these autobiographies establish this accommodation through a narrative ordering of social relations in public and private space. The home, the committee rooms of the town hall, the meeting rooms of learned societies, the podium of the public lecture theatre became symbolic sites of benefit to others; in turn, those others would bear witness to the author's success. Such spaces also demonstrated the author's ability to cross boundaries with increasing confidence and authority. From the first, possibly awkward steps between home and school and the initial stumbles into work, the author began to move more freely between the hearth, the office, the committee room, while taking time to travel and even to explore the empire. It is precisely this ability to cross boundaries that identified the individual as a part of a broader, but bounded, middle-class culture.

The life stories considered here suggest that what it meant to be male and middle-class needed to be negotiated. Through the narratives of self-help, the gendered separation of spheres and homosociable belonging, the middle-class autobiographer could create a sense of self which appeared to negotiate conflicting public and private pressures: business was successful, one's family contented and one's public duties recognised by the society of local notables. Still, despite rhetoric and narrative as the controlling element of life writing, many writers struggled to smooth over the cracks and tensions involved in staking a claim to the social power associated with the narratives of belonging from which middle-class masculinity was assembled. Some such tensions were more easily accommodated than others. The nervous breakdown could be used to confirm masculinity in which duty is pursued relentlessly and with little regard for one's health.[15] The Liverpool cotton broker and later Liberal MP Samuel Smith narrated his breakdown as a result of the pressure of maintaining business in Liverpool, political life in London, constituency work in Wales, family life in Scotland and reform campaigns through the country. In his autobiography, *My Life Work* (1902), Smith reaffirmed his useful masculine agency by taking a trip to India that then became the landscape for his contemplation on the nature of progress, a move that perhaps suggests that travel to more 'exotic' locations was often undertaken after an illness, a breakdown or in retirement, possibly as a way of reaffirming masculine identities that had been challenged.

Perhaps because of the importance of social relations to male middle-class identity, conflicts with others and the fear for one's reputation associated with failure were less easy to narrate. Although, as we have seen, Bessemer's autobiography was presented to his readers as a clear example of 'the law and progress which evolve social and moral results from material discoveries and inventions', his narrative of progress was punctuated with anxieties over his failures.[16] Bessemer was as well known for his successes, particularly the Bessemer processor, as for his failures, in particular the Bessemer saloon ship. Bessemer had to use his money to shore up the struggling Bessemer Saloon Ship Company in 1872. The company failed when the saloon ship crashed into the pier at Calais on its first trip. Bessemer attempted to maintain his narrative of 'self culture' by blaming his failures on the cynicism of others. He countered the popular opinion that the ship failed because of the hydraulic system Bessemer had designed. To do so, however, he positioned himself outside the events he described. In discussing the difficulty of writing about failure, conflicts and struggles without 'appearing to be self assertive', Bessemer stated:

> I must either for ever remain under the stigma of this supposed
> failure, or I must combat that erroneous impression by placing
> unreservedly the leading facts of the case before the public, and thus
> bring home, even to the untechnical reader, evidence that no fair
> minded person can hesitate to accept.[17]

Despite this appeal, Bessemer was unable to pick up his story. He
finished his life story in 1897 after outlining his version of the saloon
ship affair of 1872 and he died a year later, in 1898.

The following sections consider the way self making and the symbolic
spaces associated with separate spheres and homosociability were used
to construct middle-class identity. Whilst the stories told easily challenge
any notion of a middle-class identity premised on a unity of interests and
a shared economic or professional status, they do suggest that narratives
could be used to constitute a self-culture bounded by a class ontology: a
shared discourse of self and society that was not always available to
others. Yet, as the example of Bessemer demonstrates, the narrative of
self-help was not always stable: there were occasions when the narrative
of self making broke down to reveal the fractured status of class and
gender identities and the role of narrative in constructing agency. A
consideration of these 'fissures' demonstrates the association between
discursive and social aspects of masculinity and affords an insight into
middle-class identity.

The Public Function of Private Space

While studies have pointed to the broad social base of a cross-class
masculinity it is clear that, whatever the discursive consistencies in self-
representation, masculinity is 'problematic, fraught with conflicts and
anxieties'.[18] Yet evidence of diversity and 'fracturedness' brings into
sharper focus the attempts middle-class men made to create a coherent
representation of self. Life writing was an important strategy in attempts
to create such coherence. Tosh has argued that, although middle-class
masculinity was constructed in relation to the home, work and all male
association, these three arenas could lead to struggles over competing
demands.[19] In life writing, success for the middle-class man was represented by the author's ability to negotiate these different demands. To
achieve this, many life stories used public and private life as symbolic
spaces, brought into the narrative at key stages in plotting the rise of the
exemplary self.

The act of writing itself was an expression of the middle-class man's
ability to negotiate boundaries. Although usually written in retirement at
home, the autobiography was often presented in prologues as a way of

continuing one's public work. Herbert Preston-Thomas's autobiography, *The Work and Play of a Government Inspector*, published in 1909, begins with a preface written by the MP John Burns, establishing the work as a further contribution to the debate on 'the problem of modern poverty'.[20] The Liberal MP and Liverpool businessman Samuel Smith used his life story to 'keep alive his influence' and 'to speak of great questions I can no longer advocate in Parliament or on a platform'.[21] Still the personal dedication of autobiographies was often to wives and children. Despite the stated public purpose of Smith's autobiography, it was nevertheless dedicated to the memory of his wife, 'my companion and helper in all good works' and his son, 'the most unselfish character I ever knew'. A story of exemplary masculinity required the careful negotiation of familial affection and public duty: each needed to be seen in the right place at the right time. Similarly, in the autobiography, *The Memories of Llewelyn Turner* (1903), the author, the successful proprietor of a Welsh slate mine, included this heartfelt dedication of his life story: 'To my dear wife and loving companion, my comforter in sickness and in health, whose affectionate kindness to me in numerous illnesses I desire to acknowledge by dedicating to her this book of reminiscences of a long public life ...'[22] The dedication acted as an acknowledgment of her contribution to his success and her bounded presence confirmed this success.

In many of these texts the social power of middle-class men was premised on divisions between the public and the private. As recent work has demonstrated, the dichotomy between these two spheres was impractical and often impossible.[23] But the narrative of separate spheres was a key aspect of Victorian male authority however difficult the distinctions were to maintain. Whilst their public lives were the focus of the autobiography the private was brought in occasionally to serve a public function in demonstrating the professional success of the author. Marriage and the domestic, when mentioned, were often presented as a consequence of professional and material success. Although Bessemer did not wait to become established before marriage, he nevertheless stated his assurance in retrospect that the decision to marry 'was a step which I had taken in the full confidence of youth that I should, in time, be able to carve out for myself a name and a position in the world worthy of her to whom my life was henceforth to be devoted'.[24] Wives could also be used to demonstrate success but the narrative space afforded depended on the professional status being claimed. As Robbie Gray's work demonstrates, ministers were more likely than other groups to refer to their 'exemplary wives'. This is perhaps unsurprising given the importance of domestic life to 'the persona of the good pastor'.[25] More typically, wives and children were often brought in toward the end of a life story as unnamed companions in leisure time. At the same narrative stage, domestic surroundings might be recounted and even pictures included of decorative interiors as a way of describing domestic satisfaction without describing private relations.[26]

Whilst this careful demarcation of the spousal relationship might help the author to avoid any complexities involved in integrating her story, it also perhaps suggests accepted conventions in life writing. As already seen, Samuel Smith dedicated his story to the memory of his wife and son but the preface, written by Smith himself, stated that 'Things essentially private are rarely touched upon, and only when necessary to the general narrative'.[27] The 'general narrative' is, on the whole, an account of his public activities, work as a local councillor and later as an MP, a record of his opinions on the matters of the day such as Irish Home Rule and bimetallism and a narrative space to continue his campaigns for social reform. Smith described his marriage and domestic life in harmony with his public activities: 'Though business was engrossing and sometimes anxious by day, all was peace and quietness in the evening, and I look back with pleasure to many volumes read aloud by my wife, and to delightful visits from family friends.'[28] Still the death of Smith's wife Melville was less easily accommodated. Smith described his anxiety over his wife's failing health in 1892, and his fears of losing 'my helper and counsellor in all my public work'. But his account of her illness and death, which forced a withdrawal from public life, was interrupted by Smith's desire to speak also about the second Home Rule Bill. He described being called back from parliament to attend his wife but added with regret, 'I missed the debate on the introduction of the second Home Rule Bill, and did not hear the wonderful speech in which the Grand Old Man of 83 expounded it for two and quarter hours … I just managed to get to London to vote on the Welsh Suspensory Bill (the first stage of Disestablishment), but was recalled by another crisis in Mrs Smith's illness'.[29] The death of Melville Smith resolved Smith's narrative dilemma and the record of his public life was restored. As he stated, 'I came back resolved to seek relief in the performance of public duty'.[30]

The carefully prescribed public nature of the life story may well also explain why mothers are largely absent from the narratives. Again, it appears mothers were associated with a private life that had no place in a record of public work. The lawyer Edmund Parry hints at this in his autobiography, *What the Judge Saw* (1912). He gave factual details about his mother but quickly followed with, 'But I do not propose to write of my mother in these pages, since I could do no justice to the grace of her memory, and the dim vision of it is my own affair'.[31] When mothers did appear in narratives they tended to be vehicles for discussing matters of religion. For example, the technical instrument maker

Thomas Stanley made little reference to his mother in his autobiography, *His Life and Work* (1911), beyond that she taught her children the Lord's Prayer and made sure they said it every night.[32] This association of morality and spirituality with the feminine may explain the declining tendency for men to recount their spiritual life. Spiritual matters were often a central aspect of self in the earlier autobiographies. William Tanner's *Memoir*, printed for private circulation in 1868, established his life story as 'a means of giving lasting influence to a life so singularly devoted to God'.[33] But, by the late nineteenth century, the narration of belief was carefully controlled. An interesting insight into this shift can be seen in the story of Samuel Smith. Religion was firmly embedded in Samuel Smith's life. He experienced a conversion in 1861 which influenced the direction of his life's work and, in particular, his campaigns for temperance and against cruelty to children. Nevertheless he acknowledged the problems with writing about matters of belief: 'it is difficult for anyone to speak of his spiritual history; indeed it is hardly becoming'. In the end he falls back on established narratives: 'It was the old story: "Once I was blind, now I see".'[34]

It is possible that these silences reflected uncertainties about the significance of femininity, female relations, domesticity and religion to public codes of masculinity. Nevertheless authority over the feminine could be publicly performed through the narrative ordering of wives and children, perhaps even religion, in distinct spaces. In sharp contrast, fathers were given considerable narrative space.[35] This is perhaps unsurprising given that fathers, and through them other male relations, acted as the agents who introduced sons to work, profession and public life. Through their relationship with fathers, authors could narrate their own coming of age, their own emerging masculinity. At the same time, however, the narrative treatment of the father–son relationship could undermine these very claims to masculinity. The paternal relationship could demonstrate a bridge to independent masculinity, the inheritance of character and the support of a well-disposed gentleman. But evidence of paternal patronage could sit uncomfortably with claims to independent masculinity.

Fathers appeared in many narratives to provide a link with the past (family history) and a bridge to the future (the emerging self) and a bridge between the private world of the family and the public sphere. Largely without exception, these narratives began with a genealogy that charted the male line, usually from the author's father, identifying the skills and talents the author associated with him in ancestors. In a particularly exaggerated example, no doubt encouraged by Smiles as the editor of his *Autobiography* (1883), Nasmyth journeyed back as far as thirteenth century Scotland for evidence of his engineering potential.[36]

The skills passed down throughout the generations were then brought into sharper focus when the author narrated circumstances that demonstrated an early ability in their later career. While talents might be 'inherited', fathers were the agents who noticed and cultivated these early abilities in many of these successful men. Nasmyth claimed to have used his father's lathe to explore his talent for engineering in making spinning tops for his friends at school. Bessemer's father allowed him to explore his 'intuitive instinct' for modelling in his workshop using his molten metals and casts. Both fathers also gave their sons access to male social networks by allowing them to join in conversations about work with other businessmen.[37]

Rather than interrupting narratives of self making, the patronage of a father, his friends and other male relations could be used to confirm the author's exemplary struggle. Smilesean heroes like Nasmyth were not of humble origins. Nevertheless Smilesean self making offered a useful subplot for middle-class men, enabling them to accommodate images of successful independent masculinity to dependence on others for support. Smiles argued that it was impossible to purchase any form of 'self-culture' and, given that comfort could easily lead to self-indulgence, 'the glory is all the greater of those who, born to ample fortunes, nevertheless take an active part in the work of their generation'.[38] Self-help could be recast as the struggle to justify paternal support and to follow the good example of one's father with the successful move to independent masculinity. Samuel Smiles edited Nasmyth's autobiography and, as one would expect, it demonstrated a particular surety in the narrative application of 'self-help'. Nasmyth acknowledged the help and support of his father and the inspiring and useful role his father's network of friends provided. Still such support did not interrupt narratives of self making. Nasmyth only referred to his father's good example in encouraging his success. The rest was put down to his own resourcefulness and hard work.

On the other hand, there is evidence in the autobiographies of some resentment over fathers who failed to recognize their sons' potential or the nature of their character. Praise and admiration for one's father could be combined with resentment over his authority and perhaps guilt for feeling resentful. The Liverpool merchant William Forwood (b.1840) admitted in his *Recollections* (1910) to being inspired by his father's love of 'hard work' yet he also resented the fact that he refused to allow him to attend university. Forwood disliked the career his father carved out for him but he did it and threw himself into public work for interest and pleasure.[39] The technical instrument maker William Ford Stanley praised his father as 'honest and upstanding' but he resented having to leave school at 14 to shore up his father's failing business. He expressed even more resentment that his father failed to appreciate his invention of a wheel with metal spokes for tricycles that was subsequently patented by someone else. Still Stanley holds back from open criticism of his father, simply blaming his 'lack of business sense'.[40]

The close association between work and masculinity made describing occupations that the author did not consider to reflect his true character difficult. Some authors spoke of the 'duty' to take on their father's profession despite feeling their skills and qualities suited them for other careers. For example, in his autobiography, *Mid-Victorian Memories* (1914), the barrister R.E. Francillon recorded his resignation to a legal career with some ambivalence, 'I had been trained for the Bar almost from the cradle; I was my father's son; all the ambition I ever had was bounded by, my associations had for years been bound up with, the bar'. On the death of his father, Francillon for the first time felt free and dumped his legal career for a literary one.[41] George Harris, in his *Autobiography* (1888), told how he ran off and joined the Navy in a bid to avoid his future in his father's office of solicitors. In maintaining the narrative of the inheritance of character, he did so with reference to a seafaring grandfather. Nevertheless, despite his best intentions, Harris ended up working for his father. Again ambivalence, at best, describes Harris's representation of encounters with his father about his future:

> As I was sitting in my bedroom late one evening by the fire at the commencement of January, 1834, my father came to me, and, having shut the door, said, 'Oh, George, we have been thinking of you joining us,' and then he told me that he had arranged with his partner, Mr Wise, that I should be admitted into the firm, which, indeed, Mr Wise, was, I believe, the first to propose. I thanked my father for the offer, to which I, of course, assented; but I remember very well thinking at the time how few young men to whom such a proposal had been made would have been so little elated by it.[42]

Accounts of filial rebellion were rare outside of literary autobiography.[43] Harris stepped back from expressing open resentment despite expressing 'surprise' that his rather had no insight into his character. But, in such cases, lack of choice could sit rather awkwardly with claims to masculine independence. Still writers like Harris and Forwood described a certain type of self-help in their accounts of their struggles to pursue their interests. As Harris explained to his readers, he knew early on that he wanted to become a great writer, painter or orator; as such, 'All that I have ever cared about of getting on at the bar or obtaining position; or wealth, or reputation, was subservient to these, and to enable me to attain them'.[44] His struggle was to pursue knowledge that his father did not value while working in a job he did not particularly enjoy. His success is confirmed in the literary associations he describes in the second half of his life story.

The narrative space given to fathers in part reflected the close association between fathers, sons and work.[45] Indeed these stories demonstrate how important fathers were in the introduction of sons to public and professional life, a key aspect of masculine identity.[46] Perhaps because of this, some middle-class men appear to find difficulty in constructing a narrative which condemned fathers they felt had failed them and, at the same time, asserting their successful move into public life. Most authors applauded their father's good example, usually in relation to their 'hard work', and many clearly appreciated the support they had in setting themselves up in a trade or profession. But this relationship appears to be one in which a certain amount of tension emerged. The father and son relation had the potential to expose the vulnerability of many in the Victorian middle class. Many inherited little except the responsibility to live up to their fathers, which they largely had to do on their own merit.[47] Thus, while submission to parental authority was a traditional value, the need to strike out independently was also necessary.

In the life writing of middle-class men, self-help could be used to accommodate the tensions between submission to authority and individual will, and to smooth the difficult transition from childhood to work and public life. It could be used to narrate a personal struggle to pursue one's own interests and desires without paternal support or to describe the struggle of Smilesean heroes like Bessemer and Nasmyth to follow their father's example and repay paternal support with successful independence. To do so, self making acknowledged 'others' as exemplars, role models or even, as in the case of Harris, as agents who frustrated desires and, in so doing, inspired greater determination. But, in turn, success was represented in the author's ability to head their own family and to define networks of friends and acquaintances of their own making. In a particularly extreme example, Nasmyth's successful self making was symbolised in his narrative through the retelling of a visit by his father to his work rooms in Dale Street, Manchester: 'He could still see his own lathe, driven by steam power, in full operation for the benefit of the son'. Whilst Nasmyth acknowledged his father's role in his success, successful self making was nevertheless demonstrated in his ability to introduce his father to the networks he had cultivated while establishing his business in Manchester:

> His [Nasmyth's father] fame as an artist was well known in Manchester, for many of his works were possessed by the best men of the town. I had the pleasure of introducing him to Brothers Grant, John Kennedy, Edward Lloyd, George Murray, James Frazer, William Fairbairn, and Hugh and Joseph Birley, all of whom gave

him a most cordial welcome, and invited him to enjoy their
hospitality.[48]

As this example suggests, self-help might be a tool for accommodating
independence and dependence but successful self making was confirmed
by the individual's ability to define his own network of like-minded men.

A Community of One's Own

Distinctions between public and private in narratives of self-making
were some of the strategies used to accommodate the tensions and
contradictions that underlay middle-class masculinity. They were also
actively employed in defining a community of one's own. Such narratives
functioned to demonstrate the author's success and notability through
his association with other successful and notable men. Here male friends
and associates were brought in to bear witness to the author's
achievements as a mature masculinity was realized in the description of
a community of like-minded men.[49] Still details about the nature of
companionship were usually absent. Instead successful self making was
symbolised by a shift in the form of autobiographical writing: details of
childhood encounters and early struggles through which the self emerged
are superseded by accounts of public activities and littered with pen
portraits of the great and the good in one's town or profession. The
narrative detail shifted to a focus on the author's contribution to local
and sometimes national governance, their involvement in social reform
activities, attendance at learned societies or interventions in learned
debates. But these activities were retold in forms that made direct
reference to a wider middle-class public culture. The professional, public
and learned activities of successful middle-class men were represented in
pen portraits, after-dinner speeches and letters to and from other
significant men or institutions, reviews in periodicals and letters to
newspapers, which were inserted into the narrative life. These rituals of
recognition emphasised the author's contribution to contemporary
debates about society and confirmed that the author had 'made it' into
the society of his choosing. Aspects of character associated with the self
were reflected and admired in other notables. A web of narratives was
created that represented the author and his associates as agents of
progress and change. In this way life stories could describe a reciprocal
relationship between self making, professional development and reforming society.

As Julie Codell has argued with reference to artists' life writing in late
nineteenth-century and early twentieth-century Britain, the emphasis

given in texts to like minded men was a key strategy in the formulation of a professional identity.[50] An emphasis on associations with other men of note could create a sense of the shared knowledge and collective values associated with being a professional man and the disciplining of self-interest necessary to inclusion in a wider community. There are certain differences in the kinds of communities middle-class men define: barristers tell of their associations with other barristers and judges sometimes through a recall of significant case histories. Perhaps because of uncertainties over their professional status, the life stories of business-men preferably told of their associations with other men of commerce and trade in the council chamber or the learned society rather than the place of business, thus ensuring that a due emphasis was given to the social consequences of their success. Despite the particularities of work or profession, a claim to professional status could be cultivated through the accommodation of individual and collective identity and the negotia-tion of commercial and community interests in life writing.[51] More often than not this was achieved through the integration of autobiography and biography in key narrative spaces.

Rather than denying the importance of society and community to the individual self, success for the middle-class man lay in the ability to define this society through friends and acquaintances.[52] This subtle shift is rhetorically demonstrated in the move towards biography in life writing. As Trev Lynn Broughton has argued, 'the act of reminiscing about others was inextricable from the process of remembering the self'.[53] The use of biography as a didactic tool in the nineteenth century was well established. Referring to what Bahktin called 'rhetorical double-voicedness', Amigoni has demonstrated the way that biography was used as a 'disciplining discourse' in which one speaker represents the voice of the subject addressed and the topics with which that voice had been associated.[54] The particular 'power' of middle-class autobiography was its ability to represent a range of constituencies and voices. The slip between autobiography and biography, references to after-dinner speeches which applauded the author and which the author composed to applaud other notable men, create a sense of dialogue and exchange that was central to and in a sense constitutive of middle-class public authority. Yet these forms of representation closely policed the boundaries of the communities they defined by creating a close associa-tion between the authors and the spaces they described. The shift between biography and autobiography placed the author in a network of narratives about businesses, professions, local governance and social reform. In turn, as Joyce has argued, new narratives were created, in particular, of the civic or the profession, to provide a setting for these networks.[55]

Local space emerged in life stories as a relational setting for the performance of middle-class identity. This process both influenced and was influenced by wider discourses. Many of these autobiographies reflected and contributed to a wider culture of civic remembrance that was played out in local papers in the mid-to-late nineteenth century. Many local papers produced their own series on local worthies and newspapers and periodicals commissioned autobiographical writing that interlinked people and places. In the life histories and local histories presented in newspapers and autobiographies, the emphasis was on the progress associated with community-based local governance: employment, professionalism, moral instruction and, overwhelmingly, public works. In these broader narratives, self making was presented as remaking society. The autobiography of the Cornish industrialist Sir Richard Tangye, *One and All* (1889), provided an interesting example. Tangye's autobiography emerged from a series of short biographies of 'self-made men' that were commissioned by *The British Workman* in 1889. Tangye was asked to provide details of the 'early life and later career' of a 'captain of industry', in relation to the Cornwall Works in Tangye's adoptive town of Birmingham and to include details of his public campaigns for technical education. When Tangye's story was republished as an autobiography, further details of Tangye's early life in Cornwall were recorded. The publisher argued that the narrative of struggle and triumph would make 'an excellent and popular volume' with a special interest to Cornishmen who would relish general details of 'social and industrial' change with specific reference to Cornwall.[56] The ritual of associating one's self with a changing locality, and the notion that one writes the autobiography to remember a place, were rhetorical devices used to stake a claim to notability.

The changing locality, be it market town or city, or, as for many lawyers, the metropolis, provided more than the setting for a description of the author's public and professional life. The interlinking of biography and autobiography through the inclusion in the life story of extracts from local papers, speeches given in the local council chambers and references to after-dinner speeches given at local events, placed the author in relational settings, akin to Bourdieu's habitus, which helped construct an identity of the author as male and middle-class.[57] Henry Aspinall called his autobiography, *Birkenhead* (1903). He hoped his life story would inspire 'simple pleasure' in his readers, yet he spoke of a 'duty to record' his life story and the history of his hometown of Birkenhead as one of its oldest residents.[58] His 'chatty, little volume, reminiscent of my native town', in particular its 'progress from a small rural hamlet', was also a record of the sacrifices Aspinall himself had made to aid this progress. Aspinall's membership of a variety of local organisations, from the local Cricket Club to the Ferry Committee, was emphasised through the inclusion of extracts applauding his good works, but his biographical and descriptive account of the work of others in the development of Birkenhead, in particular the Lairds and the Jacksons, placed his own work in the context of other 'great men' who reformed the city.[59]

The self-made man was a central narrative in stories of middle-class men but success was also defined in putting aside one's own desires for the good of the community. In this way, middle-class men's auto-biography presented an alternative version of heroism in which progress was the result of the small but regular actions of modest men. In this way, through their life stories, middle-class men constructed themselves as agents of historical change. Forwood presented his work on Liverpool council as an important part of history:

> A great city – its people and its institutions, as seen by a contemporary, presents incidents that do not specially appeal to the historian, who is more concerned with the larger features and events which mark its growth; but those incidents may serve as sidelights upon the movements and the spirit of the times, and woven around the outlines of a life which had been threaded in the weft of its activities, may afford a background to bring into more prominent relief and give juster proportion to the characters and the actions of the men who have built up its prosperity.[60]

Forwood's dialogic history presented a relational location which enabled him to represent himself, his contemporaries and his home town. It demonstrated how a male middle-class identity was premised on a society and contingent on one's ability to speak for that society. The lawyer R. Francillon crafted a self-conscious attempt to chart the changes of the nineteenth century. Calling his autobiography, *Mid-Victorian Memories*, his text revelled in the democratization of print culture and asserted the greater cultural authority of the 'nobody', someone perfectly placed to reflect the spirit of the times.[61]

This symbiosis between biography and autobiography demonstrates the way that middle-class autobiography constructed the relational location which narrated a sense of self and society. The rhetorical dynamics established between the individual and the community, and the town and profession, was a mechanism for mapping change. In defining communities of participation, the author could show that he had a place in history. The role of the exemplary life in explaining change had been recognised by Smiles; however, by the late nineteenth century, this was more self-consciously explored in the view of history as the active agency of men. In their own self making, these men also defined the ways in which they mastered landscapes and contributed to change. Thus the representation of carefully controlled accounts of discussions and debates with notable others was used to construct a heroic image of everyday middle-class masculinity.

Conclusion

The writing of an autobiography in the late nineteenth century was a social act. As Malchow has argued, the written word was often used by the Victorian middle class as a form of communication that appeared intimate and confessional but which was in fact 'distant and controlled'.[62] As I have argued here, control was attempted through narratives of self-help, the separation of public and private and homosociability. These narratives could be used to present a successful self which balanced the different demands of family, work and society. In these narratives the significance of others to successful masculinity could be acknowledged while individual agency could be presented as shaping society. Despite the attempts to use these narratives to bring together gender and class identities these stories demonstrate moments when the story slips and the author displays awkwardness and anxiety in, for example, narrating failure or in talking about one's private life. More often than not, these slippages demonstrate the disjuncture between narrative and social agency, and the fractured nature of class and gender, but they also serve to bring into sharper focus the importance of a coherent ontology in staking a claim to middle-class masculinity.

Certainly, in the broader history of the Victorian middle class, the life story demonstrates the significance of locality and profession to a sense of self and community; however it also shows that expressions of the self and society commonly drew on a much wider range of cultural references. In the overwhelming focus given to public activities and the company of like-minded men in networks that moved between the domestic, the town and, on occasion, the nation, middle-class men's life writing reflected and informed a broader middle-class culture. These same emplotments, however, functioned in the texts studied here to delimit and define a middle-class male self through the society he inhabited. The intertwining of the life story with the stories of other people and places, one's family, other like-minded men, the history of a town or the development of a profession, placed the self at the centre of a network of narratives about self and society. At the same time, the movement of the authorial 'I' across boundaries of public and private, time and place were strategies of order and control, albeit ones that were not always successful.

Notes

1. This work is the result of a project undertaken with the late Robbie Gray who deserves credit for stimulating discussion of the issues addressed.
2. For a recent overview, see the introduction in R. Dekker (ed.), *Egodocuments and History: Autobiographical Writing in its Social Context since the Middle Ages* (Rotterdam: Erasmus University, 2002).
3. An important exception here is H.L. Malchow, *Gentlemen Capitalists: The Social and Political World of the Victorian Businessman* (London: Macmillan, 1991). As the title suggests, this study uses a biographical approach to study the social forces at work in the lives of businessmen. Critical rereadings of the Victorian 'men of letters' have reconsidered the relationship between autography, biography and the narrative strategies through which autonomous masculinity is defined. For example, see Trev Lynn Broughton, *Men of Letters, Writing Lives: Masculinity and Literary Auto/Biography in the Late Victorian Period* (London: Routledge, 1999); V. Newey and P. Shaw (eds), *Moral Pages, Literary Lives: Studies in Nineteenth-Century Autobiography* (Aldershot: Scholar, 1996) and L. Marcus, *Auto/biographical Discourses: Theory Criticism, Practice* (Manchester: Manchester University Press, 1994). Other works have considered the life writing of marginalised people, workers, women and the colonised: for example, M.J. Corbett, *Representing Femininity: Middle-class Subjectivity in Victorian and Edwardian Women's Autobiographies* (Oxford: Oxford University Press, 1992); J. Swindells, *Victorian Writing and Working Women* (Cambridge: Polity Press, 1985) and D. Vincent, *Bread, Knowledge and Freedom: a Study of Nineteenth-century Working Class Autobiography* (London: Europa, 1981).
4. In particular, see Marcus, *Auto/biographical Discourses* and D. Amigoni, *Victorian Biography: Intellectuals and the Ordering of Discourse* (Hemel Hempstead: Harvester, 1993).
5. P. Lejeune, *On Autobiography* (Minneapolis: University of Minnesota Press, 1989), pp.172–3.
6. See R. Gray, 'Self-made men, self-narrated lives: male autobiographical writing and the Victorian middle-class', in *Journal of Victorian Culture*, 6 (2001), 290.
7. The term 'discursive consistencies' is taken from P. Lejeune, *On Autobiography*, 172–6. See also R. Gagnier, *Subjectivities; A History of Self-Representation in Britain, 1832–1920* (Oxford: Oxford University Press, 1991); P. Joyce, 'Introduction', *Democratic Subjects. The Self and the Social in Nineteenth Century England* (Cambridge: Cambridge University Press, 1994), pp.161–76; see also D. Vincent, *Bread, Knowledge and Freedom*, pp.197–203.
8. V. Sanders, '"Fathers' daughters": Three Victorian anti-feminist women autobiographers', *Mortal Pages, Literary Lives*, 153–71.
9. M.R. Somers and G.D. Gibson, 'Reclaiming the epistemological "Other": Narrative and the social construction of identity', in C. Calhoun (ed.), *Social Theory and the Politics of Identity* (Oxford: Blackwell, 1994), p.73.
10. P. Joyce, *Democratic Subjects*, p.172.
11. S. Smiles, *Self-Help* ([1859] London: Sphere, 1968), pp.13–14.
12. Ibid, p.9.
13. H. Bessemer, *An Autobiography* (London: 1905), anonymous preface.

14. J. Tosh, *A Man's Place: Masculinity and the Middle-class Home in Victorian England* (New Haven: Yale University Press, 1999), p.2.
15. John Tosh recently made this point in a conference paper, 'Masculinities in Britain, 1800–1914', *Journal of British Studies* symposium, Sussex University, 2003. I am grateful for permission to refer to this.
16. Speech from Abraham Hewett, who introduced the Bessemer process in the United States, given to the London Iron and Steel Institute 1890; reprinted in the prologue to Bessemer's autobiography.
17. Bessemer, *Autobiography*, p.326.
18. C. Machan, 'The construction of masculinity in Victorian autobiography', *Nineteenth-Century Prose*, 26: 2 (1999), p.12.
19. Tosh, *A Man's Place*, p.6.
20. H. Preston-Thomas, *The Work and Play of a Government Inspector* (London: Backwoods and Sons, 1909).
21. S. Smith, *My Life Work* (London: Hodder and Stoughton, 1902), preface.
22. L. Turner, *The Memories of Llewelyn Turner* (London: Isbister and Co. Ltd., 1903).
23. L. Davidoff and C. Hall, *Family Fortunes: Men and Women of the English Middle-class, 1780–1850* (London: Hutchinson, 1987), Prologue.
24. Bessemer, *Autobiography*, p.42.
25. R. Gray, 'Self-made men', pp.302–3.
26. See also Julie Codell, The *Victorian Artist. Artists' Lifewritings in Britain, c. 1870–1910* (Cambridge: Cambridge University Press, 2003) pp.196–9.
27. S. Smith, *My Life Work*, preface.
28. Smith, p.87.
29. Smith, p.301.
30. Smith, p.304. See S. Garton on the disjuncture between public and private grief in 'The scales of human suffering: love, death and Victorian masculinity', *Social History* 27: 1 (2002), 40–58.
31. E. Parry, *What the Judge Saw* (London: Smith, Elder and Co., 1912), p.18.
32. W. Ford Stanley, *His Life and Work,* ed. R. Inwards (London: Crosby, Lockwood and Co., 1911), p.21.
33. W. Tanner, *Memoir* (London, 1868), preface.
34. Smith, p.37.
35. There is, however, little discussion of the author as father. See Tosh, *A Man's Place*, p.79.
36. J. Nasmyth, *Autobiography*, ed. S. Smiles (London: John Murray, 1885), pp.1–15.
37. J. Nasmyth, pp.45, 50, 87, 98; and Bessemer, *Autobiography*, pp.6–11, 41.
38. Smiles, *Self-Help*, p.22.
39. W. Forwood, *Recollections of a Busy Life* (Liverpool: Henry Young and Sons, 1910), pp.2, 20.
40. Ford Stanley, *His Life and Work*, pp.10–18, 23.
41. R.E. Francillon, *Mid-Victorian Memories* (London: Hodder and Stoughton, 1914), pp.118, 126.
42. G. Harris, *Autobiography* (London: Hazell, Watson and Viney, 1888), p.41.
43. Tosh, *A Man's Place*, p.121.
44. Harris, *Autobiography*, p.25.

45. But, despite the importance of fathers to the future of their offspring, their role and their private duties and public responsibilities with regard to their children were rarely discussed. See Tosh, *A Man's Place*, p.79.
46. In Malchow's study, three of the four examples of Victorian businessmen he considered were set up by their fathers. See *Gentlemen Capitalists*, p.343.
47. L. Krenis, 'Authority and rebellion in Victorian autobiography', *The Journal of British Studies*, 18 (1978), 109–10.
48. Nasmyth, *Autobiography*, 219.
49. As Tosh says, full masculinity was the 'gift of ones peers', (*A Man's Place*, p.3).
50. Codell, *The Victorian Artist*, p.104–9.
51. Ibid, p.106.
52. See M. Danahay, *A Community of One*, p.28.
53. Broughton, *Men of Letters*, p.25.
54. Amigoni, *Victorian Biography*, pp.20–23.
55. P. Joyce, *Democratic Subjects*, p.176.
56. R. Tangye, *'One and All': An Autobiography* (London: S.W. Partridge and Co., 1889), preface.
57. P. Bourdieu, *Distinction* (London: Routledge and Kegan Paul, 1984), pp.169–72.
58. H. Aspinall, *Birkenhead and Its Surroundings* (Liverpool: Liverpool Booksellers' Co., 1903).
59. Ibid., preface.
60. Forwood, *Recollections*, ch 1.
61. Francillon, *Mid-Victorian Memories*, p.1.
62. Malchow, *Gentlemen Capitalists*, p.2.

CHAPTER FOUR

Male Masochism
A Model of Victorian Masculine Identity Formation

Martin A. Danahay

Masochism was a common and disturbing feature of Victorian masculinity. Victorian male masochism was marked by a sublimated anxiety that made it impossible for the male subject to recognize his complicity in his self-inflicted pain. This pain was acknowledged only at the margins, in diaries and letters, but not overtly in public utterances. Rather than recognise the psychic pain that they were causing themselves, Victorian men would look 'outward' and find compensation for their own inner pain in idealised images of the other. This chapter will focus, not on obvious forms of masochism such as those chronicled in the work of Krafft-Ebing[1] (who coined the term) for example, but rather in the psychic self-lacerations of such Victorian figures as Thomas Carlyle, John Stuart Mill and Arthur Munby. These males show a persistent aversion to acknowledging their own desires, and are thus unable to recognise their self-inflicted pain. Masochism is for them an accepted part of male identity.

Masochism as a mechanism makes 'pain appear to come from elsewhere' and thus facilitates the repression feelings of depression and anxiety.[2] Rather than take account of the way in which Victorian masculinity itself constrained men to self-repression and self-inflicted pain, such feelings could be managed by projecting them. Projection defined in psychoanalytic terms is a 'process whereby a painful idea or impulse is attributed to the external world'.[3] Arthur Munby, John Stuart Mill and Thomas Carlyle exemplify this process by making projection an integral part of their own identity formation. Such projections helped them externalize corrosive feelings of insecurity or depression and make them appear to come from outside the psyche.

The classic tale of male masochism is of course Leopold von Sacher-Masoch's *Venus in Furs* (1870) after whom Richard von Krafft-Ebing named the syndrome. Krafft-Ebing claimed that Masoch created the category through his fiction and created a category that was previously unknown to science.[4] I will argue that Masoch's narrative actually only codifies a common feature of Victorian masculine subjectivity that was prevalent throughout the period. I am not the first in using the story to characterise masculine subjectivity through masochism; Kaja Silverman has carried out an extensive analysis in her book *Male Subjectivity at the Margins*, especially in her chapter on 'Masochism and Male Subjectivity'.[5] I will build upon her insights into masculinity to suggest the peculiarly Victorian aspects of Masoch's narrative and its implications for male subjectivity. Masochism, I argue, is not a marginal and esoteric fetish, but a central heuristic for understanding Victorian male identity formation.

Silverman uses Freud's essay on 'The Economic Problem of Masochism' to analyse the mechanism of displaced desire that undergirds this 'perversion'. I put 'perversion' in quotation marks because, as I will argue and Silverman's analysis makes clear, this condition is simply an extreme form of heteronormative Victorian masculinity. As Silverman says, the male masochist 'acts out in an insistent and exaggerated way the basic conditions of cultural subjectivity, conditions that are normally disavowed'.[6] The masochistic fantasy thus represents the mechanisms that make normal masculine subjectivity possible, albeit in a hysterical and exaggerated form that makes explicit what is usually implicit in conventional narratives.

I will trace this masochistic narrative through diaries, photographs and letters rather than directly through autobiographical narratives. Like many theorists, I believe that the formal distinctions between autobiography, biography and fiction obscure the cultural assumptions about identity that inform them.[7] From the perspective of contemporary critical theory, the boundary between autobiography and fiction is permeable; it is one of the many binaries that have been deconstructed in the critique of autobiography as a genre. Unlike Clinton Machann, I would not attempt to define autobiography as a genre, seeing the issue rather in terms of a model of identity that can be found in any text.[8] Machann draws a boundary between autobiography and diaries or journals because there is no retrospective controlling narrative and they are meant primarily as 'private documents' and not for publication.[9] However, as Mary Evans argues, the growth of what we now term 'autobiography' is marked by an 'increasingly problematic negotiation between the public and the private' and the inclusion of more and more of the 'merely' private concerns not only of the famous or noteworthy but also of ordinary people.[10] From Evans's perspective autobiography is an 'impossible' genre because it has no boundaries. In this volume, Martin Hewitt and Matt Cook both use diaries as a way of understanding autobiography and issues of identity.

Having said that, it must also be recognized that for the Victorian male the boundary between 'public' and 'private' was crucial to identity formation. The masochism that I will describe as a common feature of

Victorian masculinity is expressed in 'private' venues like diaries, letters and journals much more readily than in published, formal auto-biographies. The divided masculinity of the Victorian period was not just fissured along gender lines, but also in terms of 'private' sentiments and public display. Thus a figure like Thomas Carlyle would privately admit his difficulties with writing, while in his published pieces extolling all forms of labour as heroic and ennobling.

An example of this fissure can be found in John Tosh's *A Man's Place*. Tosh makes a convincing argument that 'the domestic sphere ... is integral to masculinity'.[11] Through a careful reading of the diaries and letters of Victorian men, Tosh argues that his subjects negotiated compromises between the public ideal of masculinity and the private 'domestic affections'. In Tosh's account, Victorian men were deeply involved in domestic life as husbands and fathers. Tosh goes on to admit, however, that Victorian middle-class culture was 'constructed around a heavily polarized understanding of gender' that was more extreme in the Victorian period than before or since.[12] This polarisation was most strongly registered in popular texts and images in which stark contrasts were represented between the male and female, and the public and the domestic. Thus for the Victorian male there was a radical separation between the private 'domestic affections' and the public performance of masterful masculinity that was expected as part of heteronormative identity. Popular imagery reinforced this division even while men in private negotiated compromises between ideology and practice.

Given this polarisation, diaries and letters thus become depositories for traces of masochistic libidinal energy that can find only oblique expression in published autobiographies. I will therefore use diaries and letters to analyse the masculine identity, and then read this model back into autobiographies such as John Stuart Mill's and published texts by Thomas Carlyle. I will also suggest that much contemporary use of Masoch's story as a model of masochism is too concerned with reading it in terms of a Freudian model of the Oedipal complex and castration anxieties, and thus erases the class basis of *Venus in Furs*. The class issue is, I would argue, crucial in understanding what marks this as a nineteenth-century narrative steeped in the social deployment of codes of dominance and mastery, especially of upper-class men over lower-class women.

To recap *Venus in Furs* briefly, in Masoch's narrative Severin von Kusiemski meets a woman called Wanda von Dunajew, and as their relationship develops he becomes her slave and encourages her to beat and humiliate him. This summary of the plot, however, does not do justice to its multilayered complexities. To begin with, Severin is not the initial narrator; we are introduced to Severin by another narrator who has a dream of a 'Venus in Furs' and goes to Severin to tell him about his strange experience. In Severin's house he sees a painting of 'Venus in Furs' and is then given the text based on a journal called *Confessions of a Suprasensual Man*, written by Severin himself. It is this text that tells the story of the relationship between Severin and Wanda, and this is in fact a mediated autobiography that, like the confession of Dr Jekyll in *The Strange Case of Dr. Jekyll and Mr. Hyde*, is encased in other narratives. Like Stevenson's text, Masoch's conceals and reveals desires that are unacceptable for a respectable male. While desires could be 'confessed' in diaries and journals, they could no be expressed overtly and must be revealed encased within layers of narrative.

Gilles Deleuze in his analysis of *Venus in Furs* is concerned primarily with the separation of sadism from masochism, arguing that Freud conflated the two.[13] He does, however, note the aesthetic aspect of the narrative, noting the way in which 'the woman torturer freezes into postures that identify her with a statue, a painting or a photograph'.[14] In the initial dream an immediate confusion is created about the status of the Venus, who is at once a statue and a real woman who sneezes and complains of the cold. In Severin's narrative itself Wanda is identified with a statue of Venus which he embraces as if it were a real woman. Given that this the narrative begins with a dream, and that in hindsight we know that Masoch was idealising his own life, the text is signalling here its affinities with the Pygmalion myth. Deleuze identifies the key to Masoch's text as 'suspense' and argues that this accounts for the number of references to paintings, statues and photographs in the text, but his analysis is most accurate when he states that 'women become exciting when they are indistinguishable from cold statues in the moonlight or paintings in darkened rooms'.[15] Masoch represents through this eroticisation of statues and paintings the male process of creating an idealised other as an aesthetic object and then turning this other into a force who dominates and ultimately enslaves him.

I have argued elsewhere that the Pygmalion myth, rather than that of Narcissus, is the best vehicle for understanding male Victorian writers' and painters' representation of masculine desire.[16] The foremost exemplar of the Pygmalion process is Dante Gabriel Rossetti who in his poetry and painting represented idealised images of women in terms of his own desires. In 'The Orchard-Pit', Rossetti gives his purest expression of male masochist subjectivity. In a prose accompaniment to the poetry he represents it as a recurrent fantasy of his fictional narrator who says that 'men tell me that sleep has many dreams; but all my life I have dreamt one dream alone' and that

> This dream shows me no strange place. I know the glen, and have
> known it from childhood, and heard many tales of those who have

died there by the Siren's spell. I pass there often now, and look at it as one might look at a place chosen for one's grave. I see nothing, but I know that it means death for me.[17]

Rossetti invokes the dream as does Masoch, and represents the woman as both enticing and deadly for the male subject. In fact, even more than a dream, Rossetti turns representing what is usually termed the 'femme fatale' into an obsession, which parallels the fetishistic aspects of masochism.[18] He obsessively represents a woman who is both alluring and overpowering, so that love becomes a question of subjugation to an idealised female figure. He encodes a similar mixture of desire and threat in his own poem and painting of Venus, who holds out an apple but also threatens with a dart that will cause 'wandering of his feet perpetually'.[19] While Rossetti does not imagine his Venus in furs, he does imagine her as controlling the male through her sexuality. The obsessive quality of Rossetti's lovely but deadly dream woman accords extremely well with Freud's account of the death drive and the compulsion to repeat.[20]

However what I wish to emphasize here is the way in which the male creates a fantasy figure through art or literature who externalises desires or fears that cannot be acknowledged directly. The Pygmalion myth is as appropriate for *Venus in Furs* as it is for Rossetti because Masoch's narrative records the process of a man creating his dream woman who is likened to a statue coming to life. It has not been noted hitherto that *Venus in Furs* represents a long socialisation process in which Wanda is turned into the ideal subject of Severin's fantasies. At several points Wanda complains that all she wants to do is kiss Severin, not whip or degrade him; in this she is trying to articulate an ideal of love as pleasure rather than pain and as a meeting of equals. For Severin, and for Masoch, however, love is linked to pain, domination and subordination, and this is played out particularly in class terms. He fashions Wanda into an ideal woman in the image of his own desires in his retelling of the Pygmalion myth.

In retrospect it has become possible to recognise the autobiographical basis of *Venus in Furs*. Wanda Sacher-Masoch in her *Confessions* revealed that the story was a fictionalised account of her own relationship with her husband.[21] While Leopold von Sacher-Masoch did not write his own autobiography to document the private basis of the story, he created an aesthetic version of his own experiences in *Venus in Furs*. It is revealing that he did not write an overt autobiography; however much Masoch may have wished to publicise his own erotic adventures, he chose to represent his experiences as fiction. Even such a sexual renegade as Masoch could not bridge the division between the public and the private overtly, but instead presented an idealised version of himself and his wife in the narrative. Rather than acknowledge his own desires publicly, he represented them in an idealised form in *Venus in Furs*, and had his protagonist renounce finally what he knew were publicly unacceptable desires. At the end of *Venus in Furs*, Severin is 'cured' of his desire to be dominated.

Masoch's contribution to the Venus myth is to dress her in fur. Apart from the obvious fetishism of having a woman dress in fur in an external sign of her pubic hair, the presence of fur also raises class issues. Wanda is an upper-class woman who as the narrative progresses becomes more and more aristocratic (and is increasingly identified with Catherine the Great) while Severin becomes a servant and ultimately a slave. The narrative thus links masochism to the class system and normalises the domination of one person by another as a natural part of the social order. This aspect of the narrative is signalled at the beginning by Severin threatening to beat a servant girl for his own pleasure. His perverse desire to be dominated has been replaced by a more acceptable desire to express his domination of women of lower social class rather than by an aristocratic 'Venus in Furs'.

The problem for male Victorian subjectivity lay in the necessity to be always dominant and masterful, at least in public. This view was codified in its most extreme form by Ruskin in 'Of Queens' Gardens' in his classic delineation of the different 'spheres' of male and female activity:

> The man's power is active, progressive, defensive. He is eminently the doer, the creator, the discoverer, the defender. His intellect is for speculation and invention; his energy for adventure, for war, and for conquest, wherever war is just, wherever conquest necessary.[22]

While this is an extreme formulation, it has profound implications for the psychic economy of men in the Victorian period. In Ruskin's schema, a man, whether he likes it or not, is in a permanently aggressive, externally directed state. Constantly ready for battle, the male is forever scanning the horizon seeking targets to attack, and countries to occupy, or looking for ways to defend the domestic space. The male psyche is, in Ruskin's view, a machine designed for external aggression that is as incapable of escaping its psychic programming for warfare as is the female mind of escaping the domestic sphere. The male is defined in terms of constant activity and the potential for violence. Introspection, rest and leisure play no part in this image of the ideal male consciousness.

Arthur Munby, who publicly wàs a conventional Victorian male, registers most strongly the contrast between the 'masterful' Victorian masculine subject and private experiences of insecurity and a desire to be dominated. Arthur Joseph Munby (1828–1910) was the eldest son of a York solicitor. He took a degree at Cambridge and was called to the bar, but never practised law, securing instead a sinecure position with the Ecclesiastical Commission, where he worked from 1858 to 1888. Munby met Hannah Cullwick (1833–1910), a working-class woman who had moved from Shropshire to London to work as a domestic servant, in 1854 and, after a long, clandestine relationship, married her in 1873. Munby kept a diary for most of his life, and collected photographs of working-class women. He also asked Cullwick to keep a diary. Munby bequeathed his diary, Cullwick's diary and his photographs to Trinity College, Cambridge library under the condition that they not be opened until 1950. Selections from Munby's diaries have been published by Derek Hudson in *Munby: Man of Two Worlds: The Life and Diaries of Arthur Munby*[23] and Cullwick's diaries have been reprinted in their entirety in Liz Stanley's *The Diaries of Hannah Cullwick, Victorian Maidservant*.[24]

Munby never revealed his relationship with Cullwick during his life. He published many poems, such as *Dorothy: A Country Story*, that in retrospect can be seen as autobiographically based as they play out the fantasy of the relationship between an upper-class man and a lower-class woman. Like Masoch, Munby represented his fantasies as fiction rather than admitting their relationship to his private life. Munby, rather than turn Cullwick into a 'Venus in Furs' made her into a 'Venus in Dirt'. He had Cullwick remake herself in the image of his own ideal of the working-class woman, obtaining an erotic charge from the result of her labour. He reverses Sacher-Masoch's model, and rather than worship an image of an upper-class woman in furs, he worships an image of a working-class woman begrimed by dirt.

Munby was obsessed with working-class women, and it was the image of women at work, especially if the work involved dirt and muscles, that most attracted him. The labour of working-class women was for Munby the antitype of male intellectual work. Munby sought in working-class women a resolution of many of the same anxieties that inform Carlyle's celebrations of work as an ideal. Munby's desires from the Victorian perspective were deeply perverted, yet his perversity reveals the dynamic of mainstream Victorian male consciousness. Far from being perverse, Munby is actually a very useful figure for understanding the relationship between Victorian male subjectivity and work.

Munby is a fascinating figure because he rebelled against what Sussman refers to as 'normative bourgeois masculinity' that enforced 'compulsory heterosexuality and compulsory matrimony'.[25] In this chapter I have adopted the term 'heteronormative' to indicate this set of ideas. Munby's illicit desires placed him outside the mainstream masculine identity of his period, but his abnormal position led him to question conventional masculine identity in fascinating ways. Munby managed to subvert masculine orthodoxy by fetishising working-class women as the epitome of the noble and heroic worker. While this would have been labelled as perversity in its time, it actually affords a unique perspective on the gender and class basis of the Victorian doctrine of work.[26]

Munby was not secure in his masculine subject position, which supposedly gave him power over dependants and 'inferiors'. He admired Hannah Cullwick's prowess and muscular power; the inverse of these statements is his awareness of his own relative lack of strength,[27] and therefore of his own proximity to a feminine subject position in the Victorian gender system. Seeing Cullwick and other women performing physical labour helped anaesthetise the disturbing implications of their muscular physical power by confirming his mastery over them. Munby's need for domination and 'mastery' is a symptom of his anxieties concerning his own class and gender status.

Munby and Cullwick both performed their rejection of conventional gender roles in their scheme to dress Cullwick up as a man and have her pose as Munby's personal servant.[28] Although they eventually rejected this possible configuration of their relationship, Munby had Cullwick photographed in men's clothing. This is Munby's version of the homoerotic subplot enacted in *Venus in Furs*, when Severin is beaten by a man as the climactic scene of masochism in the story. Munby and Cullwick would collaboratively transgress gender lines and adopt conventionally 'masculine' and 'feminine' roles by having Cullwick dress as a male servant, signalling the transgressive nature of Munby's desires in terms of both class and gender. However they dropped this piece of role playing and reverted to more conventional gender roles eventually, just as Masoch disavows homoeroticism in *Venus in Furs*.

Cullwick also transgressed gender norms by deriving satisfaction from her own power. Cullwick was proud of her own muscular strength, and the fact that she could pick grown men up; she derived power and a sense of autonomy from this conventionally 'masculine' aspect of her body. Munby enjoyed being picked up and 'petted' by Cullwick and assumed a relationship with her that both infantilised him and made his position to her one of passivity and dependence. The photograph of Cullwick in men's clothes thus demonstrates the way in which they privately negotiated supposedly fixed public gender norms.

The strongest form of counteridentification and subversion of his gender identity for Munby occurs in the realm of work, particularly manual labour. This is why hands were such an important locus of class and gender identity for him, as they were for Victorian culture generally.

Munby spent most of his time at work writing reports, letters and poetry, occupations which left his hands free from callouses. When he compared his hands to those of Cullwick or other working-class women he was comparing the gender implications of their respective kinds of work. Munby makes the connection between his fetish and work explicit in one striking diary entry in which he compared the sumptuous surroundings of a dinner being served to him, Dante Gabriel Rossetti, F.W. Burton and other members of Munby's literary and artistic circle:

> The glass, the china, are all antique: the dinner, elaborate and refined, is handed round by a single female servant; a robust, comely young matron, whose large strong hands, used to serving, contrast with the small hands of her master, used to pictures and poems.[29]

Munby's connection, and that of the other artists and writers around him, to a particular occupation implicitly feminises them. The gender identifications and disidentifications in Munby's diary entries relate directly to forms of labour and their effect on the body. For Munby his work made him feminine and he compensated for this by idealising the signs of manual labour on working-class women's bodies. Munby fetishises the signs of physical labour in the working-class women he had photographed because of their connection to strenuous work and the way in which, particularly in the case of women mine workers, they transgressed gender lines by wearing men's clothing. The calloused hands and muscles that Munby admired in these women were marks of strenuous physical labour recorded at the level of the body that aligned them with men's work. They are the locus of all his anxieties about his own work, and his doubts about his masculine status as a worker. Munby frequently complained about his lack of aptitude for work, and his feelings of oppression at having to practise law:

> This is not a Diary of moods and 'experiences:' else I might say much of the wretchedness and selfdespair I have gone through this week – and all, or chiefly, because of some law business I had in hand! The practice, though not the grand and general principles, of Law is most hateful to me, from natural inaptness & from the miserable associations of home. Perplexed among its dry hideous subtleties, ever afraid to bring one's little knowledge to bear, for fear of some unsuspected trap which nothing can evade – one feels degraded by this, and by the hypocrisy one has to maintain.[30]

This is one of the few moments where Munby does in fact directly address work and identity. Interestingly he claims that this is not a 'diary' in the sense that we would think of such a text; this is not the place for an exploration of his own psyche but rather a more documentary approach to his ramblings around London in search of working-class women. This is one of the few points where Munby actually talks about his own work rather than working-class labour. Legal work for Munby acts as the focus of his anxieties about his own autonomy and efficacy as a masculine subject. Law is for him associated with his home, and his damaging emotional and financial dependence on his father. Munby felt acutely his lack of income, and his consequent need for supplements from his father, who seems himself to have been preoccupied to an unusual extent with his finances. Clarke has noted a similar anxiety in Carlyle vis-à-vis his father, who carried out manual labour; for Carlyle manual labour became the idealised form of work, and one that implicitly devalued intellectual labour.[31] The law seems also for Munby to have brought to the surface his anxieties about his own intellect and competence that left him feeling 'degraded' and hypocritical. He clearly felt himself unsuited to the role of a masculine professional. These anxieties became less pronounced when he finally found an undemanding job with the Ecclesiastical Commission.

Men were conventionally supposed to derive power and identity from their work. In the division of the Victorian world into the private and the public, the private realm was represented as mostly 'feminine' and domestic and the public 'masculine', although as Elizabeth Langland has demonstrated this division did not work in practice, only in theory.[32] Far from experiencing work as a source of power and masculine identity, Munby instead was tormented by feelings of inadequacy. Work did not reinforce his masculine identity; instead it made him doubt his efficacy as a worker and as a man.

Munby's fetishising of working-class women can therefore be seen as an imaginative compensation for his own feelings of inadequacy, and his attempt to square his own experiences with the Carlylean ideology of the sanctity of labour, an ideology that he himself espoused fervently. Munby felt that work ought to be, and was for most people, a redeeming and ennobling enterprise. He calls work carried out by Cullwick, for instance, 'noble and sanctified'.[33] For him, however, work provided no satisfaction, and in fact made him feel insecure and unhappy. He therefore, in compensation, idealised the labour of the working classes as a sanctifying undertaking and tried to fashion Hannah Cullwick in his image of work as a redemptive activity.

A similar process of idealising a feminine figure is to be found in John Stuart Mill's *Autobiography*. Mill's well-documented 'mental crisis' seems as much a crisis of introspection as anything, especially given that his response was to formulate his 'anti-self-consciousness' doctrine that proscribed analysing his own mental processes. To become introspective turned him into a 'paralysed intellect' and he determined instead to fix his mind on 'some other object' external to himself.[34] Later this 'object' became Harriet Taylor, whom Mill turned into a paragon of femininity so that he could claim that 'my objects in life were solely those which were hers'.[35] While Mill does not have Taylor dress in furs, he turns her into an ideal woman before whom he can abase himself.

Mill enacts on a psychic level the drama of Masoch's *Venus in Furs*. While Mill does not seem to have had a taste for whips, he was, like Masoch, acutely aware of the power basis of Victorian gender relationships. This is made clear in his essay on 'The Subjection of Women' where he discusses the power relationships between men and women in Victorian society and asserts that Victorian men want 'not a forced slave but a willing one'.[36] The idea of a 'willing slave' is exactly the masochistic ideal in *Venus in Furs*, and the perversion of the situation comes from a male placing himself in the subjected position most naturally occupied by a woman. Mill's own subject position vis-à-vis Taylor made him acutely aware of power issues in the formation of gender in Victorian society.

The common denominator between Mill, Munby and Masoch is the binary of domination/subordination. Munby and Cullwick similarly enacted the power relations between them when she posed as a slave and called him 'massa'. Masoch also shows his protagonist at the beginning dominating a serving woman, while the bulk of the narrative is about a male abasing himself. Preserved in this process is the binary of domination and subordination, with one or the other partner having to be dominant. Conventionally the male was dominant, but Munby's masochism led him to subordinate himself to the image of working-class women.

Work was supposed to provide the arena in which men were to prove themselves as the Ruskinian ideal of the 'doer and creator' rather than passive and feminine. Munby subverted this model by idealising working-class women as strong, and himself as implicitly weak and passive. The model of male subjectivity presented by Masoch and Munby as 'masochistic' provides the key to understanding the contradictions in the foremost exponent of the 'Gospel of Work', Thomas Carlyle. Carlyle admitted in a letter, 'Writing is a dreadful Labour, yet not so dreadful as Idleness'.[37] This sentence shows both the reality of work as 'dreadful' as opposed to the ideal represented in such texts as *Past and Present*, and the function of 'idleness' as the binary opposite of work that is both its nemesis and the term that allows masculine subjectivity to exist in its masterful form. It was only in private that Carlyle would acknowledge the gap between ideology and reality.

Carlyle in his letters expressed a masochistic attitude toward his body that was intimately associated with depression. Whenever Carlyle felt depressed he would exhibit a series of illnesses that would cause him to take medicine that would exacerbate his symptoms. Carlyle 'felt degraded by his misfunctioning "bowels", for which he took "pills" and "castor oil"'.[38] These remedies would make him even worse and the psychic symptoms would become inextricably linked with worsening physical discomfort so that in Kaplan's words he 'could no longer detect the real source of his pain'. Kaplan ascribes Carlyle's confusion to an inability to distinguish mind and body, but what appears here more strongly is a desire to punish the body by making it feel a pain equivalent to the psychic distress that Carlyle was experiencing. Sussman has noted this same 'dis-ease' that Carlyle felt in his revulsion at the male body, although he does not make the connection directly to Carlyle's 'misfunctioning' bowels.[39] Carlyle clearly had antagonistic feelings toward male bodies in general, and his own body in particular.

Kaplan is a very perceptive biographer of Carlyle and my task here, thanks to his excellent work, is to bring together some of his remarks to map out Carlyle's masochistic tendencies. Kaplan at one point refers to Carlyle's 'angry dialogue' with Victorian society that had 'been deeply internalized' and ascribes this to Carlyle's vision of 'the world as an extension of self rather than self as an extension of the world'.[40] It is difficult to see what Kaplan means by 'self' and 'world' here, but placing his remarks in the context of Ruskin's words about men and battle gives more substance to this characterisation. Carlyle expressed his anger in a generally violent and hostile denunciation of his age, but this anger was a redirected form of the aggression he expressed toward his own body. As Sussman notes, 'Carlyle's language consistently conflates the physical and the psychological' and the boundaries between his own body and his image of the social were amorphous.[41] Carlyle in general followed Ruskin's dictum that he constantly be ready for battle externally, but when depressed this hostility would be directed inward and at his 'misfunctioing' bowels. Carlyle would take medicines that exacerbated his bodily complaints as a way of punishing himself in the same way that he usually railed against Victorian society with his rhetoric. Depression brought on by not working (or 'idleness') was therefore to be avoided at all costs.

Carlyle's antidote for psychic pain was the 'gospel of work,' just as the anti-self-consciousness doctrine was for Mill. The pain that Carlyle ascribes to not working was equally present in the 'dreadful labour' of writing; only by turning idleness into a state worse than working could Carlyle make it seem an attractive alternative. Work as an 'active' undertaking along Ruskinian lines leads men to focus on work to avoid an internal fire. Although 'only through work could he feel useful and whole again',[42] his experience of work was of distress and difficulty, and quite frequently depression. As he said, it was a 'dreadful labour'.

Writing for Carlyle was, in Marxist terms, alienated labour. While we tend to think of 'alienated labour' as a working-class phenomenon that is best represented by the factory, this is only the most extreme forms of alienated labour in the Victorian period. Marx thought that the working classes were the most exploited by the capitalist system and thus were the class most likely to rise up against the hegemony of capital. Alienated labour, however, can be found in any class under capitalism, but the specific ideology of that class may militate against recognition of exploitation.[43]

This is true of writers as a subset of intellectuals. Carlyle was unable to recognise his own work as alienated and this led to a twofold compensation. He exalted the compulsion to work into a divine edict rather than a form of work organised by a capitalist system, which he in other contexts denounced as Mammonism and the definition of people by 'cash payment'. He also idealised manual labour as an unalienated activity that would ennoble the worker and raise him to a higher level of existence. The figure of Abbot Samson in *Past and Present* becomes a wish-fulfilment figure for Carlyle, uniting the act of writing with an idealised image of labour. The community of monks and their leader is an overdetermined site of nostalgia for Carlyle.

Carlyle's criticism of the 'cash nexus', quoted approvingly by Engels, is not a criticism of capitalism per se but a criticism of materialism which he sees as a threat to his transcendence of his own alienated labour. As David Amigoni has argued, Socialists later in the century 'were able selectively to appropriate and mobilize discourse from Carlyle's contradictory rhetoric' and thus read him as a radical writer.[44] Such a reading, however, necessarily suppressed Carlyle's essentially masochistic relationship to the male body.

Carlyle's criticism of capitalism is based, not on an indictment of social organisation, as is that of Marx or Engels, but on a denial of the male body.[45] This connection becomes explicit when a typical Carlyle rant about the Corn Laws veers into Mammonism, and then from there to the body. Carlyle says that Mammonism 'is not the essence of his or my station' but 'the adsciticious excrescence of it; the gross, terrene embodiment of it'. Money and Mammonism for Carlyle reinstate the material conditions of existence, especially the body, which for him is connected with embodiment as a pathological or morbid condition.

The idea of the 'terrene' as the return of the repressed body recurs when Carlyle once again invokes the 'monster' of idleness and writes about the Caribbean in terms of the 'merely pumpkinish and terrene'.[46] Rather than the idle aristocracy at this point in *Past and Present*, his target here is the 'pretty man' of the Caribbean who, in Carlyle's tropical fantasy, has only to lie in a hammock all day and eat pumpkins. Obviously calling the Caribbean male 'pretty' feminises him, and indicates that racial and gender categories are both implicated in Carlyle's tropical fantasy. For Carlyle the British creation of a plantation system in the Caribbean has rescued the area from swamps and pestilence and introduced an era of God-like work. The Caribbean was an area of 'waste and putrefaction' before the empire, the invocation of waste recalling Carlyle's representation above of the body as 'excrescence'. This is simply an imperial version of his attempt to escape from embodiment and find refuge in an idealised image of work and the transformation of nature through human labour. In Carlyle's idealised empire, the divine interference of British work has banished the demon idleness and the threat of 'terrene' embodiment.

The contradictions in Carlyle's positions have been characterised by Norma Clarke (echoing Wordsworth) as 'strenuous idleness'.[47] Clarke provides an excellent analysis of the contradictions in the phrase: 'strenuous' denotes a male world of validation through hard work and 'idleness' a female world of leisure.[48] Leisure for Carlyle represented 'an unproductive self-torture' that only work could cure. As Clarke's phrase 'self-torture' suggests, introspection and idleness were unbearable states for Carlyle that a self-denying emphasis on toil was supposed to combat. Carlyle had to reject the idle as a symbol both of the feminine and of the Caribbean, and turn them both into abject images expelled from his own psyche. Along with 'idleness', however, goes any notions of introspection or self-examination. Carlyle insists on work as an antidote to any introspection and the spectre of depression that could follow.

Rather than 'strenuous idleness', Carlyle represents in *Past and Present* a 'monstrous idleness' that is a projection of his deepest fears and desires. If Sussman is correct in his assertion that Victorian masculinity was based on 'manliness as self-regulation',[49] then its opposite, an unregulated, idle and profligate state held tremendous attraction for Carlyle. Such an existence for Carlyle was the object of both fear and desire and his tropical fantasies of the Caribbean encode this fear and desire most obviously. Life on a plantation was very different from this fantasy, of course; it was purely a concoction of Carlyle's imagination as a zone of idleness and licentiousness that he denied himself.

Carlyle anathematises figures who must carry the burden of his own unacknowledged depression. Carlyle's imagination is peopled by figures which represent the psychic pain that he cannot himself directly acknowledge and must externalise through such figures as the 'pretty man' of the Caribbean. Gender and racial differences help confirm the masculine subject as white, male and dominant and thus assuage the pain and anxiety of the 'dreadful labour' of writing. The unacknowledged subversive desires which Munby expressed through his idealisation of working-class woman Carlyle represents through demonised figures such as the Caribbean man.

While contemporary theory has worked to deconstruct binaries, Victorian men were caught at the ideological level between stark dichotomies such as male and female, and dominant and subordinate. The emphasis upon being the 'doer and creator' created tremendous pressure to deny feelings of insecurity and anxiety that found expression in 'deviant' forms and in diaries and letters. Masoch's text represents this binary where the protagonist is either in a position of power over working-class women or subordinate to women for whom he is a slave. To read these narratives in purely Freudian terms, however, is to lose sight of the class basis of Victorian society which triangulated masculinity, femininity and class. Contemporary readings of such narratives tend to focus on the gender implications of the masochistic relationship, but it is in the final analysis the class basis that is crucial.

This binary is represented in Masoch through metaphors of heat and cold. While the conventions of love upon which Masoch is drawing used images of freezing and burning, in a tradition that dates back to Petrarch, in *Venus in Furs* the contrast indicates the power binary that informs his text. There are only two choices available, to be masterful or subordinate, and the text moves from one to the other just as it moves between heat and cold. This binary exists because the relationship is expressed in class terms as well as gender terms, and the class system naturalises the idea of one person having power over another. Rather than lover and beloved, the text eroticises the relationship between mistress and servant. This is what marks it as a particularly nineteenth century version of a relationship caught in a system of binary opposites in terms of power. The most erotic relationship in Victorian terms is one in which class domination is part of sexual play.

Silverman gives an excellent analysis of the mechanics of 'disavowal' as a typically male form of self-defence, particularly against castration anxiety.[50] Rather than appeal to theories of male castration anxiety, however, in the Victorian period the disavowal is motivated by fears of subordination provoked by the class system. Since Victorian men were conventionally supposed to be masterful in the class sense of the term, all feelings that subverted this mastery were disavowed and projected onto both female and working-class others. They had to be either 'masters' or 'servants' (Severin in *Venus in Furs* spends a great deal of time playing the role of servant). Texts by Victorian men thus switch between desire for and fear of mastery and subordination. Masoch in *Venus in Furs* simply gives the most extreme version of this common narrative.

Far from being an aberrant psychic mechanism, therefore, masochism appears as a psychic self-defence against feelings of anxiety and inadequacy. Rather than acknowledge the 'I' that experienced these emotions, Victorian males would disavow these feelings and express them only 'at the margins' in Silverman's terms, in diaries and letters. The masochistic mechanism is a defence mechanism, one of disavowal that makes pain appear to come from somewhere else. The pain that could not be recognised directly is externalised onto an idealised image of the other, whether a racial, gendered or class other. Masoch's text, with its frequent invocations of statues and paintings, shows the aesthetic process at work in creating these idealised images. In hindsight it can be seen how much autobiographical content is involved in the creation of such a narrative, but given the radical division between public and private in the period the desires encoded in such texts could never be acknowledged directly.

Notes

1. Richard Von Krafft-Ebing, *Psychopathia Sexualis, with Especial Reference to Contrary Sexual Instinct: a Medico-Legal Study* (Philadelphia: F.R. Rebman, London 1893).
2. Nathan Constantin Leites, *Depression and Masochism: an Account of Mechanisms* (New York: Norton, 1979), p.14.
3. Jack Novick, *Fearful Symmetry: the Development and Treatment of Sadomasochism* (Northvale, NJ: Jason Aronson, 1996), p.98.
4. Krafft-Ebing, *Psychopathia Sexualis*, p.86.
5. Kaja Silverman, *Male Subjectivity at the Margins* (New York: Routledge, 1992), pp.185–213.
6. Silverman, *Male Subjectivity*, p.206.
7. In my approach to the genre I have been influenced by Jacques Derrida on 'La Loi du Genre/The Law of Genre', trans. Avita Ronnel, *Glyph* 7, 202–32 (repr. Baltimore: Johns Hopkins Press, 1980), the theoretical work of Sidonie Smith and Julia Watson in *Getting a Life: Everyday Uses of Autobiography* (Minneapolis: University of Minnesota Press, 1996) and the introduction to Leigh Gilmore's *Limits of Autobiography: Trauma and Testimony* (Ithaca, NY: Cornell University Press, 2001).
8. Clinton Machann, *The Genre of Autobiography in Victorian Literature* (Ann Arbor: University of Michigan Press, 1994).
9. Machann, *Genre of Autobiography*, pp.4–5.
10. Mary Evans, *The Impossibility of Auto/Biography* (New York: Routledge, 1999), p.12.
11. John Tosh, *A Man's Place: Masculinity and the Middle-Class Home in Victorian England* (New Haven: Yale UP, 1999), p.4.
12. Tosh, *A Man's Place*, p.46.
13. To further complicate matters, Gilles Deleuze maintains that sadism and masochism belong to totally different orders of discourse and should not be confused with one another in 'sadomasochism'. Deleuze argues that 'the

woman torturer' from Masoch cannot be labelled 'sadistic' because she belongs entirely to the 'masochistic' order of discourse. See Gilles Deleuze, *Masochism: And Coldness and Cruelty & Venus in Furs*, trans. Jean McNeil (New York: George Braziler), 1971, p.42.

14. Deleuze, *Masochism*, p.30.
15. Deleuze, *Masochism*, p.61.
16. Martin Danahay, 'Mirrors of Masculine Desire: Narcissus and Pygmalion in Victorian Representation', *Victorian Poetry*, 32:1 (Spring 1994), 35–54.
17. Dante Gabriel Rossetti, 'The Orchard-Pit', in *The Works of Dante Gabriel Rossetti*, ed. William M. Rossetti (London: Ellis, 1911), pp.607–8.
18. James Eli Adams has detected a similar pattern in Kingsley's *Alton Locke*, where he sees 'the pleasures of abasement'; see especially the paradoxical autonomy gained through abasement to a dominating, upper-class woman: *Dandies and Desert Saints: Styles of Victorian Masculinity* (Ithaca: Cornell University Press, 1995), p.147.
19. Rossetti, *Works*, p.210.
20. See Deleuze, *Masochism*, pp.97–105; Silverman, *Male Subjectivity*, p.58.
21. Wanda Sacher-Masoch, *The Confessions of Wanda von Sacher-Masoch* (San Francisco: Re/Search Publications, 1990).
22. John Ruskin 'Sesame and Lilies', in *The Works of John Ruskin*, ed. E.T. Cook and Alexander Wedderburn (39 vols) (London: G. Allen, 1903–12).
23. Arthur Munby, *Munby: Man of Two Worlds: The Life and Diaries of Arthur Munby*, ed. Derek Hudson (London: John Murray, 1972).
24. Hannah Cullwick, *The Diaries of Hannah Cullwick, Victorian Maidservant*, ed. Liz Stanley (New Brunswick: Rutgers UP, 1984).
25. Herbert L. Sussman *Victorian Masculinities: Manhood and Masculine Poetics in Early Victorian Literature and Art* (Cambridge: Cambridge University Press, 1995), p.5.
26. Jonathan Dollimore uses the term 'perversity' to construct a theory of 'sexual dissidence'. Munby is, in Dollimore's terms, a 'sexual dissident' like Oscar Wilde. See Jonathan Dollimore, *Sexual Dissidence: Augustine to Wilde, Freud to Foucault* (Oxford: Clarendon Press, 1991).
27. As Stallybrass and White point out, 'Munby worshipped Cullwick's physical strength and contrasted it to his own puniness and whiteness'. See Peter Stallybrass and Allon White, *The Politics and Poetics of Transgression* (Ithaca: Cornell University Press, 1986), p.156.
28. For a discussion of the kind of subversion implied in Munby and Cullwick's performance of gender identity, see Judith Butler, *Gender Trouble: Feminism and the Subversion of Identity* (New York: Routledge, 1990) and Marjorie Garber, *Vested Interests: Cross Dressing and Cultural Anxiety* (New York: Harper, 1992).
29. Munby, *Man of Two Worlds*, p.297.
30. Munby, *Man of Two Worlds*, p.54.
31. Norma Clarke, 'Strenuous Idleness: Thomas Carlyle and the Man of Letters as Hero', in Michael Roper and John Tosh (eds), *Manful Assertions: Masculinities in Britain since 1800* (London and New York: Routledge, 1991).
32. See Elizabeth Langland, *Nobody's Angels: Middle-Class Women and Domestic Ideology in Victorian Culture* (Ithaca: Cornell UP, 1995).
33. Munby, *Man of Two Worlds*, p.329.

34. Mill, John Stuart, *The Autobiography of John Stuart Mill*, (New York: Columbia University Press, 1924), pp.100, 170.

35. Mill, *Autobiography*, p.171.

36. John Stuart Mill, 'The Subjection of Women', in *Collected Works of John Stuart Mill* (Toronto: University of Toronto Press, 1984), p.271.

37. Thomas Carlyle, quoted in Fred Kaplan, *Thomas Carlyle: A Biography* (Ithaca: Cornell University Press, 1983), pp.151–2.

38. Kaplan, *Carlyle*, p.63.

39. Sussman notes perceptively that for Carlyle 'sickness is associated with a slackening of psychic control' as it was for the Victorians generally. See Sussman, *Victorian Masculinities*, p.23.

40. Kaplan, *Carlyle*, p.403.

41. Sussman, *Victorian Masculinities*, p.19.

42. Kaplan, *Carlyle*, p.350.

43. Mary Poovey has discussed the relationship between men's alienated labour and their idealisation of women's work in *Uneven Developments: The Ideological Work of Gender in Mid-Victorian England* (London: Virago, 1989).

44. David Amigoni, *Victorian Biography: Intellectuals and the Ordering of Discourse* (New York: St Martin's Press, 1993), p.72.

45. James Eli Adams has an intriguing discussion of the Victorian male body in the context of Walter Pater in *Dandies and Desert Saints*.

46. Carlyle, *Occasional Discourse*.

47. Clarke, 'Strenuous Idleness', pp.25–43.

48. Clarke, 'Strenuous Idleness', p.26; James Eli Adams also notes the effects of the 'feminisation of intellectual labour' in *Dandies and Desert Saints*, p.2.

49. Sussman, *Victorian Masculinities*, p.11.

50. Silverman, *Male Subjectivity*, p.45.

CHAPTER FIVE

Promoting a Life
Patronage, Masculinity and
Philip Meadows Taylor's *The Story of My Life*

Trev Lynn Broughton

I

Memoirs by and about official personnel in nineteenth-century 'British' India are not, at first glance, an appetising prospect for critical enquiry. Noting that memoirs of the British in India were overwhelmingly hagiographic in purpose, Benita Parry comments: 'Because few corporate bodies have written of themselves with quite the same self-congratulation couched in flatulent prose as did the Indian Civil Service, one is bound to remark on how many Anglo-Indian officials were preoccupied with rank and advancement.'[1] One of my purposes in this chapter is to question the inevitability of the relationship this implies between genre (colonial hagiography), tone (self-congratulation) and theme (rank and advancement). I want to suggest ways in which this conjunction between promotion as biographical publicity, self-promotion and career promotion may have been a matter of historically specific struggles over the definition of manliness even, or perhaps especially, when the writers and readers involved were themselves Anglo-Indian officials.[2]

As eminent Indian civil servant and historian William Wilson Hunter acknowledged in 1897, the very terms of the typical official career in India were at odds with the 'manly narrative' which might nerve others to personal struggle and self-sacrifice. If Anglo-Indian biography, according to Hunter, was largely restricted to 'sectarian memoirs' and 'the more disastrous panegyrics of filial piety', this was at least in part attributable to those two cornerstones of the unreformed service: 'patronage and seniority'. Knowing the right people and waiting one's turn for promotion were par for the course; drawing attention to oneself by unusual feats of daring, endurance or initiative were not. 'All seniority services,' Wilson remarks, 'are jealous of exceptional success.' In the military, the seniority principle was at least tempered by 'the battle field and the brevet', a system which could acknowledge de facto advancement in the ranks with honorary titles and distinctions. The Indian Civil Service, on the other hand, sanctioned 'no such short-cuts to greatness, and [...] regarded brilliancy of any sort with a coldly

distrustful eye'. In a caustic formulation, Hunter ascribes the weak
state of mid-Victorian Anglo-Indian memoir, and by extension of
the unreformed service itself, to a kind of male subjectivity which
subordinated invigorating homosocial rivalry and the desire to excel
among men to dogged careerism and family loyalties:

> Its *esprit de corps* was the *esprit de corps* of aunts, sisters, and
> cousins; a family feeling which bound with feminine withes many a
> strong man's hands, but which had little sympathy for talent without
> relatives, and made no defence for it if it fell.[3] (p.58)

We cannot then automatically attribute the cultural salience of Anglo-
Indian life-writing to a Victorian appetite for tales of heroism and
success in exotic places: the published lives of British administrators in
India often commemorated careers hemmed in, or even thwarted, by the
constraints of working within an impenetrable hierarchy. In any case,
success in one's vocation was only one facet of the masculine ideal, and
its significance relative to domestic virtue on the one hand and bonds of
allegiance among men on the other was, as John Tosh has shown, under
constant revision.[4] At stake in disputes about rank and advancement in
nineteenth-century 'British' India and, I will argue, in the production
and reception of the memoirs of Anglo-Indian officials, was a more
fundamental concern with competing ideals of colonial masculinity.
E.M. Collingham has characterised the nineteenth-century transition in
styles of British government in India as that between the 'nabob', the
ruler whose mode of authority was 'open to Indian influences, and
aspects of Indian practice' and the 'sahib', an increasingly anglicised
figure who in more or less subtle ways preserved his distance from his
Indian subjects and operated in a 'British idiom'.[5] But was the new
'sahib' notion of masculinity, based on (British) domestic values and a
secure (British) career ladder – a model in which the personal hardship,
cultural affronts and risk to health and comfort of simply 'being in India'
were to be construed as heroism enough – sufficient either to meet the
challenges of Empire or to fulfil the fantasy of racial superiority required
by the emergent late-Victorian imperialist project?

Such concerns about the class, gender and 'racial' implications of
changing models of colonial masculinity, were, I suggest, evident in the
reception of Philip Meadows Taylor's posthumous *The Story of My Life*
(1877).[6] Located squarely in the world sketched in Davidoff and Hall's
Family Fortunes, Taylor's provenance was not the Anglo-Indian elite, but
the provincial middle-class whose members made, and frequently lost,
fortunes in trade, or attempted to establish its sons in the professions or
the civil service.[7] The failure in business of Taylor's father in 1815–16
meant that he had to make his own way in the world with relatively little

formal education behind him. Having scrambled his way through various unpromising openings, he was sent in his teens to India and found himself working as a glorified shop-boy in Bombay. The intercession of a cousin, Mr Newnham, Chief Secretary to Government at Bombay, finally procured him a commission in the army of the Nizam of Hyderabad, which was to be his base for the next 34 years. While working his way up through a series of increasingly responsible (and increasingly administrative) postings, Taylor also found the time to begin writing. During Taylor's only furlough to Britain in the late 1830s, another cousin, the distinguished *Times* leader writer Henry Reeve, busied himself on his kinsman's behalf, helping him launch his first (and still most widely read) novel, *Confessions of a Thug* (1839) and introducing him to a glittering acquaintance that included many of London high society. While there Taylor received a commission from one of Reeve's early employers, the *British and Foreign Quarterly*, for an article on India, and thus began his moonlighting career as a journalist. On Taylor's return to India, Reeve encouraged him to write to him by every mail on Indian affairs and, guiding him carefully as to the correct political tone to take in his commentaries, managed within a short time to establish him in the role, and with the stipend, of a 'special correspondent' to the *Times*. Though Taylor achieved considerable fame and success as a novelist,[8] his location on geographical peripheries of colonial influence, and his ambiguous position as a military officer (but only indirectly a servant of the Crown), seem sometimes to have undermined the authority of his writings on Indian affairs and history: his 'special correspondence', for instance, had to be anonymised and its origins carefully disguised.

The Story of My Life, written towards the end of Taylor's retirement to England on health grounds and published in two volumes shortly after his death, has many of what we now recognise as the typical characteristics of Anglo-Indian narrative: picaresque structure, sublime scenery, accounts of 'exotic' superstition and custom, and the usual admixture of pigsticking and other bloodsports.[9] Though in many ways formulaic, the work retains the immediacy and boastful enthusiasm of the letters home, mainly to his parents, upon which it was based. Though Taylor was marginal to many of the more 'glamorous' scenes of action – he missed out, he claims, by a whisker on exposing 'Thuggee' to the West (I, pp.88, 113) and played only a distant role in the suppression of the 1857 revolt – he nevertheless conveys the excitement and satisfactions of a varied and challenging career, whether it was facing down what he saw as corruption and dissipation in 'native' courts, improving water supplies and roads, reforming revenue collection or balancing the books of the district in his control. His private life is dealt with scantily: his happy marriage to Mary, the daughter of one of disgraced Hyderabad banker William Palmer's Indian unions, was cut short by her early death, and his consequent separation from his two surviving daughters is treated poignantly but fleetingly.[10]

The disappointments he does relate at length are mainly in consequence of his appointment as a 'local' officer of the Nizam of Hyderabad, at a time when rapid promotion, good pay and pension, sick leave and furlough entitlements (as opposed to the 'spoils' of India), had come to be regarded as the rightful perks of the 'covenanted' servants of the East India Company (I, pp.89, 116 and *passim*).[11] The frustrations of his career were aggravated by the structural incongruities of his 'local' status, which in turn compromised the *Story*'s moral certitudes. That he was answerable in varying degrees to the people of the areas in his charge, to the Indian noble families to which they were (at least theoretically) subject, to the Nizam of Hyderabad and his ministers, and via the British Resident to the East India Company and the English Crown – all of which constituencies were usually at loggerheads – put a strain on the sense of moral purpose necessary to a heroic narrative (I p.184 and *passim*). That the land-revenue he was charged with collecting mainly went, not to civic improvements or rural welfare but towards the costs of the European-officered Contingent of which he was a member, only added to his narrative difficulties (II p.63).[12] The *Story*, like many of Taylor's novels, depicts a subject 'open to the heteroglossia of colonial life', to borrow Nancy L. Paxton's phrase. It inscribes, moreover, a colonizing subject profoundly divided in his allegiances, and, by virtue of his location in the lower (and more racially integrated) 'uncovenanted' ranks of the administration, often bewildered and disillusioned by the policies and prejudices of the ruling elite.[13]

Taylor's *Story*, then, is a colonial memoir proccupied with rank and advancement, a memoir, furthermore, far from innocent of the self-congratulation Parry discerns in the self-writing of Anglo-Indian administrators of the Victorian period. Yet it also bears traces of earlier, less hide-bound models of colonial masculinity: the Indianized nabob with his mixed-race household, the colonial adventurer living on his wits. What challenges, and what satisfactions, might such a narrative, poised on the historical, cultural and social brink between competing ideals of Anglo-Indian manhood, offer to a late-Victorian readership still to some extent traumatised by the 1857 revolt and its aftermath?

II

This was the battleground on which Henry Reeve, Meadows Taylor's

cousin and executor, mounted his campaign to promote Taylor's autobiography. Four years Taylor's junior, Reeve came from the same
provincial middle-class background, though he was more closely
connected to its literary elite. Although his father, a physician, died in
1814, Reeve was nevertheless able to use family connections to gain a
solid and cosmopolitan education and, as Clerk of Appeals to the Privy
Council (and later Registrar), and as senior leader writer on the *Times*
and then editor of the *Edinburgh Review*, attained an influence and
power over Victorian political affairs (national and international)
unsurpassed outside the Cabinet.[14] Despite his own stellar career, Reeve,
as we have seen, had long kept a friendly eye on the fortunes of his older
but less prosperous cousin.[15] He had also, as a widowed father himself,
interested himself in the motherless Taylor girls, watching over their
education on their father's behalf. In return, he received a steady supply
of Indian 'news' and a grateful dedication in Taylor's monumental
Students Manual of the History of India.[16]

Henry Reeve was, from their long correspondence, only too aware of
the absurdities and disappointments of his cousin's career: indeed he had
drawn extensively on this intelligence in his own writing on 'The
prospects of India' in the wake of the Mutiny of 1857.[17] Faced, in 1877,
with the task of providing a Preface to Taylor's narrative, Reeve confined
himself to two 'considerations' which Taylor's modesty had kept out of
the main narrative. The first is Taylor's achievement in self-education.
The exigencies of his work prompted him to become proficient in land
surveying and engineering, in geology, botany and archaeology, and in
Indian languages and legal systems; the need for constructive leisure
trained him in painting, music and, of course, authorship. His feats as an
autodidact are not offered 'by way of panegyric', but because a young
Englishman embarking on an Indian career 'with this book in his pocket'
may learn by Taylor's example 'what may be done, in the course of a
single life' for the improvement of self and subject race (I, viii–xi). The
moral is the more important because the corporate culture of young
Anglo-India is changing: 'The world grows more methodical, and
routine takes the place of individual effort', so that even so modest an
'adventure' as Taylor's is fast becoming impossible (I, xviii). The second
lesson Reeve draws is the importance of 'gentleness and sympathy'
towards the people of India: qualities in which, for all its benefits of
peace and civilisation, British rule has been 'sometimes wanting'. The
mutual respect Reeve ascribes to Taylor's relations with 'the natives' has
implications for the future: 'The sphere of his power and influence was
not wide, at least in comparison with the vast extent and population of
the Indian Empire; but as far as it extended they were complete' (I, xiii).

It remains for Reeve to explain why, given his innate strengths as an administrator, Taylor's sphere was so moderate. He went to India long before the days of 'Indian examinations and Competition Wallahs' (I, vi) and perforce started his Indian career where he ended it: in the Nizam's service. The very circumstances that called forth his 'energy and perseverance' – his 'independen[ce] of the patronage of the great Company or the authority of the Crown' (I, vi) – kept from him the more lucrative and influential posts jealously withheld by the established civil and military services.[18] Towards the end of the Preface, Reeve acknowledges that Taylor's public rewards were considerable ('the pension of his rank in the British service' and various 'honourary distinctions'). Even as he does so, however, he quietly drops Taylor's honorific title 'Colonel' in favour of his actual rank of 'Captain', thus leaving uncertain whether Taylor's efforts have yet been adequately remunerated (I, xvii).[19]

If there is an element of condescension in Reeve's sponsorship of his kinsman's narrative, it is perhaps because he is conscious that Taylor's was, after all, 'only a drop in the ocean of good services' to India, as one reviewer pointed out.[20] There is, too, an element of calculation in the patronising tone: Reeve is attempting to engage the sympathy and interest of a middle-class Anglo-Indian readership sufficiently secure in its prestige to enjoy acknowledging the merits of an admittedly minor brother-in-arms. Two letters affixed to a British Library copy of *The Story of My Life*, written 22 years after its publication, reveal not only that the volumes were still in circulation among the retired Anglo-Indian community of Lymington, Hampshire, but also that Reeve's gloss on Taylor's career had stuck. In the first, Thomas Turton delightedly recognised in the *Story* a brief cameo of himself at ten years old being boxed on the ears by Taylor for cheeking his mother ('he was the first person who had ever struck me a blow!'). Another correspondent, W.H. Burton, who served in the Nizam's dominions shortly after Taylor's retirement, found the story 'somewhat sad':

> the sad part of the story is that notwithstanding Col Taylor's long, toilsome, and responsible and withal successful service of 36 years successful that is as regards the work he did for the British Govt. he did not get to the top of the tree in the Civil Dept – nor even higher than to become a Deputy Commissioner on R[upee]s 1200 or R[upee]s 1500 a month. Yet he deserved far better treatment.

Taking his cue from Reeve's Preface, Burton goes on to attribute this failure to Taylor's exclusion from patronage: his status as a 'friendless adventurer – viz. As one not belonging to either the Civil or Military service of the late E.I. Comp.y'. He then cites two examples of Taylor's having been passed over for promotion in favour of Company men, including Patrick Caddell (who later edited Taylor's letters to Reeve). Burton argues that, though Taylor received the pension of a brevet Colonel when he retired, this barely compensated for his having been deprived of the Nizam's pension while he was serving in a British District: 'a most nefarious proceeding of Lord Dalhousie's'.[21] The letter neatly illustrates Parry's point about the sensitivities attached to status and advancement, but especially to the issue of pensions. It suggests, too, that Reeve's 'spin' on the *Story* met understanding and sympathy from its Anglo-Indian readership.

III

Though they varied in length from thirty-two pages to two lines, the reviews and notices of *The Story*, particularly those in periodicals susceptible to Reeve's influence (such as his own *Edinburgh Review* in October 1877 and *Blackwood's* the following month) picked up and enlarged upon the hints Reeve had left about Taylor's professional frustrations. Reviewers adopted a consistently deferential tone towards, in the *Fortnightly*'s phrase, 'a great Indian administrator on a small scale'.[22] Consistent, too, was their celebration of Taylor as a 'type' of colonial manliness: 'soldier-administrators, rough and ready in conception and daring in execution, but with small respect for form and little fear of constitutional restraints before their eyes'.[23] Taylor, in other words, was remembered as a relic of the days when 'India was India' ([Allardyce], 'Anglo-Indian Soldier and Novelist', p.577): when the relatively ramshackle state of British administration allowed scope for initiative, courage and energy. Taylor's demise is thus taken to mark a watershed in the history of colonial masculinity: the breaking of 'a link between the past and present of India' (ibid., p.575).

Yet despite their relish for Taylor's successes, most commentators agreed that his rewards did not keep pace with his achievements, nor his responsibilities with his powers. If, as the *Westminster Review* conceded, his book were a little 'self-complacent', this could be forgiven an 'old man who has distinguished himself without due reward'.[24] This they attributed, as Taylor and Reeve had done, to the unlucky circumstance of his employment by the Nizam of Hyderabad rather than the Company or Crown, and his consequent exclusion from the charmed circle of the 'covenanted' services. *Blackwood's* emphasised that the career offered by the Nizam's service was 'strictly local and limited', and that 'the social position, the pay, privileges, and pension of the Nizam's officers, were on the whole inferior to those under the Company'. Even though the Nizam's contingent was eventually transferred to the Indian army, entitling Meadows Taylor to the privileges of a British officer, it was too late to rescue his career: 'He had been too heavily handicapped by his position as a "local" officer to get up in time to the winning-post' (ibid., p.587).

Though Taylor's narrative was praised for its intrinsic qualities – its picturesque scenes, its romance, freshness and 'honesty' – it was commended to the public above all for the lessons it offered to the rising generation of Anglo-Indian officials. Effectively the Taylor case afforded two challenges to the existing administrative elite in India. The first, expounded by *Blackwood's*, pitted Taylor's vigorous pursuit of opportunity, his ingenuity and initiative, against the creeping mediocrity of an increasingly routinised bureaucracy: 'ability and zeal are not lightly to be set aside, even though they may not be tied up in red-tape or stamped with the magic impress of the "covenant"' (ibid., p.575). Others may bulk more largely in Indian history, but they 'had their work cut out for them' (ibid., p.591) whereas Taylor's peculiar capacity was 'for cutting out work for himself' (ibid., p.578). The dominant administrative culture was a peculiar mix of traditional 'Company' elitism and promotion by seniority on the one hand, and codes, regulations and standardised training on the other. Such arrangements might increase efficiency, might even mitigate abuses, but did they not blunt the appetite for individual responsibility and action, replacing the manly adventurer with a cadre of effete time-servers? And were such protocols an adequate substitute for 'sympathy, kindliness and consideration for the people of India'?[25] The *Westminster* reviewer put it bluntly: 'Not being a servant of the Company, or of the Imperial Government [...] [Taylor] was obliged to treat natives humanely.'[26]

The second line of argument, relentlessly pursued by the *Edinburgh* reviewer G.T. Chesney, extrapolated from Taylor's exclusion from the centres of British power in India a critique of the covenant system itself. Like Allardyce in *Blackwood's*, Chesney stressed that Taylor's position outside the recognised Indian services debarred him from rising to high office. Though the worst excesses of 'Company' patronage had been eliminated, automatic promotion by seniority ensured that plum jobs were still reserved for covenanted officers. Thus, when he retired, Taylor was 'merely' in charge of a district, 'to which comparatively humble preferment every "covenanted civilian" is entitled to succeed in ordinary course, without displaying any merit whatever' ('Story of an Indian Life', pp.520–21). But the iniquities of the system were not restricted to professional gate-keeping. The covenant itself was simply the oath of obedience, probity and loyalty to which senior members of the recognised (civil and military) services subscribed. What it represented in practice, as Chesney laboured to point out, was an exclusive career path and a package of advantageous conditions of service: conditions which, as the nineteenth century progressed, were liberalised to include furlough and sick leave entitlements, generous pension arrangements and financial security for widows and orphans. Covenanted service, in other words, was being redefined to conduce to loyalty to homeland and to (European) family. Its provisions were designed to preserve a mid-Victorian middle-class ideal of white masculinity against the trials and temptations of the East.

And it was a closed shop. For 'uncovenanted' servants the leave rules, for instance, were far more stringent, assuming 'robuster state of health, a more rapid recovery from sickness, and a less strong desire to revisit their native land' (ibid., p.551). That the 'degrading' and 'ludicrous' pension and leave entitlements of these workers were 'incongruous and absurd' (p.535) was the more serious in face of the huge extension of Indian administration in all lines: 'engineers, forest and telegraph officers, education inspectors, and so forth'. Was this massive body of skilled workers, 'to which almost every family in England has furnished a member' and distinguished by 'education, training and ability', to be treated no differently from 'the humblest native officials, to be numbered by tens of thousands, who naturally do not want to come to England or to send their families there?' (ibid., p.535). The *Edinburgh* thus used Taylor's *Story* as a pretext to invoke an aggrieved underclass of Anglo-Indian workers deprived, by virtue of 'class prejudice' (p.550), of some of the essentials of British bourgeois masculinity: health and wholesome leisure, respectability in old age and the ability to visit, support and identify with 'home'. The danger, left implicit, was that in such circumstances the growing population of uncovenanted Europeans would 'go native', take Indian mistresses or wives and breed Eurasian children, thus blurring the boundaries between governing and governed which the emergent ideology of Empire sought to enforce. For Taylor, Chesney asserted, the disabilities associated with uncovenanted service meant that, when he lost his wife, he 'had to' send his children to England, remaining in India until retirement 'a solitary Englishman, finding solace only in official labour' (p.541). Discreetly passing over the fact that Taylor's wife was Eurasian, Chesney implies that if Taylor, though poorly recompensed for his services, had escaped the worst consequences of being 'clubb[ed] up' (p.535) with native officials, it was no thanks to the British government.

That two reviews of the same *Life*, published only a month apart, should have produced such divergent accounts of the gender, race and class politics of colonial masculinity in India reflects the high cultural stakes and recognised ideological costs involved in the transition to late Victorian modes of imperial governance. The rhetorical urgency with which reviewers addressed issues of rank and advancement, along with related conditions of service, suggests that the discussion of such matters in and around life writing involved more than the personal self-aggrandisement of a ruling elite. 'Nothing matters,' as Kipling would put it eleven years later, 'except Home-furlough and acting allowances.'[27] The level of complexity at which the debate was conducted suggests, too, that such questions could command an informed and discerning audience among a general middle-class readership.[28] Questions about who deserved public recognition and why resonated far beyond the differentiae of rank.

What the *Edinburgh* and *Blackwood's* commentaries had in common was a willingness to deploy life writing in the service of political critique; indeed there was an implied threat in the *Edinburgh*'s recommendation to the families of future administrators 'of whatever class' (pp.521, 553) of a work which, by the review's own account, illustrated a 'chronic source of discontent' which 'need only to be brought prominently under the notice of proper authority to be set right' (pp.534–5). *Blackwood's* plea was more modest: that Taylor's achievement should, once put before the public, 'meet with a generous recognition' (p.591). Collectively the reviews posed a challenge to their readers: it was obvious what Taylor had done for the Empire, and what the example of his *Life* might do for the imperial imagination. What would the Empire now do for him?

In different ways, both the *Blackwood's* and *Edinburgh* reviewers amplified Reeve's Preface, with its respectful tone and muted critique of Indian service, into fulsome praise for Taylor and full-blown denunciation of the institutional prejudice he had faced. Since Henry Reeve was editor of the *Edinburgh* and William Blackwood was publisher of *The Story of My Life*, neither the warmth of Allardyce and Chesney's recommendations nor the lead they took from Reeve should surprise us. An editor must necessarily cultivate a wide literary acquaintance, so to be accused of feathering one's own nest by favouring one's friends' books was something of an occupational hazard. In the case of Reeve's sponsorship of Taylor, the hazard was compounded by his family connection with Taylor, his literary executorship and his sponsorship of Taylor's literary career. [29] At this stage, however, Reeve's championing of his late cousin's book took him into murkier waters still.

IV

On 12 February 1878, William Wilson Hunter copied to Blackwood and Reeve a letter he had written from India to Sir Erskine Perry of the India

Council in London. His letter discussed Meadows Taylor in terms eerily close to those already in circulation:

> I have learned quite accidentally that Miss Meadows-Taylor is in straitened circumstances. As a Bengal civilian, I had been painfully impressed by her father's posthumous 'Story of my Life.' I could not help contrasting the rewards which come as a matter of course in the covenanted service with the scanty promotion earned by his long and exceptional labours. Though technically an 'uncovenanted officer,' Colonel Meadows-Taylor held what are now styled 'covenanted' appointments, and yet he had no chance of reaching more lucrative posts, nor is there any pension for his daughter after his death. But it is rather as a man of letters than as an official that I venture to ask your Council as to whether it might be possible to do something in the matter. [...] '[His works] form a most salutary reminder that Indian administration is not, and ought not to be, merely a matter of system, but one of individual knowledge. [...] I believe that I am only one among hundreds of Indian officials who owe their first awakening to this fact to Colonel Meadows-Taylor's writings. Surely it must be possible to do something for the daughter of a common benefactor of this sort?[30]

Did not Taylor's 'rare literary excellence' and the devotion of his 'whole life and leisure to Indian subjects' provide sufficient grounds without any need to relax the rules for uncovenanted service, or creating an 'inconvenient precedent'? On this signal, though 'hat[ing] to ask the Government for favours, especially for my own family', Reeve sought Perry's permission to forward Hunter's letter to Lord Lytton, the Governor-General of India and 'an old friend'.[31] On 29 April, Lord Lytton wrote to Henry Reeve agreeing with his estimation of 'the value of Meadows Taylor's life and work in India' and recognising the 'exceptional claims of the two ladies, on whose behalf you have written to me, to the grant which I regret to hear they require'.

> Their case is rather a difficult one to deal with, owing to the fact that nearly the whole of Meadows Taylor's life was performed, not in the service of the Government of India, but in that of the Nizam's Government [...]. In my own opinion, however, the claim of these ladies may be fairly admitted on other grounds furnished by their father's eminence, not only as a literary man, but also as an administrator, and the fact that his work, though not performed in the service of the Government of India, has been, and is, in various ways, unquestionably beneficial to India.[32]

Lytton reported that he had the 'concurrence of my council' to an annuity of £100 to both of Meadows Taylor's daughters from the Indian revenues, subject to the agreement (for which Reeve had simultaneously lobbied) of the Secretary of State and *his* council at the India Office. The pension was duly granted on 30 June 1878.[33]

The reception of Taylor's *Story* allows us glimpses of an energetic and skilful campaign, one which drew on all Reeve's resources, both literary and political. The effort and discretion needed to transform preferred reading into desired outcome was considerable. From the timing of publication, the procuring of a sympathetic and serviceable press reception, the judicious distribution of complimentary copies, the selective lobbying at the highest levels of Indian government on two continents, to the pressing home of specific, limited claims in the face of carefully orchestrated 'public' support, Reeve appears, in concert with Blackwood, to have ventriloquised his special pleading and turned the cultural capital of Taylor's *Life* into a regular income for his daughters.

As we have seen, 'patronage', along with 'seniority', was one of the values William Hunter saw as inimical to manly biography. Although the East India Company had, until the mid-1850s, been the greatest source of middle-class patronage in Britain outside the government, by the publication of *The Story of My Life* the formal channels of patronage had given way to competitive examination and a meritocratic ethos. Yet the legacy of the system continued to be felt, not only in the influence of great Anglo-Indians and their families, but in well-oiled mechanisms of informal patronage. As historian J.M. Bourne notes, 'patronage in the form of "second-order resources", strategic contact with other people', continued to flourish as a social medium, cementing relationships characterised by 'inequality, reciprocity and intimacy'.[34] The concerted reception of Taylor's *Story* neatly illustrates this diffusion of patronage, while at the same time suggesting that the relationship between these new modes of patronage and competing styles of colonial masculinity was complex and shifting. Those attempting to broker patronage on Taylor's behalf had to tread warily between constructions of merit based on independent, self-fashioning 'nabob' style manliness and a 'sahib' model of masculinity that was deserving because dutiful, obedient and loyal to the crown. 'Patronage and seniority' may have been unfavourable to heroic biography, but biography could and did channel (and, I would argue, even constitute) patronage.

That life writing was both a means and an end of patronage is highlighted by the textual fate of the annuities episode. Given the lengths to which he went to remain in the background of the transaction, it is striking that, three years after Reeve's own death, the annuities episode figures in John Knox Laughton's *Memoirs of the Life and Correspondence of Henry Reeve* (1898), where Governor-General Lytton's letter agreeing to the pension stands as the only sustained reference to Meadows Taylor in two massive volumes of barely digested correspondence. Like much of the rest of Laugton's biography, the letter serves to illustrate the extent and confidential nature of Reeve's acquaintance with notables in the worlds of national and international affairs, his tact and effectiveness as a negotiator and his philanthropy and consideration towards the unfortunate. The effect, needless to say, is to reduce Meadows Taylor's status vis-à-vis Reeve to one of abject dependence.

Three years later, another voice is raised, annexing another slice of the credit for the pension, this time to William Wilson Hunter. In his 1901 biography, Francis Henry Skrine describes how Hunter 'look[ed] after' Colonel Meadows Taylor on his last sojourn in India: 'Poor old man! It is fifty-two years since he entered the Haidarabad Contingent as a subaltern, and he has now become so blind and paralytic that he is carried about like a child by his daughter and a faithful Irish valet.'[35] It is Skrine, underlining Hunter's 'rare degree of sympathy for others' who describes how perusal of *The Story of My Life* impelled him to 'press the claims of Colonel Meadows-Taylor's daughter on the special considera-tion of the State'. In this version, it is 'greatly to Hunter's credit' that he, though a member of the covenanted services, 'should have felt the injustice of these galling class distinctions'.[36] By recounting in detail Hunter's 'chivalrous intervention' on Taylor's behalf – his correspon-dence with Perry and networking with Reeve – Skrine demeans both Taylor (who, as we have seen, is portrayed as incapable of looking after himself or his daughters), and Reeve, whose special pleading behind the scenes for a family member is thereby brought into the public domain.[37]

V

How does the 'spinning' of Taylor's *Story* nuance our understanding of Victorian life writing? First and foremost, the complex role of life writing as a 'technology of identity' should not lead us to overlook the plain fact that many, if not most, lives were published to make money, for publishers as well as for writers or their descendants. My analysis of Reeve's campaign illustrates the level of calculation and planning that could go into achieving the desired effect. The book sold well,[38] and its warm reception among influential readers secured a small but regular income for Taylor's daughters within a very short time of publication.

One could simply dismiss the episode as an instance of the monetary advantage of having friends in high places. The case also suggests, however, that the relationship between financial gain and identity was necessarily convoluted. If Taylor's autobiography seems at first glance an uncomplicated hymn to rugged colonial manhood, its context of reception tells a different story. In this context life writing was used at once to critique and initiate patronage; to celebrate masculine independence while forging obligation; to affirm and contest existing understandings of the balance between imperial endeavour, corporate loyalty and kinship bonds in the constitution of Anglo-Indian masculinity. In the delicate business of establishing Taylor's deserts without demeaning his manhood, life writing both revealed and mitigated the fragility of masculinity as a construction.

Furthermore a life was produced and consumed within a volatile intertextual field that embraced competing understandings of gender, class and 'race' as well as evolving perceptions of public and private as generic proprieties. The fact that it is possible to piece together the financial fate of Meadows Taylor's daughters from a series of late Victorian and indeed twentieth-century biographies, rather than from private papers or government minutes, suggests the episode may have relevance to the gendered history of Victorian life writing and, by extension, to masculinities as cultural formations. In order to grasp the significance of life writing for the reproduction of gender, I would suggest, we need to move beyond exclusive concentration on 'the text', and to a study of life writing as a complex and multifarious cultural field. If we want to use Victorian autobiography and biography as a means of understanding the workings of gender over time, we should look beyond the historical boundaries of the individual life and explore the afterlife: the way life writings are deployed and redeployed as a way of managing masculine reputations beyond the grave while mediating the needs, and protecting the sensibilities, of families from one generation to the next.

Acknowledgment

I would like to thank Liz Buettner and Ellen Carpenter for their invaluable suggestions, as well as the organisers and participants in the Locating the Victorians conference, and the members of the University of York Gender and History group.

Notes

1. Benita Parry, *Delusions and Discoveries: India in the British Imagination, 1880–1930* (London and New York: Verso, 1998), pp.32, 48.
2. The term 'Anglo-Indian' has, since the last years of colonial rule, come to refer to the people of 'mixed race' formerly known as 'Eurasians'. For clarity I retain the usage adopted by my Victorian sources, using 'Anglo-Indian' to refer to Britons living and working in India. See Elizabeth Buettner, 'Problematic Spaces, Problematic Races: Defining "Europeans" in late Colonial India', *Women's History Review* 89:2 (2000), p.293.

3. William Wilson Hunter, *The Thackerays in India, and some Calcutta Graves* (London: Henry Frowde,1897) p.58.

4. John Tosh, 'What should historians do with masculinity?', *History Workshop Journal*, 38 (1994), 179–202.

5. E.M. Collingham, *Imperial Bodies: the Physical Experience of the Raj, c.1800–1947* (Cambridge: Polity, 2001), pp.7–10 and *passim*. A fascinating account of the changes in colonial masculinity in India can be found in Mrinhalini Sinha, *Colonial Masculinity: the 'Manly Englishman' and the 'Effeminate Bengali' in the Late Nineteenth Century* (Manchester: Manchester University Press, 1995).

6. Philip Meadows Taylor, *The Story of My Life*, ed. his daughter, pref. Henry Reeve, 2 vols (London and Edinburgh: William Blackwood 1877). Further citations appear in the text.

7. Leonore Davidoff and Catherine Hall, *Family Fortunes: Men and Women of the English Middle Class, 1780–1850* (London: Hutchinson, 1987).

8. His first novel, *Confessions of a Thug* (1839) became a best-seller and is still in print today. For discussions of Taylor's literary works, see David Finkelstein, *Philip Meadows Taylor (1808–1876): A Bibliography* (Queensland: University of Queensland, 1990), and Nancy L. Paxton, *Writing Under the Raj* (New Brunswick, NJ and London: Rutgers University Press, 1999).

9. See Sara Suleri, *The Rhetoric of English India* (Chicago and London: University of Chicago Press, 1992), pp.30, 82; C.A. Bayly, *Empire and Information: Intelligence Gathering and Social Communication in India, 1780–1870* (Cambridge: Cambridge University Press, 1996) p.172.

10. Glimpses of married life can be found in *Story*, I, pp.107, 114. For a sense of the distress and anxiety occasioned by Taylor's separation from his daughters one must turn to Patrick Cadell (ed.), *The Letters of Philip Meadows Taylor to Henry Reeve* (London: Geoffrey Cumberlege, Oxford University Press, 1947), pp.118, 157–8, 194–5, 205. A vivid account of the Palmer family, and of the cosmopolitan Deccani society into which Taylor married, can be found in William Dalrymple, *White Mughals: Love and Betrayal in Eighteenth-Century India* (London: Harper Collins, 2002).

11. The term 'covenanted services' referred to the senior branches of the British civil and military services in India. The reference was to the covenants executed in England by which members of these services, selected and appointed in the metropole, engaged to subscribe to pension funds, not to accept presents, and so on. See L.S.S. O'Malley, *The Indian Civil Service 1601–1930* (London: John Murray, 1931), pp.83–4.

12. On land revenue as 'the determining discipline through which the conquerors "knew" Indian rural society', see Bayly, *Empire and Information*, p.151. On the relationship between land revenue and the Hyderabad contingent, see Gobind Singh Mansukhani, *Philip Meadows Taylor: A Critical Study* (Bombay: New Book Co., 1951), pp.10–11, 13.

13. Paxton, *Writing Under the Raj*, pp.30, 122.

14. For assessments of Reeve's career, see John Knox Laughton, *Memoirs of the Life and Correspondence of Henry Reeve*, 2 vols (London: Longman, Green, 1898); Joanne Shattock, 'Showman, Lion Hunter or Hack: The Quarterly Editor at Midcentury', *Innovators and Preachers: the Role of the Editor in Victorian England*, ed. Joel H. Wiener (Westport, Conn. and London: Greenwood Press, 1985), pp.161–83.

15. Reeve appears, for instance, to have arranged for the private circulation of Taylor's letters on the Indian Mutiny among family and friends. See 'Letters from Meadows Taylor Esqu. Deputy Commissioner of the Ceded Districts in the Deccan Written during the Mutiny, Printed for Private Circulation' (London: John Edward Taylor, 1857). For evidence of Reeve's avuncular interest in the Taylor girls, see Cadell, *Letters*.

16. London: Longmans, Green (1877).

17. [Henry Reeve], 'Prospects of the Indian Empire', *Edinburgh Review*, 198: 217 (Jan. 1858), 32.

18. This was a concern the cousins had shared: Reeve had commented publicly on the moral and political consequences of the disabilities facing unconvenanted Europeans in India in 'Prospects', p.42.

19. The autobiography was published as that of 'the late Colonel Meadows Taylor'.

20. [Alexander Alladyce], 'An Anglo-Indian Soldier and Novelist', *Blackwood's Magazine*, 121: 744 (Nov. 1877), 587. Further citations in the text.

21. See British Library Shelfmark W8-8179. The Turtons and Burtons were well-known Anglo-Indian families: see E.M. Forster, *Passage to India* (1924; reprinted Harmondsworth: Penguin, 1978) p.66.

22. 'Books of the Month', *Fortnightly Review*, 22: 131(Sept. 1877), 730.

23. '*The Story of My Life*, by the Late Colonel Meadows Taylor,' rev. in *Calcutta Review*, 67: 107 (1878), xxvi.

24. 'Contemporary Literature', *Westminster Review*, 53: 109 (Jan. 1878), 285.

25. [G.T. Chesney], 'The Story of an Indian Life', *Edinburgh Review*, 146: 300 (Oct. 1877), 553. Further citations in the text.

26. 'Contemporary Literature', 285.

27. Rudyard Kipling, 'Thrown Away', in Andrew Rutherford (ed.), *Selected Stories* (Harmondsworth: Penguin, 1987), p.41.

28. The continued success since its publication in 1863 in *Macmillan's Magazine* of George Trevelyan's fictionalised account of life as a 'Competition-Wallah' testified to a public appetite for insight into the impact of recent reforms and for reassurance about corporate probity, and to concern about the domestic drawbacks of an Indian career. See *The Competition-Wallah* (London: Macmillan, 1895), pp.127–30 and *passim*). For debates contemporaneous with the publication of Taylor's *Story*, see Lyon Playfair's 'The Indian Civil Service' and Arthur James Balfour's 'Reply', *Fortnightly Review*, ns, 22: 131 (Sept. 1877), 115–25 and 244–58.

29. See G. Le Grand Jacob, *Taylor's Students Manual of Indian History and the Edinburgh Review* (London: Kegan Paul, 1877), *passim*. For a similar instance in Reeve's career, see Laughton, II, pp.98–102.

30. Francis Henry Skrine, *The Life and Letters of Sir William Wilson Hunter* (London: Longmans Green, 1901), p.281.

31. Skrine, *Life and Letters*, pp.282–3.

32. Laughton, II, *Memoirs and Correspondence of Henry Reeve*, p.259.

33. Ibid. Significantly a year later Lytton ordered that uncovenanted service be reserved for 'natives of India', a category understood to include 'Indians proper and the domiciled [European] community'. See Edward Blunt, *The I.C.S.: The Indian Civil Service* (London: Faber and Faber, 1937), p.50. Presented as part of a process of 'Indianisation' of administration, and as in part a response to a vocal 'native' lobby, the move had the effect of hardening class distinctions between governors and subjects, while coding

as effects of 'race' power differences between the governing elite and an increasingly heterogeneous and overlapping population of 'native', Eurasian and resident European workers (see Buettner, 'Problematic Spaces', p.284 and *passim*). Buettner points out that ability to travel to and from the metropole at intervals became a key marker of 'European' identity at a time when other distinctions, such as skin colour, were becoming unreliable as proofs of status (p.281).

34. *Patronage and Society in Nineteenth-Century England* (London: Edward Arnold, 1986), pp.5, 56.
35. Skrine, *Life and Letters*, p.252.
36. Ibid., p.282.
37. A footnote cites as the authority for this outcome 'Letter from Mr. William Blackwood to Miss Meadows-Taylor, dated 18th December 1878' (Skrine, p.283). The fact that the whole annuities episode is retold as a postscript to Henry Bruce's 1920 edition of Taylor's *Story of My Life* (Oxford: Oxford University Press), in which his daughter Alice Taylor appears to have collaborated extensively, suggests that she may have been involved in the circulation of information about the campaign to later biographers.
38. See Finkelstein, *Philip Meadows Taylor*, p.16.

CHAPTER SIX

Excursive Discursive in Gandhi's *Autobiography*
Undressing and Redressing the Transnational Self

Julie F. Codell

Gandhi's *Autobiography: The Story of My Experiments with Truth* (1925) remains understudied by scholars.[1] When it is cited, often very briefly, it is for historical and biographical content, rather than for its literary values.[2] Yet Gandhi adored English literature and regretted giving it up for politics. Eighteen of his twenty recommended books to his Indian readers were western.[3] The most profound influences were Carlyle's *Heroes and Hero-Worship* and Ruskin's *Unto this Last*, which Gandhi paraphrased in Gujarati in 1908 in nine instalments in the South African *Indian Opinion*, a newspaper he published. He commends them in his *Autobiography*, along with Tolstoy, Thoreau, Plato, Max Nordau, Edward Carpenter, Mazzini and modern Indians Dadabhai Naoroji and Romesh Chunder Dutt.[4]

To address one possible *rapprochement* between Carlyle and Gandhi, I will examine Gandhi's *Autobiography* as an adaptation of Carlyle's *Sartor Resartus* in Gandhi's obsession with clothes as signs of change and multiple identities.[5] My argument is that *Sartor Resartus* offered Gandhi ideals, themes and metaphors of clothes and wanderings with which to help him fashion an Indian national self as a transnational identity, beyond parochial regional and caste hierarchies inherent in traditional Indian identities.

Gandhi's sartorial transformations coincide with his arrivals after long voyages between Britain, India and South Africa which mark transitions between sections of his text. A long trip or passage begins each section of the text, complemented by sartorial decisions and anxieties in which Gandhi struggles which changing and conflicting identities. He is a perpetual wanderer for over twenty years, as perambulating and displaced as Carlyle's Teufelsdröckh, described metaphorically as the Wandering Jew making his 'perambulation and circumambulation of the terraqueous Globe'.[6] This may have resonated with Gandhi's auto-biographical emphasis on diasporic and intercolonial travel, and with his radical revision of the very British practice of the excursion. Roland Barthes's examination of the excursion also inflects my reading of

Gandhi's possible meanings, extending the excursion into a global jaunt, as I will later argue. Wandering gave Gandhi the opportunity to test ideas against experiences, experimenting in the world's laboratory. His intriguing subtitle, *My Experiments with Truth*, is a conceit with a Carlylean ring, yoking science and religion through the irony of finding spiritual truth through laboratory experiments, a suggestion that critiques both religion as dogma and science as universal and material.

Victorian Gandhi

Victorian science and religion underpinned Gandhi's spiritual quest, and he partook of British ideals of self-help, reformism, hygiene and public health. He described England as 'the land of philosophers and poets'.[7] Gandhi's religious examination of Hinduism and Buddhism was largely the product of his time spent in Victorian London with Britons interested in these religions.[8] Many of his ideas about chastity and vegetarianism were reinforced by scientific justification in books he read in London.[9] While raised as a vegetarian, he discovered a philosophy articulated by British authors to justify this diet, and he joined the London Vegetarian Society.[10] People he met in London between 1888 and 1891 may have included James Routledge, former editor of the Calcutta *Statesman*, who exhorted others to love truth and help the poor. Routledge advocated handloom weaving and land labour (Hay, 'M.K. Gandhi' 1987, p.80). At teas of the Humanitarian League, Gandhi heard discussions about causes he later championed (ibid., p.94).

Gandhi's autobiographical self is Victorian in several ways. He was influenced by Victorian writers and thinkers, the time period of most of the *Autobiography* is Victorian and he is a colonised subject whose identities are British and Indian. His expression of his hybridity and identity changes are reflected in the structure of his text around two series of events. One is travel, between India and England and then between India and South Africa. These trips begin and conclude each section of his book. The second series, coinciding with his travel, is his changing attire. With each trip, Gandhi changes his clothes, gradually transforming his identity in the process from British dandy to various Indian identities (for example, Parsi) until he finds an Indian identity that fits his philosophy at the moment he decides to return to India for good. Each change is an undressing (he wears fewer clothes each time), and a redressing in both senses of the word: he re-dresses literally and redresses or corrects his ways making reparation for his past selves. In this decades-long process, he digests and deploys conflicting, dialectical cultural norms until he 'dresses' in a coherent but bricolaged Indian *and* transnational identity without regional or religious attire.

There are literary connections between Gandhi's process of undressing and redressing and the clothes philosophy of Carlyle's *Sartor Resartus*.[11] Carlyle's influence has not received scholarly attention but Gandhi read Carlyle with much appreciation. Geoffrey Ashe mentions Carlyle's influence several times.[12] B.R. Nanda notes the appeal to Gandhi of Carlyle's Mohammed facing 'humiliations and hardships'.[13] It was through Carlyle that Gandhi discovered Mohammed, as did the Victorians in general.[14] Gandhi was inspired by Carlyle's report of Mohammed doing his own cobbling and darning; he also read Carlyle's *French Revolution* and was impressed by Carlyle's view of the suddenness of the hero's appearance, a view shared by Tolstoy, another of Gandhi's favorite authors. Gandhi's diasporic wanderings, like Mohammed's, underlined his difficulties finding a vocation. His many hardships echo Carlyle's heroes' self-abnegation, dilemmas, wanderings, lack of vocation, timidity and shyness, and their stutterings and silences that signify their purity, innocence, credibility and authenticity.

Gandhi mentions Carlyle several times in his writings and letters. In 1908, on his experience in jail, he writes, 'I had intended to complete the translation of one of Carlyle's books and another of Ruskin'; he claimed that, if he served his entire jail sentence, 'I might have been able to complete my translation of the books of Carlyle and a book of Ruskin'.[15] Writing in 1909, Gandhi comments on his jail reading of 'Tolstoy, Emerson and Carlyle' and commends Carlyle's *French Revolution* as a 'forceful book'.[16] Gandhi quotes Carlyle's description of Parliament as the 'talking shop of the world'.[17] When his friend Hermann Kallenbach was leaving South Africa, he was given 'the complete works of Carlyle' by the President of the Cantonese Club.[18] To his son Manilal in 1912, Gandhi writes, 'I have with me what your Carlyle says on this. Only recently I read in it some profound observations, which I shall reproduce for your benefit some other time.'[19] He cites Carlyle's observation 'that the fool and the scoundrel go always hand in hand'.[20] In 1921, Gandhi wrote, 'I can still read with love some of the writings of Carlyle and Ruskin.'[21]

Carlyle shared with Ruskin and Tolstoy the advocacy of austerity, simplicity and respect for all kinds of labour that Gandhi applied to his ideals of community. Carlyle complained that the Industrial Revolution left Lancaster weavers in a state like that of 'a colony of Hindoo weavers squatting in the heart of Lancashire' ('Signs of the Times', p.3). Gandhi's vision of making one's own clothes as a form of resistance to the Raj applied Ruskin's and Carlyle's perceptions on the devastating effects of industrialism on rural and working-class labourers. Carlyle in *Past and*

Present wrote, 'All work, even cotton-spinning, is noble.'[22] Gandhi's *Autobiography* applies a metaphoric political economy (Carlyle's 'dismal science' and Ruskin's 'bastard science') and a notion of national identity rooted in personal morality in harmony with Carlyle's and Ruskin's views of the relationship between individual character and national character. Gandhi, like many Victorian critics, viewed the problems of modernisation in moral, rather than in strictly political or economic terms, sharing 'a sense of moral earnestness ... deep anxiety about the ethics of personal life and of public roles', including the nature of duty and altruism, as Judith Brown points out (Brown, *Gandhi: A Victorian Gentleman*, 1999, p.78).

In his *Autobiography* Gandhi echoed many Carlylean themes, such as the preference for silence over speech ('all deep talent, is a talent to *do*, and is intrinsically of silent nature', *Latter-Day Pamphlets*, no. V, 'Stump Orator', p.6; 'No grand Doer in this world can be a copious speaker about his doings', p.11).[23] Gandhi was often incapable of speaking, embarrassed to do it, and usually tongue-tied at the most inopportune moments. Just as the prophet's difficulties in speaking becomes a mark of his authenticity in Carlyle,[24] Gandhi, humiliated by an inability to speak in public that damaged his law career, discovered his own mission of self-abnegation and sacrifice out of what others needed, like Carlyle's heroes.[25] Carlyle's many themes of house building, repentance, journeys, the quiet life, anti-materialism, living by necessity alone, abstinence, control of all appetites, frugality, duty, nationalism, religion as a leveller of class and compassion are all themes taken up in Gandhi's text, too (Ashe, p.42). Carlyle, too, admired the 'self-abnegating' and was always ready to 'proclaim his defeat';[26] Gandhi in his autobiography seems at times to confront Carlyle's masculinised militant Mohammed with a non-violent asceticism that Carlyle also idealised. Dominant themes of Gandhi's autobiography, such as abstinence, self-deprecation, poverty and wandering, are echoes of Carlyle's construction of Mohammed (*Autobiography*, p.159).[27] Almost as dyspeptic as Carlyle, Gandhi focused on his body as essential to his identity for being both the *obstacle* to his purity (for example, desires, lust) and the *vehicle* for virtues (for example, celibacy, vegetarianism).

But Gandhi's biographical subjectivity incorporated and also critiqued Carlyle. Gandhi promoted as manly virtues, moral and bodily purity, celibacy, self-restraint, non-violent disobedience, all virtues manifest 'in the life of duty'.[28] Courage meant being 'warriors of the spirit', while the use of physical force was cowardice.[29] Gandhi's self offered ways 'to create new ideals of Indian manliness, and also a vision of a spiritually powerful Indian woman'.[30]

Gandhi's *Autobiography*: Intercolonial Dialectics of the Self

Gandhi points out in the foreword of his autobiography that the genre is thoroughly western and dangerously dogmatic. He insisted he was not writing a 'real autobiography', but one recording his 'experiments' with truth, a narrative of a tentative life, constantly on trial (*Autobiography*, p.xxvi).[31] As C. Yadav argues, Indians considered self-portraiture 'bad manners'.[32] Gandhi's own spare, austere writing style repudiated the flowery language and rich phrasing of much English-educated Indians' writings (Iyengar, p.272), making his style less self-indulgent.

Gandhi's autobiography was serialised weekly in Gujarati in *Navajiyan* and in English in *Young India* and then reissued as a book in 1925. *Young India*, one of Gandhi's papers, had a readership of almost 40 000 by 1922 when Gandhi went to jail, from where he began writing his text.[33] Gandhi's autobiography, then, was a newspaper story and in that regard entered the arena of politics, gossip, editorialising, and entertainment of this bricolaged medium, a site coherent with Gandhi's own often disrupted autobiographical trajectory, full of mis-directions, discoveries of new vocations conflicting with a 'normal' life. His own unfolding disrupted his domesticity, professional duties, career goals and role as scion of his family. Brown describes Gandhi's *Autobiography* as 'erratic and often confusing if the reader is seeking some clear chronological development or reasoned analysis ... there is no "conversion experience" as a landmark ... his experience was more a process of deepening enlightenment and discovery, influenced by a multiplicity of sources which reinforced each other'.[34] It was written at a time when Gandhi was somewhat marginalised; imprisonment between 1922 and 1924, combined with illness, kept him out of politics in which he had been active from 1920 to 1922. The *Autobiography* marked a quiet period when Gandhi worked on his growing Sabarmati ashram in Ahmedabad and witnessed the failure of his 'moral politics', hurt by growing internecine violence.[35]

Gandhi's autobiography is western in more than genre. It is marked by a scientific format of experiments on diet, celibacy, self-control and community living that Gandhi tried on his own body. This experimentation, as Alter notes, employed 'hypotheses gleaned from the margins of Europe', in which science was defined as a body of knowledge 'outside of ideology, history, and culture', despite being 'implicated in a complex genealogy of power and knowledge',[36] making science 'a peculiar discourse in the transnational context of late imperialism' (Alter, p.22). Gandhi blurred lines between rational empiricism and subjective experience, converging these modes of knowing (Alter, p.xii). He believed experimentation could be employed by all Indians to change themselves and ultimately to decolonise their bodies (Alter, p.27). Alter notes that Gandhi's notion of health was physical and moral, very Victorian; individual Indians could practise 'total self-control' and thereby attain for India 'the moral fibre to rule itself' (Alter, p.139) necessary to become a nation. Like a scientist, Gandhi claimed that his conclusions were not final but always open to re-experimentation, diluting his own authority.

Tradition, too, was folded into Gandhi's autobiography. Joanne Waghorne argues that Indian autobiography borrowed other forms of story telling from classic epics to present 'a special ritual process whereby daily life experience is transmuted into a truly religious experience'. In this way 'experience is not the monopoly of a few'; epic narrative in its performative narration or story telling elides with individual autobiographical meanings of its teller and listeners.[37] Richard Fox argues that the distinction between the supposedly unique western self and Asian conceptions of the self grew in 'the colonial situation', and was not sociological or anthropological, but was a political set of identities.[38] Whatever the blend of cultural sources, Gandhi's experiment offered a unity of practice and permitted a discontinuous, fragmented, constantly changing self, open to experience. His discontinuous, self-critical persona emphasised process over goal, inner life over outer appearance, and change over stability.

Gandhi's wanderings were not linear but dialectic, back and forth from India to England to India to South Africa, back and forth between India and South Africa for twenty years, then moving to India and wandering all over a country that was his birthplace but largely unknown to him. Gandhi's intercolonial and dialectic self, cultivated out of his experiences in Britain, South Africa and India, permitted him to try on Victorian identities of the Briton, the Anglicised Indian and the untouchable.[39] Out of these bricolaged identities that were the products of colonialism, Gandhi wrote his autobiographical identity within, and emerging from, layers of colonial and colonised selves. Gandhi's self was not really a hybrid, but a dialectically created identity that did not evolve simply from Anglophile to resistor in progressive steps, but went back and forth psychologically and geographically. His identity began in mimicry and ended in a carnivalesque rejection of the Indian social and British imperial orders. He critiqued Victorian masculinity with his non-violence, reiterations of his failures, inabilities and humiliations, and his identification with the lowest social groups, assertions and identifications diametrically opposed to hegemonic Victorian heroic masculine autonomy and individualism, and to hegemonic Indian colonial or caste identities.

Undressing and Redressing the Self: Clothed Identities Exposed

Writing his identities through clothes, Gandhi seems affected by Carlyle's *Sartor Resartus* (1836), which sold at least 69000 copies by 1881. Its popularity and Gandhi's references to, and affection for, Carlyle, make it likely he read it.[40] In his experiments with self-control, self-development and self-examination, Gandhi is close to Carlyle's *Sartor Resartus*'s dialectical self-questionings of variant aspects of selfhood, a mutual criticism or dialectic of the 'masks' of selfhood, until through 'their critical action a new self is gradually defined and a new kind of self-questioning literature is born'.[41] Carlyle's metaphors for philosophy are bodily ones: 'the inmost Pericardial and Nervous Tissue, which ministers Life and warm Circulation to the whole' (*SR*, p.172). In his near obsession with 'self-introspection' and everyday life – hygiene, clothes, sex, eating or fasting, educating children, abstinence and frugality, cleaning latrines – Gandhi refused to sublimate the banal and the bodily. The banal opened up transubstantiated insights, while remaining banal, never 'heightened'. Gandhi politicised and philosophised through mundane, all-too-intimate details of everyday life. His advocacy of everyone's participation in domestic activities transformed these duties into revolutionary acts of resistance by cooking one's own food, spinning and weaving one's own cloth. This advocacy made room for women in his movement, as it also transformed him into a womanly figure. On occasion he himself referred to 'the woman in me' and was a figure of 'ambivalent gendering', as Roy points out (Roy, pp.90, 149). Gandhi's experiments also permitted him to laugh at himself and let others do the same (for example, at the haircut he gave himself), like Teufelsdröckh's humour that permitted him a cosmic embrace, diffused his stumblings and opened him to sympathy and love for his fellow humans.[42]

Colin Manlove argues that the clothes metaphor realises Carlyle's vision that 'the condition of reality is continual change and movement'. The confusions and inconsistencies in the clothes philosophy are 'an extension of the absurdities of scientific investigation' that produced 'a philosophy at once necessary and useless, full and empty'.[43] Through changes, frequently expressed regrets, and citations of his failures and embarrassments, Gandhi similarly employs inconsistencies and errors to insist that only palpable experience, not knowledge learned by rote or repetition, can teach. His own philosophy was always subject to revision through new experiences represented by changes in his mode of dress that made palpable a philosophy as inconsistent, mobile and flexible as Teufelsdröckh's.

Gandhi's travels from one continent to the other are marked by his sudden self-consciousness about apparel: 'On the boat I had worn a black suit, the white flannel one, which my friends had got me, having been kept especially for wearing when I landed. ... I found I was the only person wearing such clothes. ... The shame of being the only person in white clothes was already too much for me' (*Autobiography*, p.43). He is sensitive to the way clothes from one country are inappropriate in another and mark him as unsophisticated and backward in English eyes: 'The clothes after the Bombay cut that I was wearing were, I thought, unsuitable for English society, and I got new ones at the Army and Navy Stores. I also went in for a chimney-pot hat costing nineteen shillings – an excessive price in those days ... I wasted ten pounds on an evening suit made in Bond Street, the center of fashionable life in London', and he got a gold watch chain from his brother (p.50). Such clothes gave him the identity of a dandy in London, c.1890. Yet he was often ignorant of clothes protocol in England; he picked up another Indian's English hat in London and rubbed the fur the wrong way, angering his friend (p.44).

Frequently Gandhi mentions that he was judged by his appearance and he learns the power of clothes in the empire: 'He surveyed me from top to toe and smiled' (p.103). Clothes determined his ability to get rooms, first class tickets, and berths on boats to Natal. Upon arriving in Natal, 'My dress marked me out from other Indians. I had a frock-coat and a turban, an imitation of the Bengal *pugree* ... expensive like that of Europeans' (p.105), making a good impression in this case. In the Transvaal to get a first class ticket which Indians were denied, Gandhi planned to negotiate with the ticket agent: 'I would therefore appear before him in faultless English dress, talk to him and possibly persuade him to issue a first class ticket' (p.116). His effort earned mixed results: 'I got a letter in reply to the effect that first and second class tickets would be issued to Indians who were properly dressed', a subjective condition, not a guarantee of equal rights, in Gandhi's view (p.128).

Clothing was saturated with mutually overlapping social, imperial, class, racial and national identities and status, symbolised in the book by the turbans. Only Muslim lawyers could keep theirs on in court in London (p.107). English rules on its wearing divided Muslim from Hindu. When he was admitted to the Law Society, Gandhi had to give up his turban and 'submit to the rules of the Court with regard to the dress to be worn by practising barristers' (p.147). Gandhi considered replacing his turban with an English hat, but a friend advised against it: 'He said, "If you do anything of the kind, it will have a very bad effect. You will compromise those insisting on wearing Indian turbans. And an Indian turban sits well on your head. If you wear an English hat, you will pass for a waiter"' (p.108). Indian Christians, children of indentured servants, wore English clothes and most were waiters, a job considered low caste. Mimicry did not make Indians into Englishmen, but could be read as degraded, not professional or respectable.

One indentured servant Gandhi represented in South Africa brought the turban issue into Gandhi's consciousness from a different perspective and linked clothes to colonial practice:

> A practice had been forced upon every indentured labourer and every Indian stranger to take off his head-gear when visiting a European, whether the head-gear were a cap, a turban or a scarf wrapped round the head. A salute even with both hands was not sufficient. Balasundaram thought that he should follow the practice even with me. This was the first case in my experience. I felt humiliated and asked him to tie up his scarf. He did so, not without a certain hesitation, but I could perceive the pleasure on his face. It has always been a mystery to me how men can feel themselves honoured by the humiliation of their fellow-beings. (p.155)

The turban had the power to link diasporic Indians and overcome the separation imposed by British protocol.

Part III opens with Gandhi bringing his family to South Africa. He dressed them in Parsi clothes: 'in order to look civilized, our dress and manners had as far as possible to approximate to the European standard. Because, I thought, only thus could we have some influence, and ... serve the community. ... The Parsis used then to be regarded as the most civilized people amongst Indians, and so, when the complete European style seemed to be unsuited, we adopted the Parsi Style. Accordingly my wife wore the Parsi *sari*, and the boys the Parsi coat and trousers. Of course no one could be without shoes and stockings. ... But I can see today that we feel all the freer and lighter for having cast off the tinsel of "civilization"' (p.186). Here again Gandhi sees his dress from European eyes. Giving up dressing like an Englishman, he moves to respected Indian Parsis, a group associated with commercial interests and friendly toward the British. He adds hindsight here and divorces clothes from notions of 'civilisation' as mere 'tinsel' to insist on the importance of clothes' utilitarian values ('freer and lighter') in place of class or caste readings of attire.

Ways of handling clothing exposed conditions of servitude that fostered self-help. Gandhi noticed that the washerman had so much work and was so unpunctual that 'even two or three dozen shirts and collars proved insufficient for me. Collars had to be changed daily and shirts, if not daily, at least every alternate day' (p.212). The solution was to wash his own clothes. He also cut his own hair. Both of these were inappropriate, out-caste acts. Clothing provided a means for Gandhi's own willing servitude in personal devotion to those he admired. He helped the politician Ghosal button his shirt as if he were his valet (p.226), taking on the servant's role which Gandhi frequently impersonated.

Clothing could signify British imperial oppression in the case of maharajahs' 'oriental' dress that represented British colonial oppression (pp.229–30):

> In the Club I always found them wearing fine Bengalee *dhotis* and shirts and scarves. On the darbar day they put on trousers befitting *khansamas* [waiters] and shining boots. I was pained and inquired of one of them the reason for the change. 'We alone know our unfortunate condition. We alone know the insults we have to put up with, in order that we may possess our wealth and titles,' he replied. … Do you see any difference between *khansamas* and us? … we are Lord Curzon's *khansamas*. … If I were to attend it in my usual dress, it would be an offence.'

At Lord Hardinge's darbar, Gandhi derives a moral about the dangers of the rajahs' wealth (p.230):

> I was distressed to see the Maharajas bedecked like women – silk *pyjamas* and silk *achkans*, pearl necklaces round their necks, bracelets on their wrists, pearl and diamond tassels on their turbans and, besides all this, swords with golden hilts hanging from their waist-bands … insignia not of their royalty but of their slavery … badges of impotence … it was obligatory for these Rajas to wear all their costly jewels at such functions … they never wore them except on occasions like the darbar … jewels that only some women wear. How heavy is the toll of sins and wrongs that wealth, power and prestige exact from man!

Returning to India in the beginning of Part V, he adopted the clothes of a poor man, another disguise and masquerade (p.377):

> During the Satyagraha in South Africa I had altered my style of dress so as to make it more in keeping with that of the indentured labourers, and in England also I had adhered to the same taste for indoor use. For landing in Bombay I had a Kathiawadi suit of clothes consisting of a shirt, a dhoti, a cloak and a white scarf, all made of Indian mill cloth. But as I was to travel third from Bombay, I regarded the scarf and the cloak as too much of an incumbrance, so I shed them, and invested in an eight-to-ten-annas Kashmiri cap. One dressed in that fashion was sure to pass muster as a poor man.

He gave up travelling first class and went only third class from this point on. But he notes here that he is trying to 'pass muster as a poor man', exposing his clothes' theatrical or performative function. Clothes mark his *wearing* an identity, which is not *being* that identity. At this stage,

Gandhi's change of clothes approaches the Carlylean philosophy of clothes, finding clothes that express a divine idea, an essential self, an ideal that Gandhi strives for, as he strips himself of English, then Parsi, then hat and scarf, to appear fit for a third class railway carriage. By undressing and re-dressing himself, Gandhi participates in the Carlylean process of destroying and creating society, since Gandhi believes society is changed one individual at a time, in this case his clothes performing an identity change into the lowest caste, in order to level caste in everyone's consciousness.[44]

Eventually he discarded any religious clothing and hairstyle in England, removed his sacred thread and *shikha*, 'lest when I was bareheaded it should expose me to ridicule and make me look, as I then thought, a barbarian in the eyes of the Englishmen' (p.392). He never wore these articles in India, later, however, because he did not want to invoke a Hindu identity. His experiences in South Africa, leading and defending diasporic Indians from all castes and religions, led him to attempt to 'wear' a transnational Indian identity without marks of region or religion, while evoking aggressively the identity of the poor and untouchable in his eventual minimal dress.

For Carlyle, clothes revealed truth and changed to fit historical circumstances. These double roles resonated in Gandhi's search for clothes that symbolise his momentary, shifting identities, and his search for a final, fitting identity. Gandhi's changing philosophies and changing clothes are mutually inflected, parallel tracks. Carlyle did not believe that old clothes could simply be patched up. Rather new institutions needed to be created to avoid simply repressing forces of change, and he hailed the sansculotte vision in which 'the Clothes fly off the whole dramatic corps; and Dukes, Grandees, Bishops, Generals, Anointed Presence itself, every mother's son of them, standing straddling there, not a shirt on them' (*SR*, p.61). Clothes were impediments to recognising authority, too, so one must be stripped to be truly seen (Vanden Bossche, pp.43–4). Gandhi, too, frequently praised those in power who dressed simply, and he believed that true authority was revealed in the wearing of fewer clothes, a stripping away he himself engaged in, like Carlyle's 'denuding project' (Helmling, p.37). His friend Dr Ray's dress 'used to be nearly as simple as it is, with this difference of course that whereas it is Khadi now, it used to be Indian mill-cloth in those days' (*Autobiography*, p.231). Of another man, Gandhi wrote, 'In the Congress I had seen him in a coat and trousers, but I was glad to find him now wearing a Bengal *dhoti* and shirt. I liked his simple mode of dress, though I myself then wore a Parsi coat and trousers' (p.234). He admired a friend who told him, '"I am not a fashionable fellow like you. The minimum amount of food and the minimum amount of clothing suffice for me"' (p.74).

Gandhi's transformation resonates with *Sartor Resartus* in his themes of dandyism, social hierarchies, invocation of science, and changing identities through discarding clothes. James Eli Adams describes the paradox of the prophet sage as both ascetic and a self-displaying dandy. Adams argues that self-discipline and self-control were interwoven into Victorian masculine identities, creating ambiguities and contradictions in these identities, because 'self-discipline perplexes the binaries of active and passive, of self-assertion and self-denial', virtues often associated with femininity (Adams, p.8). In his chapter, 'The Dandiacal Body', in *Sartor*, Carlyle attacks the dandy as dependent on social approval and a self-aggrandising theatricality, but recognises that, at the same time, the dandy is a purist who carries 'a true Nazarene deportment … unspotted from the world' (cited in Adams, p.22). Carlyle pits the prophet, defined by an ascetic spectacularity, against the dandy seeking social approval.

But these two masculine identities are intimately bound in an obverse relationship. Gandhi's changing sartorial displays transform him from dandy to prophet, from 'civilised' (English, Parsi) to Carlyle's 'wild' and 'savage' ascetic prophet-as-hero (Mahatma, poor man) and from middle-class Anglicized Indian to an untouchable, in defiance of society's hierarchies and order. But, unlike Carlyle's heroic prophet, Gandhi refused to be obscure to his public or to remain outside society; instead he proposed through the writing of an autobiography to offer an experimental model for all Indians, performing his own extreme version of 'virtuoso asceticism' (Adams, p.2) through his text. And like a saint, he undressed to his loincloth in public, not as an anti-social act, but as a fundamentally social act. Gandhi remade himself in Victorian ways; he transferred 'martial courage to inner struggle' (Adams, p.7), eliminated martial force completely. His inner struggle was projected in his text into a communal struggle, neither solitary nor excessively agonistic. Experimentation offered a distancing, 'strange scientific freedom' (Carlyle's phrase) from his family ties and created a means for others to use and employ what he learned. Gandhi was a Victorian self-made man in reverse. Instead of his self as an additive construction (self-made as demonstrated by material acquisition and social status), Gandhi's self was a subtractive deconstruction-as-reconstruction, removing clothes, caste, class and even gender.

Carlyle's choice of clothing to represent revolution linked it to the Industrial Revolution, as the textile industry was the first to be mechanised, and to the French Revolution's *sansculotte* movement.[45] Hand-loom weavers were the most active in riots and social unrest, suffering economic losses in the 1820s. According to Chris Vanden Bossche (p.43), Carlyle uses the weaving of cloth, or the sewing of a suit of clothes, to represent the process of authoring beliefs and institutions. His emphasis on clothing as woven textile plays on the root of the word *text* – *texere*, to weave. Transcendental authority authors, weaves, or sews together the institutions and beliefs that constitute human society. Clothes are the medium through which the transcendental becomes visible in the finite world of human history.

The final clothes transformation advocated by Gandhi offered national unity and an imagined community through Khadi, the simple cotton cloth hand-spun by ordinary citizens and outside the British production/consumption system. Gandhi's ashram in Ahmedabad, 'an ancient centre of handloom weaving', was a site for 'the cottage industry of hand-spinning' (*Autobiography*, p.395) that promoted self-help, new identities and decolonisation (pp.489–90):

> to be able to clothe ourselves entirely in cloth manufactured by our own hands. ... It enabled us to know, from direct contact, the conditions of life among the weavers, the extent of their production, the handicaps in the way of their obtaining their yarn supply, the way in which they were being made victims of fraud, and, lastly, their ever growing indebtedness. ... All the fine cloth woven by the weavers was from foreign yarn, ... By thus adopting cloth woven from mill-yarn as our wear, and propagating it among our friends, we made ourselves voluntary agents of the Indian spinning mills.

Gandhi's definition of religion as fundamentally moral and his belief that religion and politics went together made it possible for him to turn spinning and dressing into complex religious–moral, political and economic acts of resistance with which to restructure Indian society as independent of British domination.[46] He hoped Indians could be unified by a common thread, so to speak, by Khadi clothes worn by all castes and classes, a dress utopia he envisioned. This economic independence and self-help or self-government, *swaraj* in Gandhi's term, was also homologous with Victorian self-help expressed in Carlyle's and Ruskin's pre-industrial dreams. Carlyle was sensitive to the social and cultural split that emerged from the Industrial Revolution, between those who gained wealth and power from it and those who had to bear its pain. This social and political split and its consequences created a rift for the Carlylean hero to heal by helping others form one homogeneous society through the hero's vision. Carlyle's tailor restitches new clothes from old, shaping change for evolving identities; 'representation must forever be separated from what it represents' so that conviction can become conduct but not fixed custom.[47] Gandhi also practised this through stripping off his clothes.

Gandhi's invocation of 'experimentation' affirmed his autobiography was not simply about one person but about philosophical truths, which, nonetheless, had no validity outside or apart from the experiences that led to these truths. His experimentation, then, is separate from the representation of his autobiographical self, to counteract autobiography's tendency to become sacred dogma for followers, something he was anxious to avoid. As Teufelsdröckh's re-stitching separated clothes from the person, Gandhi undresses, strips away his clothes, and examines in almost excruciating detail his body and nakedness – physical (food he eats, excretion and hygiene) and psychological (many anxieties, disruptive desires) – to test the accumulating philosophy rooted *in* the body and in *overcoming* it. Gandhi is not the signified of his autobiography (the simplistic humanistic reading of Gandhi's autobiography, as Alter shows). Neither is he writing his own hagiography, a genre that claims the self as a vehicle for a 'higher meaning'. Gandhi's end is not an ideal model for others to follow, but the experimentation process itself. Toward this end Gandhi records every one of his failures, stutterings and incompetencies with relish. Like Carlyle's philosopher, Gandhi wants to incite his readers to 'self-activity' (Carlyle's phrase) which means changing clothes, redressing social ills and finding new patterns.

In Wolfgang Iser's view, the end of cross-cultural discourse is not appropriation or assimilation but changing both cultures by defamiliarisation and the effects of one culture on another.[48] Undressing and redressing are means for defamiliarisation of cultural norms, reiterating the defamiliarisation Gandhi experienced every time he arrived in port from one country to another. Every arrival was painful, as he was often inappropriately dressed, usually overdressed, to 'pass muster'. Teufelsdröckh's task was to make clothes transparent, to reveal clothes as cultural, not as natural, and to denude clothing of its class and differentiating distinctions until all stand naked.[49] Gandhi became increasingly naked in seeking distilled 'Indian' self. As Gandhi declassed, re-cast(e) and re-gendered himself, he re-tailored and re-dressed (in both meanings) himself and others to fit a nearly naked Indian world in which many poor Indians could not clean their clothes because they had only one set to wear, a discovery he made while travelling in India to get to know his own native country and people.

Gandhi's Pleasures of the Text: Excursivity and Border Writing

By continually finding and losing his identities, Gandhi made sure his identity was always experimental. By regretting past acts and words, narrating his regret over past acts and words and his failings, and not finding Truth or god at the end, Gandhi avoids writing a transcendental life. Gandhi's anti-transcendentalism was apparent in his use of domestic life as the *mise-en-scène* for formations of autobiographical subjectivity. Carlyle's search led him to heroism, while Gandhi's led him to a kind of anti-heroism, while sharing Carlyle's belief that the socioeconomic order was not entirely separate from a transcendental order. Gandhi hoped to remake ordinary individuals into people capable of building a new social cohesion based on each person's individual, physical transformation through proper eating, sanitation, home-spun clothes, frugality and celibacy.

Teufelsdröckh's stripped away vision, clothes-less and rapt, is also Gandhi's, but the Mahatma was not willing to claim having a vision, preferring to be always on the way to it. Both Carlyle and Gandhi explore a kind of selflessness, Gandhi's to be an utter servant of others, and Teufelsdröckh's to be one with the universe, the ultimate NOT ME. Carlyle's self approaches disembodiment, while Gandhi's always remains embodied. While Gandhi, like Teufelsdröckh, increasingly stripped himself of clothes, he did not follow the philosopher into transcendentalism, but remained committed to the mundane and the bodily. Gandhi repudiated a goal; he would continue to wander without direction or teleology, within and beyond his autobiography.

Gandhi's autobiography is excursive, as well as discursive, and fits several definitions of the word as given in the *Oxford English Dictionary*: running out, escaping from confinement (writing from jail and release from family caste and ties); any body or particle in oscillating or alternating motion (travels back and forth; regrets over the past); an offshoot, branch, projection in any direction (his life as an offshoot of many fortuitous directions and encounters); an outburst, an overstepping of the bounds of propriety or custom, a freak; vagary, escapade and deviation from a definite path or course (the unexpected paths he took through circumstances and happenstances that defied customs and traditions on three continents; his ad lib acts of resistance to British rule); ramble from a subject, digression (his narrative achronological digressions to focus on particular incidents or topics that become thematic); an excursion-train to convey persons making a pleasure excursion, usually at reduced fares (his determination to travel first class in South Africa; his later choice of third class travel in India).

Gandhi's wanderings around the globe and his incessant walking that became a powerful and symbolic act of resistance to imperialism were matched by his pedestrian style and refusal to offer a coherent philosophy, recalling Barthes's notion of the excursion, that very English concept (think of Wordsworth), as a means to avoid foreclosure by an emphasis on method, rather than ultimate meaning:

> For what can be oppressive in our teaching is not, finally, the knowledge or the culture it conveys, but the discursive forms through which we propose them ... this teaching has as its object discourse taken in the inevitability of power, method can really bear only on the means of loosening, baffling, or at the very least, of lightening this power. And I am increasingly convinced, both in writing and in teaching, that the fundamental operation of this loosening method is, if one writes, fragmentation, and, if one teaches, digression, or, to put it in a preciously ambiguous word, *excursion*.[50]

Ann Game describes a stroll as a metaphor for writing in contemporary culture theory, in which the purposelessness of wandering situates the wanderer outside the system: 'To wander is to err from the straight and narrow of linearity, of the order ... distinguished from the purposive walk which is concerned with an end, a goal. ... The stroll, on the other hand, has no concern for a whole or an end; the unforeseeable excites.'[51]

Gandhi's autobiographical identity depended on excursions and on excursions in the empire. As Brown suggests, 'For Gandhi, the heart of Indian identity was not geographical location, religious tradition, ethnic belonging or shared language. Rather it lay in a common cultural identity, shared by all Indians: it was eclectic, expansive, tolerant, deriving from all the diverse groups who had made India their home'.[52] Brown's statement could be emended to refer to those 'who had made the empire their home'. It was, after all, the empire Gandhi inhabited and in which he wandered. Without the empire, he would not have been able to escape his failed practice in India, or be induced to go to England to study law and read English literature, or defend diasporic Indians in South Africa. His identity was diasporic, intercolonial and Victorian, bricolaged, never completed, always in-process. To move from an anglophile to a defender of African Indians to a resistor of British rule required an intercolonial perspective to avoid a nationalism he hated and to understand British rule in order to resist it. Gandhi applied Victorian notions of self-help, hygiene and science to Indians' very resistance to the Raj, believing that resistance required Indians to attend first to the control of their own bodies, and by Victorian standards and ideals (hygiene, work ethic, self-control of desires), in order to control their communities and ultimately their nation.

Gandhi exemplifies the ways in which imperial India constructed Indians as 'cosmopolitan and complex figures'. Sometimes considered quintessentially Indian, Gandhi was in many ways just as Victorian, 'in his ideals and concerns', long after he discarded his English clothes (Brown, 1999, *Gandhi: A Victorian Gentleman*, p.69). His intercolonial subjectivity exemplified the increasingly shortened distances between colony and metropole. Brown's felicitous phrase for Gandhi, 'critical outsider', plays on multiple meanings of critical: he was critical of the social/racial order for South African Indians, critical of both British and South African societies, critical of India to which he returned as an outsider when he was 46, and critical of empire. He was a critical outsider in all three countries.[53]

Gandhi's wanderings led him across and along borders, giving him a perspective from several sides. Emily Hicks describes border writing as 'a mode of operation ... choosing a strategy of translation rather than representation' to 'undermine the distinction between original and alien culture'. Such writing offers 'multidimensional perception and nonsynchronous memory'[54] as its authors see the world from several sides. Hicks describes border culture and writing as a space that deprives discourse of the power to dissimulate an identity, as it simultaneously opens up identity possibilities, like Barthes's excursion. In Hicks's view, border writing deterritorialises the subject and the cultural codes, so that, at times, even 'existential questions about identity and place become legal nightmares of displacement and deportation' (Hicks p.113). This applies to Gandhi's near deportation from South Africa even before his boat landed, the beating he suffered when he was allowed to disembark, and his imprisonments in South Africa and India. Gandhi discovered that codes of meaning in India had to be translated in England (why he sought scientific justifications for vegetarianism) or could not be translated back again (his legal training in England did not prepare him to practise law in India).

For Gandhi, London and South Africa offered a kind of atopia, a virtual space outside the social order, doxa or referential codes of India. In his atopia, Gandhi could change clothes, undress, redress and take on multiple and fluid identities to fit or resist circumstances. Every fit was temporary and subject to change. Gandhi's autobiography is a translation across real, hybrid and imagined cultures and places. From multiple perspectives Gandhi could inhabit Ruskin's social philosophy as non-violence, Tolstoy's idealisation of the peasant as a vision of village India, Carlyle's Mohammed as a non-violent celibate who believed in equity among religions and Teufelsdröckh's transcendental nakedness as a new social order, a carnival of caste. But despite his transnationalism, Gandhi resisted Enlightenment idealism and universality as arms of the Raj and replaced them with material identifications with the lowly, the body, the accidental and praxis, making the everyday into the epic.

Culture is, as one critic points out, not fixed but always 'intrinsically creative, inherently improvised, and deeply felt' (Alter, p.xii) and always in states of both disintegration and reorganization. It is also, as Arjun Appadurai defines it, 'intrinsically public and inherently transnational' (cited in Alter, p.58). Gandhi fits Rosenberg's definition of a Carlylean hero, with 'a sense of duty unconnected to the institutional sources which legitimate authority in the sociopolitical world', so that the hero 'transvalues everything ... makes a sovereign break with all traditional or rational norms'. Gandhi's Carlylean 'self-assertion and self-discipline', however, led him to resist the institutionalisation of British authority through excursions, undressing and redressing, the results of which, the end of empire, might have surprised Carlyle.[55]

Acknowledgment

I want to thank Chris Vanden Bossche for his many helpful suggestions on Carlyle and related readings, Judith Brown for sharing a typescript with me and answering my queries, Julia Watson for years of help in my forays into autobiography, David Amigoni for his guidance, and the anonymous reader for very helpful suggestions.

Notes

1. I am using *An Autobiography: The Story of My Experiments with Truth*, trans. Mahadev Desai (Boston: Beacon Press, 1993); hereafter cited as *Autobiography*. Desai was Gandhi's secretary.
2. See Joan Bondurant's *Conquest of Violence* (Princeton: Princeton University Press, 1958). Geoffrey Ashe, *Gandhi: A Study in Revolution* (London: Heinemann, 1968), pp.252–4; K.V. Tirumalesh, 'Autobiography's Moment of Truth: The experiments of Mahatma Gandhi', *Indian Journal of American Studies*, 27 (1998), 15–20, applies some theoretical points about autobiography to Gandhi's text. B.R. Nanda does not index the autobiography in *Mahatma Gandhi: A Biography* (Delhi and Oxford: Oxford University Press, 1958). See also James D. Hunt, *Gandhi in London* (New Delhi: Promilla and Co, 1978); Joseph S. Alter, *Gandhi's Body: Sex, Diet and the Politics of Nationalism* (Philadelphia: University of Pennsylvania Press, 2000); Judith M. Brown, *Gandhi: Prisoner of Hope* (New Haven: Yale University Press, 1989). These uses are perfectly justified in historical scholarship. A few authors address its British or Indian literary sources or parallels, again briefly: see Meena Sodhi, *Indian English Writing: The Autobiographical Mode* (New Delhi: Creative Books, 1999); K.R. Srinivasa Iyengar, *Indian Writing in English*. 2nd edn (New York: Asia Publishing House, 1973); K.C. Yadav (ed.), *Autobiography of Swami Dayanand Saraswati* (New Delhi: Manohar, 1976), orig. pub. 1875–79; Stephen Hay, 'Digging up Gandhi's Psychological Roots', *Biography*, 6 (1983), 209–19; Joanne Punzo Waghorne, 'Case of the Missing Autobiography', *American Academy of Religion Journal*, 49 (1981), 589–603; K.V. Tirumalesh, 'Autobiography's Search for Truth: Newman and Gandhi', *The Centennial Review*, 40 (Winter 1996), 99–123; Winand M. Callewaert and Rupert Snell, (eds), *According to Tradition: Hagiographical Writing in India* (Wiesbaden: Harrassowitz Verlag, 1994); Vijay Mishra, 'Defining the Self in Indian Literary and Filmic Texts',

Narratives of Agency: Self-Making in China, India, and Japan, ed. Wimal Dissanayake (Minneapolis: University of Minnesota Press, 1996), pp.117–50. None offers a sustained literary analysis of the autobiography.

3. B.R. Nanda, *In Search of Gandhi*, p.60.

4. K.R. Srinivasa Iyengar, *Indian Writing in English*, p.251. After reading Ruskin, Gandhi founded his community of Phoenix outside Durban. Years later, Gandhi read *Fors Clavigera* (Judith Brown, 'Reading *Unto This Last* – A Transformative Experience: Gandhi in South Africa', typescript, p.17).

5. Gandhi's *Autobiography* also appears unCarlylean, too, in Gandhi's unprophetic voice, refusal to assume the mantle of authority and heroism, and feminisation of political participation and authority (Ashis Nandy, *The Intimate Enemy*, Delhi: Oxford University Press, 1983, p.52). As Parama Roy notes, Gandhi 'feminized himself', believed women were better fit for nonviolence, and legitimised women's participation in public life (Parama Roy, *Indian Traffic*, Berkeley: University of California Press, 1998, p.139). Gandhi's style was simple, unlike Carlyle's rich, free-wheeling rhetoric.

6. See G.B. Tennyson, *Sartor Called Resartus*, (Princeton: Princeton University Press, 1965), p.207; the quotation is from Carlyle's text.

7. Gandhi, *Works*, I, 42; see Stephan Hay, 'The Making of a Late-Victorian Hindu: M.K. Gandhi in London, 1888–1891', *Victorian Studies*, 33 (1987), 76.

8. Judith M. Brown, 'Gandhi – A Victorian Gentleman: An Essay in Imperial Encounter', *The Journal of Imperial and Commonwealth History*, 27 (1999), 76.

9. Authors of such books included Paul Bureau, Dr Mary Scharlieb and William Loftus Hare.

10. Gandhi, *Autobiography*, pp.48–9, on his readings, and pp.56–7 on the Vegetarian Society. See also Hay, 'A Late-Victorian Hindu', 1987, pp.87–92.

11. Thomas Carlyle, '*Sartor Resartus*' in *The Works of Thomas Carlyle*, ed. H.D. Traill, 30 vols (New York: C. Scribner, 1903–4), vol. I. Hereafter cited as *SR*.

12. Judith Brown lists Carlyle among the authors Gandhi profitably read in jail in 1908–9 (*Gandhi: Prisoner of Hope*, 63). Ashe (*A Study in Revolution*) describes the interests Gandhi had in Carlyle's Mohammed (pp.42, 86–7, 117–18, 147).

13. B.R. Nanda, *Mahatma Gandhi*, p.68.

14. Gandhi also read Washington Irving's *Mahomet and His Successors* (1845) and Maulana Shibli's biography of the Prophet, according to B.R. Nanda, *In Search of Gandhi*, p.57.

15. *The Collected Works of Mahatma Gandhi*, 100 vols (Delhi: Government of India, 1958–94), v.8, p.159. The editors have noted that the Ruskin book was *Unto This Last*, Gandhi's favourite, but failed to note which Carlyle book Gandhi had planned to translate. The second version of this quotation appears in C.F. Andrews (ed.), *Mahatma Gandhi at Work* (London: George Allen and Unwin, 1931), p.202.

16. *Collected Works*, v.9, p.241.

17. *Collected Works*, v.10, p.17. While Carlyle has often been credited with this phrase, his actual words were 'Talking Apparatus' in *Latter Day Pamphlets*, no. V, 'Stump Orator' (p.10) and 'Talking-machine' in *Latter Day Pamphlets*, no. I, 'The Present Time' (p.19). I have not been able

to trace Carlyle's comments on the fool and the scoundrel. My quotation from 'Stump Orator' are from the text on http://cupid.ecom.unimelb.edu.au/het/carlyle/latter5.htm and from 'The Present Time' from http://cupid.ecom.unimelb.edu.au/het/carlyle/latter1.htm, and page numbers cited are from their printed versions.

18. *Collected Works*, v.11, p.135.

19. *Collected Works*, v.11, p.256. There seems to be no surviving letter in which Gandhi did this.

20. Raghavan Iyer (ed.), *The Moral and Political Writings of Mahatma Gandhi* (Oxford: Clarendon Press, 1986), p.621. I have not found this reference in any of Carlyle's texts.

21. *Collected Works*, v.19, p.178. Scholars have commented extensively on Victorian influences on Gandhi. One biographer claims that in South Africa in 1893–94 Gandhi read eighty books, most of them western literature, cited in Adi H. Doctor, 'Western Influence on Gandhian Thought', *Gandhi India and the World*, ed. Sibnarayan Ray (Philadelphia: Temple University Press, 1970), p.71. See Z. Hasan, *Gandhi and Ruskin* (Delhi: Shree Publishing, 1980); V. Lakshmi Menon, *Ruskin and Gandhi* (Varanesi: Sarva Seva Sangh, 1965); Erik Erikson, 'Gandhi's Autobiography: The Leader as Child', *American Scholar*, 35 (1966), 632–46; Ruth Vanita, 'Gandhi's Tiger: multilingual Elites, The Battle for Minds, and English Romantic Literature in Colonial England', *Postcolonial Studies*, 5 (2002), 95–110; K.V. Tirumalesh, 'Autobiography's Search for Truth: Newman and Gandhi', *The Centennial Review*, 40 (1996), 99–123; Stephen Hay, 'Between Two Worlds: Gandhi's First Impressions of British Culture', *Modern Asian Studies*, 3 (1969), 305–19.

22. *Works*, v.x, *Past and Present*, p.153.

23. My source is http://www.victorianweb.org/authors/carlyle/signs1.html.

24. See David J. DeLaura, 'Ishmael as Prophet: *Heroes and Hero-Worship* and the Self-Expressive Basis of Carlyle's Art', *The Critical Response to Thomas Carlyle's Major Works*, ed. D.J. Trela and Rodger L. Tarr (Westport: Greenwood Press, 1997), p.129.

25. Regarding the hero propelled by others, see Philip Rosenberg, *The Seventh Hero: Thomas Carlyle and the Theory of Radical Activism* (Cambridge: Harvard University Press, 1974), p.192.

26. Steven Helmling, *The Esoteric Comedies of Carlyle, Newman, and Yeats* (Cambridge: Cambridge University Press, 1988), p.34.

27. Gandhi appears to have read Carlyle on Mohammed twice, in England when studying law and in South Africa about 1894 (*Autobiography*, pp.69, 159).

28. Judith M. Brown, 'Gandhi – A Victorian Gentleman', p.80.

29. After being beaten by a white mob and escaping, Gandhi refuses to prosecute them, having clarified in the press his innocence of their suspicions about him. He believed this behaviour 'enhanced the prestige of the [Indian] community' and 'proved that the Indian could put up a manly fight' (*Autobiography*, pp.196–7). Ashis Nandy argues that Indian nationalists only gained loss of self by replicating British masculinity (pp.52ff).

30. See Richard G Fox, 'Self-Made', *Narratives of Agency: Self-Making in China, India, and Japan*, ed. Wimal Dissanayake (Minneapolis: University of Minnesota Press, 1996), p.109; Brown, 'Gandhi – A Victorian

Gentleman', p.81; Roy, *Indian Traffic* p.148, citing Kishwar. British Victorian masculinity was not monolithic or untroubled. Conflicts between hegemonic masculinity and the life of the man of letters was deeply conflicted for Carlyle, as James Eli Adams points out in *Dandies and Desert Saints: Styles of Victorian Masculinity* (Ithaca: Cornell University Press, 1995), p.1.

31.   See Meena Sodhi, *Indian English Writing*, pp.48–9. The modern version of autobiography in India developed in the nineteenth century, influenced by European literatures, and required a dramatic change in the views of agency against traditional fatalism, according to N. Radhakrishnan, 'Contemporary Indian Biography', in *Life Writing from the Pacific Rim*, ed. Stanley Schab and George Simson (Honolulu: University of Hawai'i Press, 1997), p.51. Narrative language became simpler, influenced by Samuel Johnson's *Lives of the Poets* and Thomas Carlyle's *Heroes and Hero Worship* (Radhakrishnan, p.51). Early Indian nationalism, however, created many hagiographic biographies in its wake (Radhakrishnan, p.52). Gandhi's secretary, Mahadev Desai, who translated Gandhi's autobiography into English, wrote biographies, including one of St Francis (Radhakrishnan, p.54).

32.   Yadav, K.C., ed. *Autobiography of Swami Dayanand Saraswati*, p.1.

33.   Gandhi's other newspaper was *Harijan* (Iyengar, *Indian Writing*, pp.263, 272).

34.   Brown, *Gandhi: Prisoner of Hope*, p.74.

35.   Ibid., pp.176–7.

36.   Joseph Alter, *Gandhi's Body*, xi–xii.

37.   See Waghorne, 'Case of the Missing Autobiography', *American Academy of Religion Journal*, 49 (1981), 599–600. She argues that Gandhi's text 'is ultimately a new phenomenon in Indian life: a product of both an Eastern and Western environment' (Waghorne, p.589). Gandhi identified with the poor masses and incorporated Hindu narrative elisions between epic hero and ordinary daily lives that Waghorne identifies as traditional in Hindu biography. Spiritual autobiographies offered patterns of renunciation combined with active involvement 'in the religious and social situation of their times ... to reform or reshape the religious practices of their contemporaries' (Rinehart, *One Lifetime, Many Lives: The Experience of Modern Hindu Hagiography*, Atlanta: Scholars Press, 1999, p.3). Some critics compare Gandhi's text to Augustine's because of the spiritual quest; others point out his materialist themes of body, clothing, lust and illnesses. For V.S. Naipaul, Gandhi's autobiography is characterised by self-absorption that blots out external sights and activities (Sodhi, *Indian English Writing*, p.49). Vijay Mishra argues, 'Gandhi reinscribes his self in the autobiography in the generic system of Brahmanical hagiography ... the enlightened soul who has achieved *moksa* [oceanic sublime state that denies the transient world for the sake of the innermost self] ... a brilliant political stroke, even one of genius, since his life galvanized an entire Hindu world behind him' (Mishra, 'Defining the Self in Indian Literary and Filmic Texts', p.145).

38.   Fox, 'Self-Made', p.107. See Yadav, *Autobiography of Swami Dayanand Saraswati*, pp.3, 7 on other Indians' life writings.

39.   I borrow the term 'intercolonial' from Barbara Groseclose, 'Death, glory, empire: art', in Julie F. Codell and Diane Sashko Macleod (eds),

Orientalism Transposed: The Impact of the Colonies on British Culture (Aldershot: Ashgate, 1998), p.189.

40. Rodger Tarr's introduction to *SR*, p.xxxiv, mentions this figure cited by the publisher Chapman and Hall. Tarr mentions in footnote 20, xxxiv, that, by 1881, the year Carlyle died, the book had probably sold 80 000 to 90 000 copies, if earlier editions are counted (not including German and Dutch versions).

41. Albert J. LaValley, *Carlyle and the Idea of the Modern* (New Haven: Yale University Press, 1968), p.9.

42. Gandhi distances himself as narrator from the representation of himself in the past, though he does not play editor as intrusively as does the 'editor' of *Sartor* intervening in Teufelsdröckh's narrative.

43. Colin N. Manlove, '"Perpetual Metamorphoses": The Refusal of Certainty in Carlyle's *Sartor Resartus*', in Trela and Tarr, *Critical Response*, pp.31, 33.

44. See Gerry H. Brookes, *The Rhetorical Form of Carlyle's* Sartor Resartus (Berkeley: University of California Press, 1972), p.169 on Carlyle's clothes philosophy.

45. Chris Vanden Bossche, *Carlyle and the Search for Authority* (Columbus: Ohio State University Press, 1991), p.42.

46. He wrote, 'those who say that religion has nothing to do with politics do not know what religion means' (*Autobiography*, p.504).

47. Wolfgang Iser, 'The Emergence of Cross-Cultural Discourse', *The Translatability of Cultures: Figurations of the Space Between*, ed. Sanford Budick and Wolfgang Iser (Stanford: Stanford University Press, 1996), pp.248–50.

48. Iser considers Carlyle the first to engage in cross-cultural discourse across English and German, in his case.

49. Helmling, *Esoteric Comedies*, p.37.

50. Roland Barthes, *A Barthes Reader*, ed. Susan Sontag (New York: Hill and Wang, 1982), p.476.

51. Ann Game, *Undoing The Social* (Buckingham: Open University Press, 1991), p.149.

52. Judith Brown, 'The Making of a Critical Outsider', in J. Brown and Martin Prozesky (eds), *Gandhi and South Africa* (New York: St Martin's Press, 1996), p.27.

53. Brown, ibid., pp.22–3.

54. Emily Hicks, *Border Writing: The Multidimensional Text* (Minneapolis: University of Minnesota Press, 1991), p.xxiii.

55. Philip Rosenberg, *The Seventh Hero*, pp.197–8.

CHAPTER SEVEN

In the Name of the Father
Political Biographies by Radical Daughters

Helen Rogers

[I]f to any it seems that I have said too much in praise of *this man*, I trust I shall be forgiven; for he was my father. (*Memoir of John Grey of Dilston by His Daughter, Josephine E. Butler*; Edinburgh: Edmonston and Douglas, 1869, p.341)

'I wish you would let me tell things, and let me write the story of your life,' I said in chatting to my father one evening about six weeks before his death. 'Perhaps I will some day,' he answered. 'I believe I could do it better than any one else,' I went on, with jesting vanity. 'I believe you could,' he rejoined, smiling. (*Charles Bradlaugh: A Record of His Life and Work by His Daughter, Hypatia Bradlaugh Bonner*, 1894; London: T. Fisher Unwin, 1908, I, p.vii)

I therefore, with confidence, commit the record of Carlile, as a man with the highest aims, unselfish purpose, and finest motives, who gave the efforts of a noble life and high moral purpose for the advancement of truth and the benefit of his fellow-men, to an enlightened and unbiased generation. (*The Battle of the Press, As Told in the Story of the Life of Richard Carlile by His Daughter Theophilia Carlile Campbell*, London: A. and H.B. Bonner, 1899, pp.vi–vii)

Political activists in their own name and champions of the rights of women, the biographers cited above and examined in this chapter dwelt explicitly on the filial experience, but their paternal memoirs were also studies of public men and, in the case of Charles Bradlaugh and Richard Carlile, men who had 'fathered' the infidel tradition of republican free-thought. The biographies throw some light, therefore, on the much-neglected history of father–daughter relationships and on the politics of paternity and political ancestry for feminists in the mid–to–late nineteenth century.[1] They are also suggestive of the positive attractions and uses that biography held for Victorian women writers and feminists. In memorialising their illustrious fathers, it could be argued that Josephine Butler, Hypatia Bradlaugh Bonner and Theophilia Carlile Campbell had found a socially acceptable medium in which to write political history, sanctioned by the role of 'dutiful daughter' so powerfully inscribed in their culture. Internationally recognised figures,

Butler and Bradlaugh Bonner both refused requests to write their autobiographies, though Butler noted that her memoir of her husband was inevitably 'in a measure, an autobiography' since they 'were singularly united through all our life'.[2] When Bradlaugh Bonner became the subject of a biography in 1942, the foreword was careful to associate her with the conventionally feminine virtues of modesty and familial devotion: 'At no time ... did she seek distinction.'[3] Yet it would be wrong to interpret the reluctance of Victorian women to write autobiographically as a necessary act of self-effacement just as biography should not be read simply as a deferential medium through which the troubling but more authentic first-person voice struggled to be heard.

The reticence with which the Victorian woman writer approached autobiography and her apparent preference for biography has been a major preoccupation of feminist criticism and historiography. With her claim to faithfully record the lives of others, the memoirist might avoid charges of originality and egotism and thus biography was one of the few mediums that notionally conformed to the feminine codes of selflessness, deference and duty.[4] In this interpretation, the memoir offered a literary safe haven for the woman writer who fought shy of autobiography, with its preoccupation with self-making and introspection and of history, with its assertion of objective knowledge and narrative authority. Valerie Sanders proposes that, 'ashamed' to write about themselves, in composing literary memoirs, historical biographies or editing their letters, 'women writers frequently pretended they were doing something other than telling the story of their lives'.[5] Lacking the confidence and 'cultural authority' to write history, Rohan Maitzen contends that historical biography provided women with a 'useful camouflage', enabling them 'to treat serious historical material in what might at least appear to be an appropriately ladylike manner'.[6]

Examinations of women's life writing and historical writing in the nineteenth century have tended to follow the claim made by Sandra Gilbert and Susan Gubar that the masking of the autobiographical persona behind the biographical guise was one of the 'strategies of evasion and concealment' by which the woman writer negotiated a deeply patriarchal literary culture. Significantly, for the father–daughter relationships analysed in this chapter, Gilbert and Gubar see such tactics as the means by which the woman writer defined herself in relation to literary paternity. In their epic study, *The Madwoman in the Attic* (1979), they wrestled with Harold Bloom's psychoanalytic reading of literary paternity in which artistic creativity was seen as the product of a 'battle between strong equals, father and son as mighty opposites', a conflict that was marked by and born out of the 'anxiety of influence'.[7] For Gilbert and Gubar, Bloom's narrative of literary paternity all but erased the woman writer from history in the same way that nineteenth-century literary culture, 'infected' by the same patriarchal assumptions, refused to recognise her existence and worse, held femininity to be incompatible with artistic creativity. The story of the nineteenth-century woman writer was thus one of constant struggle with 'the stern literary "fathers" of patriarchy', without the legitimising presence of literary foremothers. The 'anxiety of influence' was experienced by the female artist 'as an even more primary "anxiety of authorship"' that, in Gilbert and Gubar's estimation, assailed every woman writer of the period.[8] In order to negotiate and transcend the anxiety of authorship, the woman writer resorted to strategies of evasion and concealment but 'the plot' that was the most carefully hidden was 'the woman's quest for her own story ... the quest for self-definition'.[9]

However, in her study of aristocratic autobiographers at the beginning of the twentieth century, Julia Bush has suggested that 'it would be misleading to accept the apparent selflessness of ladylike authors at face value'.[10] The same can be said of women biographers, even those writing in the early nineteenth century, for Gilbert and Gubar the heyday of literary patriarchy. In her introduction to her study of the electoral reformer, *The Life and Correspondence of Major Cartwright, edited by his niece* (1826), Frances Dorothy Cartwright conceded that 'The compiler of this work cannot plead the hackneyed excuse that she has been persuaded to the undertaking solely by the pressing solicitations of her friends', for she had determined 'to dedicate her pen to his memory' from the moment of his death as 'a necessary and almost unavoidable duty'. She admitted a degree of 'reluctance arising from the dislike of publicity', noted the approbation of friends and relatives, and warded off criticism by disavowing 'motives of personal interest' and 'literary ambition', but these protestations can be read as biographical conventions as much as the 'anxiety of authorship'. The 'compiler' identified her authorial authority with that of her subject; 'the only merit of his biographer' consisted 'in her anxiety to follow' Major Cartwright's 'diligent search after, TRUTH'. Empowered by the very values embodied by her illustrious predecessor, the dutiful niece overruled Cartwright's sanction that any 'biographical sketch' should '"not be the subject of frivolous details"' and should confine itself to '"subjects of political interest"', since 'subsequent reflection has induced her to think that whatever tends to illustrate his character, in private as well as public, cannot justly be considered frivolous'.[11] Thus the niece of the great reformer boldly redefined the modus of political biography, against the injunctions of her uncle. Likewise political principle was a commanding source of legitimacy for the writers discussed in this chapter. Biography was a form of political activism and their voices were firm and assured, betraying little evidence of 'anxiety of authorship' in any of their extensive publications across a variety of media. In contrast to the purported struggle for artistic authority and recognition between literary fathers and daughters, the filial relationships delineated by Butler, Bradlaugh Bonner and Carlile Campbell were mutually respectful, empowering the daughter to become an activist in her own right.[12]

In their ready adoption of the role of loyal and admiring daughter, the preoccupations of these Victorian biographers also contrast with those of much twentieth-century feminist autobiography which seeks precisely to identify and break free from the ideological construction of the 'dutiful daughter'. In her edited collection, *Fathers: Reflections by Daughters* (1983), Ursula Owen found that 'loyalty' was a problem for the contributors, all feminists, whose father was alive, and that several found that 'the moment their pen touched the paper they felt they were betraying their history'. These rebellious daughters still felt the urge to protect their father's image of them or keep his approval.[13] This sense of trepidation might be interpreted, however, as evidence of a very specific anxiety of authorship experienced, as Carolyn Steedman has suggested, by professional and intellectual feminists in the late twentieth century.[14] Since the beginning of the twentieth century, as Owen indicated, the father–daughter bond has been articulated largely within two frequently connected paradigms, at least within western feminism: those of the Freudian myth of the daughter's seduction by the father, and feminism's understanding of patriarchy as the institutionalised power of the father.[15] For some Victorian feminists, however, the father could represent an exemplary role-model for their own and for their readers' private and public behaviour.

Within second-wave feminism, the individual testimonies of women have been used to explode myths of femininity and to claim the common experiences shared by women as a sex. In autobiography, Julia Swindells argues, 'the "dutiful daughter" idea is a way of registering a shared experience and common condition of family duty and social restraint' which can become the basis for collective consciousness raising and a political strategy. The purpose of feminist autobiography must be to 'articulate the experience of oppression first hand as a precondition for social and political change' for, when separated from collective experience and political purpose, the personal can descend into individualism and nostalgia.[16]

Likewise, Josephine Butler perceived the political and ethical value of first-person testimony. During her crusade against the Contagious Diseases Acts, introduced in the 1860s to control the spread of venereal disease through the compulsory inspection and treatment of suspected prostitutes, Butler frequently cited the words of 'outcast' women to contest what she saw as the lies of advocates of the state regulation of prostitution. Nevertheless she was much more cautious about the political uses of autobiography than second-wave feminists. Towards the end of her father's memoir, Butler discussed the significance of John Grey's life beyond that of his own family. Given increasing male profligacy, Butler admitted, it was not surprising that some women should consider retreating from the world to form their own 'pure communities' and yet she grieved that 'good women' could 'resign' themselves to the idea 'that all men are corrupt' (p.338). Men with 'silly wives', she regretted, were too ready to think all women the same, while women with 'a sorrowful experience in their own male circle' found it difficult to 'refrain from a bitter censure of all men.' Given most people's inability 'to get beyond the influence of our own generalizations on the state of society', Butler insisted that 'It therefore all the more behoves those who have had a happy experience to speak boldly, and to testify to the existence in our English homes, not among women only, but among men also, of a purity of heart, of innocence of life, of constancy in love' (p.339). For Butler, personal testimony could reveal social and moral iniquity and injustice but it could lead also to cynicism and despair. The inspiration for moral or political agency lay not within, through personal examination, but on the contrary, without, by looking to the exemplary figure. As Butler concluded: 'the influence of one pure man is more powerful than that of a hundred impure, and [...] a whole Nineveh of corrupt persons might be in some measure redeemed from hopeless debasement by the presence of such a man as I have tried to describe' (p.341). The preference for biography over autobiography was no act of self-effacement, therefore, but rather reflected an ideal of self-culture based on the imitation of exemplary selves.

John Grey (1785–1865), brother of Earl Grey who moved the 1832 Reform Bill, was an internationally renowned agricultural reformer and prominent Liberal in the North East from whom Josephine Butler (1828–1905), educational and moral reformer and international activist against the state regulation of prostitution, imbibed her passionately Christian conception of liberalism. That Butler constructed her father's exemplary character in relation to the rise in profligacy is highly signi-ficant, for the memoir was published in 1869, the year that she would begin her crusade against the Contagious Diseases Acts. It articulated the very political, moral and family virtues that Butler promoted in her campaign against the Acts: 'It was from him,' the biographer declared, 'I first learned what *public spirit* really means' (p.49). The biography also redefined what it meant to be a public man. As manager of the Greenwich Hospital Estates in Northumberland, John Grey was not permitted to stand for Parliament, and he was frustrated that he could only 'watch and advise' from outside (p.179). Defensively Butler asserted the integrity of her father by anticipating criticisms that a man who had neither stood for Parliament nor written a book could not be said to be a 'public man'. It was precisely men, she retorted, without ambition but with integrity and purity of life, who were 'the salt of society' (p.50). It was to such men that Butler would appeal and seek to lead in the ensuing decades. Though taking an interest in national questions, Grey was first a local man, with a firm commitment to the Border country of Northumberland; Butler would pit the democratic virtues of local communities against the tyranny of state institutions again and again in her campaigns. His 'political principles and public actions' were governed by his Christian spirit, manifested in 'his large benevolence, his tender compassionateness, and his respect for the individual rights and liberties of the individual man'; 'God made him a Liberal,' the author stated, as he also made her (p.47). Butler would infuse the repeal campaign with the Christian brand of liberalism she believed her father embodied.

John Grey represented, therefore, a political role model for Butler, and for those she herself would lead: 'What an education I had under my father,' she exclaimed, 'an anti-slavery man, a Liberal, a *true* lover of Liberty, a *free* Churchman of wide sympathies, & called to constant crusades against tyranny.'[17] In composing her father's memoir, Butler sought to illustrate how his values were imbibed through the wider family; he learned his abhorrence of slavery from his mother, and from his sister, Margaretta, of 'the imperfect means of education for her sex' (pp.13–15). While Grey could move with ease between the public political sphere and the home (unlike his sister who dressed as a boy to sneak into the House of Commons), all the family participated in political debate and anticipated the 1832 Reform Act with excitement (ibid.). On its passing, Margaretta reminded John that the elective franchise was not the be all and end all of politics; 'There wants a sounder moral basis for the erection of extended liberties ... We shall have only as good a Government, as good a Church, etc., as we deserve,' she instructed; a sentiment that clearly passed through the family to Butler (pp.170–71). Delighted that Grey supported her campaign for women's education and for married women's property rights, Butler noted that 'He had indeed been so long accustomed to give his wife and daughters a share in, and confer with them on all matters of interest and importance, political, social, and professional, as well as domestic, ... That they should ever be indifferent to anything that concerned their country's good was to him the only marvel' (pp.327–9).

Grey's manliness was indicated not only by his independence of mind but by his ability to demonstrate feminine qualities of compassion and empathy: 'He was like a woman in his tenderness; like a girl in purity of mind and thought,' wrote one of Butler's sisters (p.336). Most particularly, Grey was not afraid to show his feelings. At his wife's funeral 'His grief was deeper than even we could fathom ... everybody was awed by it. The men stood behind looked frightened, and wept too' (p.294). The significance of Butler's contribution to the repeal campaign lay precisely in mixing the discourses of popular constitutionalism and liberalism with a language and a symbolics of emotion; the witnessing and the demonstration of silent grief was to be as powerful as polemic in the mobilisation of political outrage.[18]

By reflecting on her father, Butler delineated a model of character that was infused with Christian and liberal conceptions of selfhood and that could inspire and be adapted by herself and others. Some readers certainly recognised the exemplary nature of her father; Mary Somerville wrote from Naples that 'his memoir will raise the character of the nation abroad' and the Italian translation was endorsed by a preface from the country's Prime Minister.[19] Butler would return to the exemplary memoir with studies of her husband and sister, and two spiritual biographies.[20] All these studies were written in the conventions of evangelical domestic biography described by Christopher Tolley. Even the biographies of public men, such as the abolitionist Wilberforce, emphasised their place within the pious Christian family, and relatives were seen as particularly equipped to recreate as well as commemorate the exemplary life.[21] Such memoirs often had their origin in family journals or correspondence. Significantly Butler, who drew on family letters and diaries in her father's memoir, utilised this mode of representation again and again in her public campaigns, recycling extracts from her father's memoir, family journals and correspondence in subsequent histories of the repeal movement.[22]

It has been argued that the biographical format enabled women writers and historians to analyse public behaviour and events in terms of private and domestic experience. In so doing, women memoirists reoriented traditional forms of public and political history towards the social and cultural, even if at the cost of reinscribing women's association with the domestic sphere.[23] If the Christian conception of the 'good life' that underlay Butler's understanding of the exemplary life provided one such model for examining the interconnections of public and private lives, secularist conceptions of selfhood offered an alternative form of life writing that informed the biographies of two of the leading figures of the British free thought and republican movements: Richard Carlile and Charles Bradlaugh. Bradlaugh (1833–91) was President of the National Secular Society, elected MP for Northampton and, famously, was prosecuted with Annie Besant for publishing Knowlton's pamphlet on birth control. On his death, Hypatia Bradlaugh Bonner (1858–1934) took over his paper, *The National Reformer*, and became an international peace activist, as well as lecturing on political reform and the rights of women and serving as an executive member of the National Women's Liberal Council. The Bradlaughs were themselves disciples of Richard Carlile, the self-styled leader of the free press in the 1820s and 1830s. Theophilia Carlile Campbell (1837–1913) was the daughter of his second, non-legal marriage to the free thought orator and feminist Elizabeth Sharples (1804–52) but, having emigrated to America following her mother's death, she lacked the direct political mentoring that Bradlaugh Bonner received from her father.

Biography was a vital mode of secularist representation, partly because, as David Nash argues, the manner and meanings of the secularist's life and death were the subjects of intensive public scrutiny and controversy as well as intensely personal preoccupation, hence the proliferation of lives and obituaries published in the movement's press and often, as in the case of Harriet Martineau, their obsessive revision.[24] In the absence of a First Cause, the origins and development of 'character' were of particular concern for freethinkers and thus biography was privileged as a vehicle for philosophical and ethical examination and example. This was also a tradition that reified individual conscience, action and resistance. Personal testimony and defence were used to establish principles and status within the movement. Carlile's publications were littered with statements of his personal and family affairs that answered his critics and established him as an exemplary role model. As he declared of himself, 'I feel that self and principles are as near alike as any individual can be associated with any principles ... I am, in my own judgement at the very acme of that which is right, best, and of the most importance, in a political point of view.'[25] Far from offering women a deferential and unassuming medium, biography in the secularist context was combative, assertive and defensive.

Alongside their politicisation of the personal, the freethinking and individualistic nature of the republican and infidel movements encouraged more consistent support for women's rights and sexual equality and fostered a more persistent tradition of female participation than contemporary radical movements. In the 1820s, Carlile had promoted sexual equality in respect of citizenship and the right to sexual pleasure, advocating the use of birth control.[26] Disowned by his parents, having declared his atheism, the young Charles Bradlaugh was adopted by Carlile's widow, Elizabeth Sharples, who educated him with her children, and it was probably from her that he acquired his life-long commitment to the rights of women.[27] Hypatia Bradlaugh Bonner and Theophilia Carlile Campbell belonged, therefore, to one of the leading dynasties of

British radicalism. This inheritance burdened them with the imperative of political engagement, an expectation of persecution and the requirement to memorialise political struggle. The burden can be traced through this radical lineage in the name Hypatia, given by Carlile to the daughter of his first wife Jane, born in the prison cell shared by both parents while serving sentences for blasphemy and sedition. As Carlile announced in *The Republican*, his daughter would 'imitate' Hypatia, the Alexandrian philosopher murdered by the 'savages called Christians'.[28] Later, Carlile bestowed the name on Sharples, who repeatedly presented herself as a victim of prejudice and persecution, and on their first daughter, with whom the young Bradlaugh briefly fell in love, bequeathing her name to his own second daughter (Bradlaugh Bonner, I, p.19).[29] Few daughters can have been invested with such high expectations for philosophical prowess and martyrdom.

Bradlaugh Bonner and Carlile Campbell were brought up with a powerful sense of destiny, both familial and personal, and of the historical destiny of women as a sex, for their own families had played a major role in allying political and intellectual progress to the rights of women. It is striking, therefore, that their use of biography is markedly different from the kinds of historical biography developed by many women writers in the nineteenth century. While there is considerable attention to 'personal history' in the lives of Bradlaugh and Carlile, as expected in the secularist biography, they represented a direct challenge to the political assumptions that underlay conventional studies of the 'great' man or woman and, of course, the lives of royalty that were such a preoccupation of women historians.[30] Rather they drew on an alternative history of 'public men', those written within the radical and working-class movements in which life writing constituted one of the major forms (if not the predominant form) of history writing.[31] Individual life stories, and especially those of leaders, were interwoven with the history of the social or political movements they had represented, as exemplified by *The Life and Struggles of William Lovett in his Pursuit of Bread, Knowledge & Freedom, with some short Account of the different Associations he belonged to & of the Opinions he entertained* (1876). The 1880s and 1890s were marked by a surge in these histories, as many radicals neared the end of their lives or had biographies written posthumously. The memoirs of Bradlaugh and Carlile can be seen as attempts by their daughters to fix their fathers' position within the pantheon of radicalism but also to rival the autobiographies of two of the centuries' leading infidels, those of George Jacob Holyoake (1892) and Annie Besant (1893).

Bradlaugh Bonner's biography was published with and complemented by an account of Charles Bradlaugh's parliamentary struggle by fellow

MP and ally John Robertson, though the daughter's record, based on personal 'knowledge', was privileged as the more authoritative text. Bradlaugh's 'life' was the source of fierce controversy between secularists and their evangelical detractors and so the daughter's biography was designed to quash alternative interpretations that circulated before and after his death, including the claims of his own brother that Bradlaugh was an adulterer who had deserted his family. As she prepared her memoir, Bradlaugh Bonner fought relentlessly to bring libel charges against C.R. Mackay's *Life of Charles Bradlaugh, MP* (1888) and to force libraries to destroy their copy; while the British Library acceded to her request, the National Liberal Club refused several injunctions.[32] Despite Bradlaugh Bonner's efforts, the rise of sensationalist journalism in the 1880s threatened to extend exponentially the circulation of such scurrilous accusations, as Nash has shown in a fascinating examination of the competing accounts of Bradlaugh's life. Secularists would find it harder than ever to secure the meanings of the infidel life, as biography, in the rapidly changing print culture, became an increasingly uncontrollable medium.[33]

Bradlaugh Bonner's record presented itself forcefully as the authorised version of her father's life, the preface beginning with the jovial conversation in which Bradlaugh confirmed his daughter as the person best equipped to write his life. The biographer posed as a scrupulous historian, having 'spared no effort' to make her record 'absolutely accurate', but she was not prepared to let the 'facts' speak for themselves and began the record with a lie. 'The task' of preparing the biography, Bradlaugh Bonner claimed, 'has been exceptionally difficult, inasmuch as my father made a point of destroying his correspondence' (Bradlaugh Bonner, I, vii). In fact, Bradlaugh had painstakingly arranged his papers, partly to refute future attacks on his reputation, and his daughter continued to work on the archive until her death, always denying its existence. The daughter's nervousness around her father's reputation was prompted not only by the evangelical scandal mongers for, as a leading activist, she fought ferociously to ensure that the movement remained true to her father's legacy. Thus the champion of free thought attempted to stop the sale of Holyoake's critical account of Bradlaugh and threatened to resign from the Rationalist Press Association on discovering that Joseph McCabe's biography of Holyoake also questioned her father.[34] In presenting herself as a dutiful daughter and her father as a family man, the biographer was asserting her role as the inheritor of Bradlaugh's legacy and the guardian of his reputation. The record of her father's life and work was also the story of her political apprenticeship, though related with characteristic modesty and diffidence; her political initiation during the Knowlton prosecution is entitled 'An Unimportant Chapter' (II, pp.23–38).

Given the combative nature of secularist representation and that many of the attacks made on her father specifically concerned his relations with his family, it is not surprising that Bradlaugh Bonner was defensive of Bradlaugh as a father and a family man. Though he was disowned by his parents, she pointed out that 'I never heard my father say an unkind or bitter ... word about either of his parents.' The forgiving son was presented as an attentive husband. Susannah Lamb Hooper, the daughter of a metropolitan radical, and her husband were, according to Bradlaugh Bonner, devoted to each other: 'She shone at her best in entertaining my father's political friends'; he consulted and deferred to her in most domestic matters and 'My father was essentially a "home" man ... [preferring] his own fireside to that of any other man.' Domestic harmony and the complementariness of public and private lives were not to last. Countering the allegations that Bradlaugh abandoned his wife and had an adulterous affair with Annie Besant, Bradlaugh Bonner exposed the 'real' truth that her father had been too gallant to reveal: Susannah was a drunkard. Her mother's intemperance, the author confessed, 'ruined our home, lost her my father's love and her friends' respect, and was the cause of her own sufferings, unhappiness, and early death' (I, pp.49–50). Bradlaugh, by contrast, 'was gentleness and forbearance itself' but in 1870 the family was broken up, with disastrous consequences, the death of the son while boarding out. In contrast to Butler's portrayal of John Grey's manly public grief, Bradlaugh Bonner conveys her father's manliness through his contemplative and silent suffering; 'His grief for the loss of his son was intense, but he shut it up in his heart, and rarely afterwards mentioned the name of his boy, of whom he had been so proud' (I, pp. 50, 301–3).

In opening up this family 'tragedy' that 'malevolent people' had turned into a 'jest', Bradlaugh Bonner suggested that the duties of the daughter and the biographer conflict:

> I have in this chapter said all I intend to say as to the relations between my father and my mother. I shall perhaps be pardoned – in my capacity as daughter, if not that of biographer – for leaving the matter there ... It is a painful subject for one who loved her parents equally, and would fain have been equally proud of both. (I, p.51)

Nevertheless, the biographer returned to the experience of the Bradlaugh family, again comparing unfavourably her mother, the disciplinarian, with her fun-loving, playful father (I, pp. 111–18). The emphasis on Bradlaugh's commitment as a family man, and the personal sacrifice he and his family incurred in the cause of free expression, serve to underline

Bradlaugh's iconic status as martyr. But though Bradlaugh Bonner insisted she only related such domestic incidents to put to rest the 'wretched calumnies' that had plagued Bradlaugh, the narrator clearly enjoyed imparting to the reader her extremely affectionate portrait of the father who involved her in his work from a very young age as an amenuensis and assistant: 'I feel indeed as though my pen must linger over these small trifles, over these merry moods and happy moments, and I am loath to put them aside for sadder, weightier matters' (I, p.112). The intimate and confidential nature of the relationship that Bradlaugh nurtured with his daughters became increasingly that of 'rational companionship', idealised by so many advocates of equality between the sexes. He was depressed when separated from his daughters and encouraged them to write daily to him: 'I want to know every thought, every act of your lives, because ... I would keep you close to my heart' (I, p.346). When barely out of their teens, Bradlaugh gave his daughters responsibility for editing and looking after the business of *The National Reformer* during the Knowlton prosecution, though the author tactfully informed her readers that her father did not permit his daughters to attend the trial (II, pp. 19, 32).

In elaborating her own political partnership with her father (her sister Alice had died in 1888), Bradlaugh Bonner tacitly worked to marginalise the significance of Annie Besant's connection with her father, following Besant's break from secularism and conversion to theosophy and socialism. She was careful to acknowledge Besant's contribution to the movement and her political skills – her lecture on the 'Political Status of Women' was the best her father had heard delivered by a woman – but not before having established Besant as an apostate who had lost her father's confidence: 'she had disappointed him, and it would be unworthy of both not to recognise that the disappointment was very bitter, though his desire to serve her and shield her always remained unchanged'. It is difficult not to read into this account of Besant's retraction the daughter's jealous protection of her own intimate relationship with her father for, as the biographer admitted, the political partners would have married had they been free so to do (II, pp.13–15). Besant was not, however, the only feminist figure undermined by Bradlaugh Bonner's hagiographic portrayal of her father; Sharples was also curiously undervalued. In 1873, Charles Bradlaugh met Theophilia and her sister Hypatia while on a lecturing tour in the United States, 'the daughters of one to whom the English freethought party in great measure owe the free press and free platforms we use today'. Writing of the meeting to his daughters, Bradlaugh recalled, 'I could not help wondering whether, thirty years after my death, my own daughters might be in a strange land so entirely overlooked' (I, p.388). The omission of their mother, who had adopted the young Bradlaugh, suggests the side-lining of the feminist legacy even within the free thought–republican tradition.

While Bradlaugh Bonner was, in his later years, her father's closest political ally and, after his death, his most ardent defender, Carlile Campbell was burdened with the task of memorialising the father who had died in 1842 when she was six years old. Following her mother's death in 1852, secularist friends of Carlile had paid for their surviving children to emigrate to America. Theophilia subsequently married Colin Campbell, the first socialist candidate for governor of Wisconsin, but if they shared political views, it was not enough to save their marriage, which ended in divorce in 1878, the same year that she was editing a weekly newspaper in Chicago.[35] Carlile Campbell's was to be the first major biography of Richard Carlile, though Holyoake had written a short sketch in 1870.[36] Struggling to bring up three young children in poverty, Sharples had failed to accomplish her ambition of writing her husband's life and her son Julian, who might well have assumed the role of his father's biographer, was killed during the Civil War.[37] Published by the Bonner Press, the memoir may have been inspired by the record of Bradlaugh. Its purpose was to identify the ultimately successful 'Battle of the Free Press' firmly with Carlile's defiant crusade in which he served a combined sentence of nine years, seven months and one week. While Bradlaugh Bonner's biography was very much caught up in the battle for control of the secularist movement, Carlile Campbell's study was of a father who had died half a century before and of a political struggle that was more or less over. Exiled from both period and place, Carlile Campbell (p.5) portrayed her father nostalgically and romantically as 'a champion of old', 'a great educator of the people', manly and heroic.

Early nineteenth-century British radicalism tended to assert a virile, pugnacious model of manliness, in which masculinity was associated with the vigorous defence of the rights of men as *men*, though as Carlile's case demonstrates, this did not always preclude a commitment to the rights of women. From the 1830s onwards, however, radicals increasingly linked men's political and social rights to the fulfilment of their domestic duties.[38] In so doing, they can be seen as active contributors to the 'the heyday of masculine domesticity' that John Tosh has seen as reigning from the 1830s to the 1870s. From the 1880s onwards, Tosh has detected a male 'flight from domesticity', evident in the rise of adventure stories, muscular Christianity and the cult of empire, a flight paralleled by the 'revolt of the daughters', as women sought to define themselves independently of husbands and fathers.[39] Nonetheless, while some may have rebelled against the dutiful daughter role, many feminists, especially those of the previous generation, continued to insist on the interdependence of public and private virtue, and on alliances between men and women in both spheres, as indicated by the biographies of both John Grey and Charles Bradlaugh. Unconstrained by the demands of contemporary British politics, however, Carlile Campbell seems not to have been bound by the same conventions of domestic manhood and gentlemanly respectability within which Butler and Bradlaugh Bonner drew their fathers.

A divorcee herself, it is significant that Carlile Campbell did not skate over the implications of Carlile's first and legitimate family in a memoir that made extensive and unabashed use of private correspondence and papers. Dismissing his 'unfortunate marriage' as a 'fatal mistake' of youth, she reprinted the public statement, made by Carlile at the time of his 'moral divorce' and 'moral marriage' that, in maligning Jane Carlile, his wife, had scandalised many fellow radicals. 'It is an ungrateful task to criticise adversely the character of a woman who did good service (however unwillingly) on behalf of intellectual freedom,' regretted Carlile Campbell but, 'in the cause of truth individuals must suffer (pp.15–16). Carlile's relationship with the children of this marriage was often acrimonious; 'my own family do their utmost to assist my enemies,' he wrote; 'I shall beat them all' (p.202).[40] Writing to Sharples, with a biography in mind, Carlile had compared his role as a father with that of his own profligate father who died before Richard was five years old. Regretting that his public duties took him away from his young second family, Carlile confessed, 'I was born into much the same conditions I now find my children. With a father much too talented to apply himself to any of the ordinary business of life, my subsistence depended on the industry of a mother, and the kindness of relatives.' The freedom Carlile experienced as a fatherless child led him to rebel against any demonstration of paternalistic or patriarchal power, and equally his experience of being raised by a resourceful mother may have predisposed him to welcoming the political support and initiative of female reformers and to championing women's political rights: 'As a boy I had neither father nor master, nor can I bear anything of the kind as a man. With me the rights of boys and the rights of men are one and the same thing, and you know how much I advocate the rights of woman' (pp.8–9).[41]

Though Carlile and Sharples were passionately attached to each other as lovers and as political partners, parenthood was a source of conflict as well as of shared troubles. Their first child was conceived while Carlile was serving a sentence for sedition. With Carlile's conversion to Sharples's idiosyncratic radical gospel, both parents anticipated that the child would be the 'second coming' to political reform. But Sharples had to plead with Carlile to make their union and the pregnancy public, while he in turn instructed her to keep quiet and concentrate on her philosophical studies: 'Will you have me woman, or will you have me a philosopher?' she retorted; 'when our child is born; it must be the hero; I still must remain what I am, a mere woman (pp.178–9).'[42] Yet it was with her father, not her mother, that Carlile Campbell identified. Sharples's opponents ridiculed her as Carlile's vain self-advertising mouthpiece but, by emphasising her father's role as Sharples's instructor, the biographer also reduced her mother's to that of disciple. The love that Sharples lavished on Carlile in her letters was of 'the old-fashioned kind ... when women had no other avenue for their pent-up feelings or ambitions ... Even our poor Isis was only in a transitional state, and had much to unlearn and overcome' (p.169). It is possible that Carlile Campbell bore some resentment to her mother. With no legitimate claim on Carlile's estate, the family lived in barely genteel poverty after his death, and Sharples and her daughters had to resort to poorly-paid plain needlework. Sharples was probably deeply depressed: Charles Bradlaugh described her as a woman 'broken' by poverty and persecution; Carlile Campbell hints that her mother died of a broken heart (*Bradlaugh*, I, p.11; *Carlile*, p.235). After appealing to the secularist movement for support for her children, Sharples had been given a position as manager of a secularist temperance hall but though 'She could grace a rostrum, [she] failed completely as a "server of coffee"' and, to her consternation, she was not permitted to give a course of lectures on the rights of women (p.232).[43] But if the radical–secularist circles of the early 1850s had marginalised the political intervention of Sharples and other women activists, at the end of the century neither Carlile Campbell nor Bradlaugh Bonner fully recognised her significance as one of Britain's first feminist orators.

The romantic demise of Sharples, depicted in both biographies, served to illustrate the manliness of the two free thought leaders. While Richard Carlile and Charles Bradlaugh exemplified the forces of progress – we might say modernity – poor Elizabeth Sharples represented a type of woman fortunately consigned to the past. 'I have looked through the volume of the *Isis*', wrote Bradlaugh Bonner; 'it is all very "proper" (as even Mrs Grundy would have to confess), and I am bound to say that the stilted phrases and flowery turns of speech of sixty years ago are to me not a little wearisome; but with all its defects, it is an enduring record of the ability, knowledge, and courage of Mrs Sharples Carlile' (I, p.10). Bradlaugh Bonner and Carlile Campbell's dismissive attitude towards earlier styles of feminism and womanhood may alert us to the problems of tradition and generation that haunt all political movements and that were played out within the different strands of the early twentieth-century women's movement. These issues have been the subject of literary treatment by Gilbert and Gubar when, returning to the questions of influence and authority, they ask what happened to the woman writer in the twentieth century, once a tradition of women's writing had been established. Where their literary foremothers had been forced to write, 'agonistically', out of a 'powerful father–daughter paradigm', turn-of-the century writers could choose, or oscillate between, a matrilineage and a patrilineage. The 'anxiety of authorship', they argue, gave way to 'a paradigm of ambivalent affiliation'. The existence of a female tradition could be seen as empowering and legitimising but it could also provoke in the woman writer feelings of rivalry and anxiety towards her female precursors or a reproachful resentment that her literary foremothers had not nurtured her artistic creativity. This 'female affiliation complex', they contend, is exemplified in Virginia Woolf's often dismissive treatment of her foremothers, even as she sought to construct a critical history of women's writing.[44] Carlile Campbell and Bradlaugh Bonner bore little ambivalence in their affiliation; their identification was with their fathers, as parents and as political exemplars.

Posing in a number of guises borrowed from biblical and classical legend, including those of Eve and Isis, Sharples had tried to combine a language of desire with the rationalist discourses of republicanism and free thought. In her lectures and writings, Sharples frequently articulated an autobiographical voice that was both introspective and self-dramatising, a form of self-representation rejected by her daughter and by Bradlaugh Bonner but, paradoxically, often celebrated by second-wave feminism. Bradlaugh Bonner's equation of Sharples with Mrs Grundy was particularly ill-chosen, for by suggesting that women could be equal partners in marriage and in the public sphere, Sharples had attempted to extend the role of 'helpmeet' that the early nineteenth-century reform movements had constructed for women. Josephine Butler also transformed the ideal of helpmeet, suggesting that men should allow women to take a leading rather than an auxiliary role in the repeal movement. Her husband embraced the role of political helpmeet to his wife, while exemplifying precisely the manly virtues that Butler had lauded in her father.

All three biographers examined in this chapter adopted the position of daughter. It is telling that Bradlaugh Bonner and Carlile Campbell saw this role as a much more positive, liberated position than that of radical wife. As daughters, they served a political apprenticeship that had prepared them to honour and guard their father's political status. If they did not see themselves as quite equal to their heroic fathers, this was because of the exemplary status of their fathers as political champions but they were certainly equal to anyone else. They saw themselves not only as the defenders of their fathers' reputations but as the guardians of radicalism. Their voice was one of authority, not anxiety. Not all

Victorian feminists lauded their fathers, but many did. If we are to see this as anything more than the ideological internalisation of the 'dutiful daughter', we need to explore more fully the role of the exemplary figure in political identification and what for feminists constituted exemplary masculinity.

Acknowledgment

I would like to thank David Nash and Rosemary Mitchell for kindly sharing unpublished work and suggesting biographical sources. This essay would not have been written without Robbie Gray's invitation to write on the subject of exemplary lives, to whom it is dedicated, in memory of a generous and inspiring historian.

Notes

1. John Tosh tentatively discusses the differences in fathers' relationships with their daughters and their sons, and the potential for greater intimacy with daughters; see *A Man's Place: Masculinity and the Middle-Class Home in Victorian England* (New Haven: Yale University Press, 1999), p.115.
2. Butler to Fanny Forsaith, 5 March 1903, Josephine Butler Collection, Liverpool University Library, 1/1.
3. Arthur Bonner and Charles Bradlaugh Bonner, *Hypatia Bradlaugh Bonner: The Story of Her Life* (London: Watts & Co, 1942), p.vi. Although compiled mainly by her husband, the foreword was written by fellow secularist Adam Gowans Whyte.
4. Sidonie Smith, *A Poetics of Women's Autobiography: Marginality and the Fictions of Representation* (Bloomington: Indiana University Press, 1987); Mary Jean Corbett, *Representing Femininity: Middle-Class Subjectivity and Victorian and Edwardian Women's Biography* (Oxford: Oxford University Press, 1992).
5. Valerie Sanders, '"Fathers' Daughters": Three Victorian Anti-Feminist Women Autobiographers', in Vincent Newey and Philip Shaw (eds), *Mortal Pages, Literary Lives: Studies in Nineteenth-Century Autobiography* (Aldershot: Scolar, 1996), pp. 153–171.
6. Rohan Maitzen, '"This Feminine Preserve": Historical Biographies by Victorian Women', *Victorian Studies*, 38 (1995), 371–93.
7. Harold Bloom, *The Anxiety of Influence* (Oxford: Oxford University Press, 1973), p.11.
8. Sandra Gilbert and Susan Gubar, *The Madwoman in the Attic: The Woman Writer and the Nineteenth-Century Literary Imagination* (1979; reprinted New Haven and London: Yale University Press, 1984), pp.48–51.
9. *Madwoman in the Attic*, p.76.
10. Barbara Bush, 'Ladylike Lives? Upper Class Women's Autobiographies and the Politics of Late Victorian and Edwardian Britain', *Literature and History*, 10:2 (Autumn 2001), 42–61.

11. F.D. Cartwright, *The Life and Correspondence of Major Cartwright, edited by his niece*, 2 vols (London: Henry Colburn, 1826), I, pp.xiii–xv.

12. Each biographer benefited from a supportive father who encouraged his daughter's education, an experience shared by considerable numbers of female writers, intellectuals and activists from across the social classes. The relationship between Eleanor Rathbone and her father William is one example; see Susan Pedersen, 'Eleanor Rathbone 1872–1946: The Victorian Family Under the Daughter's Eye', in Susan Pedersen and Peter Mandler, *After the Victorians: Private Conscience and Public Duty in Modern Britain* (London: Routledge, 1994), pp.105–25. As Rosemary Mitchell has shown, however, the nurturing father could also undermine or frustrate the aspirations of his daughter; see '"The Busy Daughters of Clio": Women Writers of History from 1820–1880', *Women's History Review*, 7:1 (1998), 107–34.

13. Ursula Owen (ed.), *Fathers: Reflections by Daughters* (London: Virago, 1983), pp.10–12.

14. Carolyn Steedman, *Landscape for a Good Woman: A Story of Two Lives* (London: Virago, 1986), pp.17–18.

15. Owen, *Fathers*, p.10.

16. Swindells contends, 'It is when "the personal" is sunk in individualism or loses its relationship to the condition of oppression, that the project fails to have a political edge'; see 'Autobiography and the Politics of "The Personal"', in Julia Swindells, *The Uses of Autobiography* (London: Taylor and Francis, 1995), pp.205–214.

17. Butler to Fanny Forsaith, 10 July 1906, Josephine Butler Collection, Liverpool University Library, 1/1.

18. Helen Rogers, *Women and the People: Authority, Authorship and the Radical Tradition in Nineteenth-Century England* (Aldershot: Ashgate, 2000), pp.197–240.

19. Somerville to Butler, 14 October 1869, cited by Elaine Jordan, *Josephine Butler* (London: John Murray), p.89. As Jordan notes, the memoir went into two further editions in 1874 and 1875.

20. See *Recollections of George Butler* (Bristol: Arrowsmith, 1892) and *In Memoriam Harriet Meuricoffre* (London: Horace Marshall, 1901). For an illuminating examination of Butler's *Catherine of Siena* (1878), see Eileen Yeo, 'Protestant Feminists and Catholic Saints in Victorian Britain', in E. Yeo, *Radical Femininity: Women's Self-Representation in the Public Sphere* (Manchester: Manchester University Press, 1998), pp.127–48.

21. Christopher Tolley, *Domestic Biography: The Legacy of Evangelicalism in Four Nineteenth-Century Families* (Oxford: Oxford University Press, 1997).

22. For examples, see Josephine Butler, *Personal Reminiscences of a Great Crusade* (London: Horace Marshall and Sons, 1896).

23. See Bush, Maitzen and Mitchell *op cit.*

24. David Nash, '"The Credulity of the Public Seems Infinite": Charles Bradlaugh, Public Biography and the Battle for Narrative Supremacy in Fin-de-Siècle England', *Journal of Victorian Culture*, 7:2 (2002), 239–62. For Martineau, see *Autobiography* (Boston: James R. Osgood, 1877), pp.1–6.

25. *The Republican*, II (1825), 165.

26. Carlile, 'What is Love?', *The Republican* XI (1825), 545–69. The essay is reprinted in M.L. Bush, *What is Love? Richard Carlile's Philosophy of Sex* (London: Verso, 1998).

27. For Sharples, see Rogers, *Women and the People*, pp.48–79.

28. *The Republican*, VI (1822), 135–7.

29. *The Isis* (7 April 1832), 136–7.

30. Natalie Zemon Davis, '"Women's History" in Transition: The European Case', *Feminist Studies*, 3:3/4 (1976), 83–103; Bonnie Smith, 'The Contribution of Women to Modern Historiography in Great Britain, France and the United States, 1750–1940', *American Historical Review*, 89:3 (1984), 709–32.

31. David Vincent, *Bread, Knowledge and Freedom: A Study of Nineteenth-Century Working Class Autobiography* (London: Methuen, 1981).

32. For Bradlaugh Bonner's correspondence (1891–2) relating to Mackay's *Life*, see Edward Royle (ed.), *The Bradlaugh Papers* (Wakefield: Microfilm Ltd, 1975).

33. Nash, '"The Credulity of the Public"', 240–41.

34. Ibid., 248 and endnote no. 30.

35. Hypatia Cooke to Hypatia Bradlaugh, 19 February, 4 April, 27 December 1878, in *Bradlaugh Papers: Additional Items*.

36. George Jacob Holyoake, *The Life and Character of Richard Carlile* (London: Austin & Co, 1870).

37. Letter, Elizabeth Sharples to Thomas Cooper, 28 July 1849, in *Bradlaugh Papers: Additional Items*.

38. For a groundbreaking analysis of changing styles of radical masculinity, see Anna Clark, *The Struggle for the Breeches: Gender and the Making of the British Working Class* (Berkeley: University of California Press, 1995).

39. Tosh, *A Man's Place*, pp.152, 170–94.

40. Letter, 14 January 1832.

41. Carlile to Sharples, 7 December 1842.

42. Undated letter, Sharples to Carlile.

43. Sharples Carlile to Thomas Cooper, 23 April 1850, *Bradlaugh Papers: Additional Items*.

44. Gilbert and Gubar, *No Man's Land: The Place of the Woman Writer in the Twentieth Century* (New Haven: Yale University Press, 1988), 2 vols, I: pp.165–226.

CHAPTER EIGHT

The Deaths of Heroes
Biography, Obits and the Discourse of the Press, 1890–1900

Laurel Brake

Mr Horatio Brown's Life of John Addington Symonds[1] is composed with so careful and so successful a reticence on the part of the author, that it is not at first sight obvious how much its concealment of art is a conscious subtlety in art. These two volumes, containing, for the most part, extracts from an autobiography, from diaries and from letters, woven together so as to make an almost consecutive narrative ... present a most carefully arranged portrait, which, in one sense, is absolutely the creation of the biographer. ... It is a painful, a tragic book, this record of what Symonds calls 'my chequered, confused, and morally perturbed existence', and yet at the same time an inspiring, as exhilarating book, which quickens one with a sense of the possibilities of life.[2]

I awoke stiff and cold; but with calmed brain. I heard the newsboys shouting – '*Star, Special Double Murder in Westminster!*' Was I an accomplice?[3]

This chapter concerns the relationship between late nineteenth-century life writing published in serials such as newspapers, journals and the *Dictionary of National Biography* (*DNB*) and discourses of homosexuality between 1890 and 1900. It focuses on the obituaries and biographies of three gay writers, J.A. Symonds, Walter Pater and Oscar Wilde, who died in April 1893, July 1894 and November 1900, respectively. The epigraphs above indicate the complexities of different levels of participation in life writing at the moment of death, for author, reviewer and those who decide to remain silent; these include censorship, self-censorship, complicity and guilt. In particular, I explore the range of expressive strategies open to journalists/writers who wished to acknowledge and on occasion to celebrate the significance of these icons of gay life and writing in the mainstream and class press.

A notable increase of homosexual discourse in serials of diverse kinds from 1880 had developed narrative confidence, forms, tropes, language, arguments and, not least, a reading community around what Arthur Douglas called in his prospectus to the revamped *Spirit Lamp* in May 1893 'the new culture'. Indeed it appeared to thrive, relatively unaffected by the enhanced definition and wider visibility introduced in 1885 by Labouchere's addition to the Criminal Law Amendment Act, until the first public test of that aspect of the Act in 1889/90 in the Cleveland Street court case, involving a homosexual brothel. On the one hand, as compared with the reporting of the Cleveland Street story, the period of 1893–4, just before the Wilde trials, demonstrates a significant tolerance of gay culture in the public sphere and a wide range of ingenious strategies on the part of journalists. The initial treatment of the deaths of Symonds and Pater fall into this period. On the other hand, the discourse of 1893–4 pales in comparison with the explosion of the press in the spring of 1895 around the three Wilde trials, a phenomenon that constitutes both a parodic analogue of and a continuum with earlier print narratives. After 1895, the example of Wilde shows a significant reduction in both the incidence of discursive obituaries and public print spaces in which the gay community could explore and develop gay identity. Partially this is accounted for in the collapse by 1900 of magazines of the 1890s such as *The Artist and Journal of Home Culture*, the *Century Guild Hobby Horse*, the *Dial*, the *Yellow Book*, the *Savoy*, the *Spirit Lamp* and the *Chameleon*, all of which would have treated Wilde's death discursively, and some sympathetically.

The pre-trial narratives had provided Wilde with a discursive community of an alternative kind, one dedicated to the circulation and consumption of what we now call gay discourses, and he contributed to several titles, the *Spirit Lamp* and the *Chameleon* for example, and figured in others, such as *The Artist*.[4] In these high culture periodicals, not all of which were 'little magazines', what was deemed unutterable in public discourse, as exemplified in the upmarket newspaper press, was articulated through a range of strategies, while the mainstream periodical press, in diatribes against movements such as aestheticism or female suffrage in titles from *Punch* to the *Saturday Review*, frequently obliquely implied (largely satirically and figuratively) generic charges of 'effeminacy' or 'mannishness', respectively. The popular, cheap, weekly press consisting of the Sundays and, from the mid-1860s, the *Illustrated Police News* and later crime papers that had burgeoned with the growth of the cheap and new journalism,[5] had on the whole been more willing to report such 'news': they included more of it as well as more sensationally.

Certainly, before 1895, the popular press led the way in accessible reporting of this kind of news. In the columns of broadsheets such as the *Times*, for example, coverage ranged from total absence to containment: in the lengthy columns of court reports, in small news paragraphs, or a referential language which effectively obscured the nature of the case from readers (such as women and the young) unfamiliar with the codes of discourse.[6] Ed Cohen, who closely examines the reporting of the 1895 trials, notes that even in 1895, in the face of the charges against the highly public and non-obscure figure of Wilde, the newspaper discourse '(re)produced the possibility for designating Wilde as a kind of sexual actor *without explicitly referring to the specificity of his sexual acts, and thereby crystallized a new constellation of sexual meanings predicated upon 'personality' and not practices.*'[7] The coverage of the popular press in 1895 is germane to an understanding of the representation of issues of sexual orientation in the bourgeois and mainstream press, as Cohen (pp.126–209) demonstrates, by drawing on a wide range of the press for his study, including visual representations in the police weeklies.

I shall be largely examining press obits and *DNB* entries, the immediate 'aftermath' of death, the ephemeral life writing which constitutes the sources of biographies of the future, the messy scramble at the point of death to control the media and avert scandal, to fix representation and to suppress, repress and displace available meanings. The life narratives following the deaths of John Addington Symonds and Walter Pater, men who both died in the mid-1890s, whose writing and lives alike involve issues around the homosocial and homosexuality, provide a telling comparison of kinds of textual inscription of sexuality on such occasions, when the desire to document and celebrate the deceased is qualified by a wish to suppress, or at least temper, what becomes for the nonce 'information', to keep it within hegemonic boundaries of discourse. This formulation assumes that in this period disclosure of these kinds of sexual orientation is potentially scandalous, particularly as it redounds on the family of the deceased and his literary reputation and potential for future sales. Certainly it is treated by most of the life writers as though it is, but it seems clear from the coded, and what I shall read as ambivalent, life narratives in the press at this time that not all readers shared this view, with at least some constituting the addressees of the encoded available meanings. The potential for scandal is far more understood after the 1895 trials, and its worst effects may be read in the stunning silence that follows Wilde's death in 1900, when even the few obituaries seem terse and nearly all of his friends are silent.

The new legal danger after 1885 in which year the Criminal Law Amendment Act made *any* such acts between men criminal was unpropitious to any degree of disclosure in print at such a time. However it is also necessary to recognise a gap between the publicly proclaimed boundaries of immorality, and social and publishing practices familiar to and tolerated by many men. There is a further gendered dimension to such censorship, which was carried out by men in the name of the protection of women and children, just as the contents of Mudie's library is 'selected' at the time allegedly for such a reason. In the cases of

Symonds and Pater, women (sisters, wife, daughters) figure in this process of policing; these are the remaining women whose reputations are more vulnerable on this account than their dead brother, husband, father and whose desire for respectability is thus conceived in concert with the dictates of publicly acknowledged morality. In the case of Wilde, the vulnerable include not only his young sons, but his friends, lovers and other gay men alike, whose lives could be seriously affected should they be named. Last, the 'new journalism' thrived on 'news', if not sensation and scandal, as was so frequently alleged. So, to a degree, attempts to suppress scandal by family and friends and limitations on discourse through social coercion *were undermined* by the inclination of some serials and journalists to publish investigative narratives that sold copies. These life narratives, produced under pressure of time and emotion, and competing discourses of power, well illustrate the mediated nature of biographical and serial texts.

The context of Wilde's death in 1900, five years after the disclosures, scandal and disgrace emanating from the trials, is different than that of Symonds' and Pater's for friends contemplating memoirs or life writers of obits or *DNB* entries. In Wilde's case, the scandal is not potential, but is already *known and circulating* in the public sphere, now possessed of a public discourse of 'the homosexual', as an individual and a concept. In these conditions, the life writer has to struggle to secure a location for his or her work and a discourse in which the knowledge is accommodated, but which at the same time permits exposition and argument.

I shall look at a sample of obituaries from mainstream middle-class serials such as the daily *Times*, the weekly *Athenaeum*, and the monthly *Contemporary Review*. I want also to draw attention to a monthly trade paper, *The Artist*, which, between 1887 and 1894 under a single editor, had a regular stream of copy inter alia which addressed culture from a homosocial perspective,[8] and which attracted and published contributions from readers on apposite subjects. The celebration in *The Artist* of what we call gay culture extends to figures such as Symonds and Pater in their lifetimes. Upon death their status as cultural icons of gay male culture is re-enforced and inscribed positively in there, rather than chastised, regretted or suppressed as in the mainstream press.

The receptivity of *The Artist* was formative if short-lived (it abandoned this stance in the summer of 1894). However it can be read as a benchmark of positive mechanisms of gay identity in the press in the period before the Wilde trials, which is only faintly and unevenly discernible in other journals of the day. My point about the examples of Pater and Symonds is that, if scandal was averted in the mainstream press and in any instant biographies, so were models of homosocial men of letters as such generally denied definition, visibility and interpretative trajectories; furtive fragmentary allusions were the crumbs offered readers on this account. Even *The Artist*, spirited, ingenious and sympathetic, with its steady menu of explicitly homosocial material, exhibits a fallibility over this five-year period that articulates dramatically the coercive as well as the permissive environment of the first part of the 1890s.

I want to start with the representation of a series of events in connection with a male brothel which did erupt into a scandal in 1889–90, that of 19 Cleveland Street, called variously by the press 'The West-end Scandal' or the 'Cleveland Street affair'. From this multifaceted 'event', which involved the Post Office, the courts, the highest reaches of government, Parliament, freedom of the press, sundry members of the nobility and even royalty, can be seen the evasions and lacunae of the culture and public discourse in the face of the homosocial and homosexual at the onset of the 1890s. The class element of the case – the prosecution and jailing of the working-class men and the failure to prosecute the middle- and upper-class suspects – quickly becomes the principal territory of the scandal on the part of the radical press such as the *Star* and the *North London Press*, while the upper classes, in the person of Lord Euston, in turn accuse the press of libel and irresponsibility, a mere two years after Arnold's charge on behalf of the cultured classes against the 'feather-brained' 'new journalism'.

What is so striking in the serial narratives of the court reports, and the short news paragraphs, is the bracketing/containment of the nature of the business in Cleveland Street in opaque phrases and words which seek to register strong disapproval and disgust, and then the averting of the gaze, to deny the reader any further insight. In reporting the journalist Parke's defence, *The Times* writes 'The witness then proceeded to give evidence of a character unfit for publication',[9] the *North London Press* refers to the 'number of aristocrats who were mixed up in an indescribably loathsome scandal'[10] and Labouchere is reported in the *Star* as having said at a meeting in Lincoln, '"The subject was too loathsome to allude to further at a public meeting."'[11] Summing up, the judge is reported to have objected to the imputation to Euston of 'heinous crimes revolting to one's notions of all that was decent in human nature' (p.6c).

It is largely in these superlative negations (a measure of the underlying fear and suppression) that the presence of the homosocial/homosexual is registered. But the testimony of Parke's defence witness, John Saul, affords one of the few moments attentive to the questions posed by the existence of the male brothel: a detailed glimpse of the career of a male prostitute. However he is dismissed by the judge as a 'melancholy spectacle' and a 'loathsome object' (p.6c), and the testimony of Saul's recognition of Euston and their meeting is not even alluded to by the judge in the summing up. Other than this instance, the representation of the affair is completely appropriated in the press by the issue of inequitable prosecution of men under the Criminal Law Amendment Act and, as the story emerges, with the connivance of specific members of government, with the 'libel' by the press of Euston serving as a half-hearted side show in which Ernest Parke is briefly incommoded.

Nor was Kains-Jackson of *The Artist* alone in his project in the 1890s. In the one-off *Chameleon*, John Francis Bloxam, its editor, smuggles a tribute to Pater who had recently died into an obituary for J.A. Froude, similarly in a periodical whose other discourses of (homo)sexuality supply reading strategies: while Froude is represented as an imperfect historian, this is mitigated somewhat by his *style,* of which Pater is introduced as *the* exemplary practitioner. The real lament of this obituary is unmistakably for Pater whose 'battle', as defined elsewhere in a number which also includes Douglas's 'Two Loves', will continue after his death: 'To many of us who heard or read the sympathetic words with which Professor Sanday in the University church referred to Mr. Froude's death, the closing quotation, appropriate as it was, must have appeared even more strikingly applicable to Mr. Pater: "If we stop to count the falling or fallen no battle will ever be won".'[12]

I want to turn now properly to the obituary, which as a form authorises the expression of opinion and judgment more than other newspaper discourses of 'reporting'. This is also a 'turn' from public (homo) sexual 'scandal', with its full panoply of exposure in Court, the press and Parliament, to a discourse in which the avoidance of scandal is a principal constituent. That said, what is noteworthy about mainstream obituaries of Symonds (d. April 1893) and Pater (d. July 1894) is how complex and articulate they are on the subject of sexuality, in contrast with the news, Court and Parliamentary reporting of Cleveland Street. They replace the public rhetoric of barracking ('abominations' and so on) with discordant and dialogic representation of sexualities.

Neither of the *Times* obituaries – of Symonds or of Pater – refers explicitly to sexuality, though each in its way contains information in which, for those readers tutored in what I would argue by this period is a recognisable tradition and set of discourses, their homosocial culture is inscribed. Thus, though Symonds is primarily described as 'the well-known literary critic and the historian of the Italian Renaissance',[13] the identification of his work on Whitman and Michel Angelo at the time of his death signals the wealth of his work on sexuality; this is reinforced by his association with an excess of fecundity, which is characterised as the antithesis of Mr Pattison's (and George Eliot's) Casaubon. He is also explicitly praised as a 'translator' with his rendering of Michel Angelo's 'profoundly touching poetry' (which JAS argued was homoerotic). The connotations in brackets here indicate what the knowing reader would have supplied. There is also a last awkward paragraph on the existence of his daughters and his wife, Catherine, whose sole discursive affiliation here is not with her husband but with her *sister,* lamely described as 'a flower painter and author of "Memoirs of a Happy Life"'. The apparently 'objective' style of *The Times* which relegates insalubrious material like Cleveland Street so far as it is able to the Court 'reports' can depend on sophisticated reading skills of its educated and politically informed readership to understand innuendo and to decode the text.

The obituary of Symonds in the weekly *Athenaeum*[14] in April 1893 avoids lying like *The Times* ('crowned by a Fellowship at Magdalen' – in which Symonds was not confirmed after his probationary year), but was also both more informative and more critical than the daily. Both papers mention his exile (itself potentially a sexualised sign; see also the two lords Somerset banished to the continent for (homo)sexual alliances in Britain), but while *The Times* presents Symonds's exile as necessitated by 'health', the *Athenaeum* constructs it as the means by which Symonds's scholarship was necessarily undermined, owing to his lack 'of constant access to a great library which received the learned periodicals of various countries' (p.506). He is positioned thus doubly as an outsider in the weekly. This is reiterated in the obituary's criticism of his 'passion for novelty', and the force of this critique becomes clear when we are informed 'he wished always to belong to the advanced guard in matters of literary criticism – an excellent wish, but that led him more than once into quagmires' (p.506). This takes up the same point about 'excess' as *The Times*, while indicating (if with qualification) that Symonds *was* among the *avant-garde* in some respects.

The example of Symonds is distinguished from that of Pater in two main respects. Unlike Pater, Symonds left a large number of published and MSS writing on sexuality, both on his personal sexuality and on the larger field. Also, his death, unlike Pater's, was almost immediately followed by a two-volume biography, appearing in 1895 before the trials and published with the approval and indeed surveillance of his family and friends. Co-authored by Symonds himself (on whose *Memoir* it drew), it was signed, shaped and edited by his close friend and confidant Horatio Brown. It was additionally heavily censored by Edmund Gosse, so that it provided a gutted version of Symonds's life and writing, but one that did not entirely delete his friendships.[15] As the result of such a process of production of the 'life' of a gay man just before the trials, it is a good example of the perceived latitude of expression for such a project, after filtering by all of the interested parties: Symonds himself, his family, the biographer, the powerful friend and the publisher. However its inclusiveness is what is reflected in the *DNB* obituary of Symonds in 1898, which was both more frank and full than the obituaries of *The Times* and *Athenaeum* published without it, mentioning his friendships with peasants and artisans, and his attraction to Whitman's 'sentiment of comradeship'.[16] The *DNB* entry also notes that he 'snatched [Lefroy[17]] from oblivion' (p.274) and describes Symonds as 'an Alexandrian', 'most successful in treating of authors whose beauties savour slightly of decadence, such as Theocritus, Ausonius, and Politian'. While misleadingly praising Brown's 'admirable biography', it registers its censored character to discerning readers: 'embodying his own memoir and diaries so far as possible' (p.275). This rapid reading of a clutch of obituaries represents a range of gendered discourses, all of which articulate Symonds's implication in sexual experimentation in his life and writing, even if approval is withheld.

Pater, who did not have the freedom from surveillance of exile or an independent income, was both more self-policing and policed – by his sisters, his position in the university and 'England'. Thus there was only a modicum of explicit published writing by Pater, carefully controlled 'remains', and no 'authorised' biography for over a decade.[18] In this sense it might be argued that Pater and his circle's control of information set the obituary writers less of a problem about covering up. The obits of Pater are on the whole more given to praise and willing to identify his discourses of sexuality: thus the anonymous writer in *The Times* of 31 July 1894[19] begins positively, framing his subject as 'a writer of considerable originality and refinement'. It also sounds a number of Pater's 'peculiar' characteristics, 'peculiar' being a reiterated adjective – 'peculiar 'style', 'flavour' and 'caste' – which bears much of the weight of the inscription of Pater's unwholesome, gendered and sexualised style, ideas and admirers. His style is 'more opulent and luscious than is altogether consistent with absolute purity of manner'. This juxtaposed diction is balanced by an acknowledgment of the pleasures of his style, the 'linked sweetness of the carefully constructed periods' which provide 'a soothing harmony' missed 'in writers more austere' (p.10c). The author also balances the question of Pater's adverse influence 'over youthful minds of a peculiar caste' with his welcome singularity of teaching 'beauty and excellence of literature adorned by art and of art enlightened by literature for their own sakes alone'. It is a life narrative that gestures toward his sexual orientation and acknowledges the aspects of Pater's life and writing that attracted adverse criticism, but one that insists on balancing such readings with positive valuations of the same qualities, which cumulatively mount a surreptitious defence of the man and writer. It is another example of a *Times* obituary to which the educated reader might go 'full of eyes'[20] and come away with supplementary meanings.

Again the *Athenaeum*[21] is both fuller and more prone to praise and blame. This is likely to be a function of a number of factors, including the avowed dedication of the *Athenaeum* to impartiality, the longer time a weekly has to gather information, and the factor here of signature by initials which meant that the writer T.B. Scannell, a theologian who wrote for the (Roman Catholic) *Dublin Review*, was answerable to a public some of whom would recognise the author. Thus Pater's 'bold sensationalism', 'intellectual sensuousness' and 'youthful admirers' are foregrounded but his 'disciples' and W.H. Mallock are blamed, not Pater. This obituary is most notably ideologically shaped, to claim Pater for family life – 'a quiet and happy family life with his sisters' – and for a conversion on Pater's part from the supremacy of the aesthetic pleasure principle of the 1873 conclusion to the supremacy of the greatness of the subject matter of the 1889 *Appreciations*. As in *The Times*, the narrative desires of the journalist coexist with evocations of competing alternatives, but in contrast to the *Times* the dissonant alternatives neither receive approval, nor are they permitted to overweigh the sanguine 'turn' in Pater's life and writing proffered here.

Edmund Gosse appears as a gatekeeper in the dissemination of Pater's life as well as Symonds's, having penned as a friend an obituary article in the monthly *Contemporary Review* in December 1894,[22] which presumably printed it because Pater had been a contributor (as the *Fortnightly* did Lionel Johnson's extensive article on Pater). For all its religious orientation, the *Contemporary Review* accorded Pater as much space as any periodical of the day, and if Gosse tailored it to that editorial remit, appropriating Pater against himself ('he was not all for Apollo, nor all for Christ', p.810), it is the fullest portrait of Pater we have by a contemporary, one which depicted Pater's mask, sometimes of 'solemn effeminacy' while insisting there *was* a different, and ludic personage 'behind' it. Full of acknowledged gaps, Gosse's 'Portrait' seeks to close down speculation ('no letters, no diaries no impulsive unburdening of himself to associates') and to be a definitive, if not a last word. It is a controlled disclosure that he monopolised by writing the *DNB* entry which appeared in vol. 44, published a year later.[23] If Gosse's obituary essay in the *Contemporary Review* is undoubtedly an encomium, the terms of its praise only glancingly include Pater's homosocial discourses or personae, though both are undoubtedly acknowledged. Pater's youthful admirers would have to go elsewhere to seek the ramifications of Gosse's bold contention there that 'Winckelmann was the master he wanted ... and it was with the study of

Winckelmann that he [Pater] became himself a writer' (p.800). I have written at length about Gosse's Pater entry in the *DNB* elsewhere.[24] I want to observe here that, while shadowing the *Contemporary Review* article, the 1895 *DNB* life is notably deprived of Gosse's emphasis on Pater's debt to the example of Winckelmann, and of Gosse's use of Pater's contrast between Apollo and Christ as *his* conclusion about Pater. It minimises rather than celebrates his sexual orientation.

By way of comparison with these faceted and dialogical mainstream serial discourses, I want to consider briefly the more unitary gendered discourses of Kains-Jackson's *Artist*. From the period of Cleveland Street in 1889–90, Kains-Jackson had developed further ingenious tactics to include homosocial and homoerotic copy in *The Artist*, 1892 and 1893 being bumper years, in which there was much attention to Symonds, reviews and articles on his writing and work by him. Kains-Jackson's bold coverage of Symonds's death is notably free of the embarrassment of the rest of the mainstream press about Symonds's 'excesses'. At that moment in *The Artist*'s history, Kains-Jackson is apparently secure as editor, and free of such constraints. He opts for a flagrant, page-one poem (actually p.3), framed in black borders, in the timely 1 May number.[25]

The poem, as can be seen in Figure 8.1, presents Symonds as a soldier 'with a fighting pen' and as a Lover of 'Art and Nature and Youth': '"Let men be lovers," your voice rang clear'.[26] In short, he is positioned as a heroic model who 'understands' the new culture, displayed in full view of *all* of Kains-Jackson's readers, as the crucial decision to put this poem on the same page as the artists' Kalendar means that not only 'understanding' readers would see it. This tribute to Symonds is followed up in a leader (p.145) in which Symonds's death – 'loss of the one critic whose reputation was European' – is linked with the remaining 'national' critics, one of whom is Pater 'in England', who is 'left with a clear pre-eminence'. This association of Symonds with Pater is typical of Kains-Jackson's opportunism to introduce the names of figures deemed to be part of the tradition of homosexual cultural discourses. The *Spirit Lamp*, the undergraduate journal edited by Douglas, in its newly designed penultimate number of May 1893, also includes a celebratory obituary of Symonds signed by Douglas which is both personal ('he has been as much to my life as the sun to a flower') and a reminder of Symonds's contribution to the cause: 'Alas! Too, he has not finished his work, there was more to do; there were chains he might have loosened, and burdens he might have lifted; chains on the limbs of lovers and burdens on the wings of poets.'[27] However, because of its layout, it appears modest in comparison with that of *The Artist*, and is not designed to command undue attention for a readership whose views of

KALENDAR.

Information to appear here should be sent to the Editor not later than the 20th of each month.

May 1.—R. Academy Opens.—New Gallery Opens.—Arthur Croft's Exhibition at Dowdeswell's Opens.—Sale of the Jeffrey's Musical Copyrights, at Puttick & Simpson's.

May 2.—Great Sale of Old Armour at Christies.—Sending in Day Nottingham Exhibition (Local Artists).

May 5.—The Clifden Sale at Christies.

May 6.—Crystal Palace Art Show Opens.—Sale of Lord Dover's Pictures at Christies.

May 8.—Sending in Day for the Munich Exhibition of Pictures.

May 9.—Exhibition of Academy Rejected Pictures Opens at the R.A. (Royal Aquarium!) Westminster.

May 12.—The Meissonier Sale at the Gallerie Georges Petit, Rue de Sèze, Paris.—Sale of the Cassiobury Collection of Art Furniture at Christies.

May 17.—Sale of Classical Keramics at Sothebys.

May 20.—Sending in Day for the Liverpool Watercolour Exhibition.—Irish Academy Exhibition closes.—A show of Local Pictures Opens at Gloucester.—N.E.A.O. closes.

May 30.—Sending in Day Dudley Gallery.

In Memoriam

JOHN ADDINGTON SYMONDS.

*Born Clifton, 5th October, 1841.
Died Rome, 19th April, 1893*

CUIUS. ANIMAM. PROPITIETUR. DEUS.

I.

Ere ever I turn to the North again
　To a city set in the sleepy shires
In a land of sunshine and pleasant rain
　A little city of domes and spires,
I will stand awhile by an open grave
　By the friend beloved that no love could save;
Here in Rome was a sweet life slain,
Here an ending of sweet desires.

II.

" The best is Health " said the Grecian poet *
　Whose fame he honoured, whose name he bore,
" The best is Health ; " but our sad hearts know it
Ah, that we knew how nevermore
　Shall the kindest voice ever heard on earth
　Grow soft with sorrow, wax strong with mirth
How the day has come it is his to go, it
Is ours to pace the deserted shore.

* Simonides.

III.

Rome, thy name is a word of thunder
　Echoing ever along the years
Thou hast seen new gods in the house of wonder,
　Seen the birth of new hopes and fears;
　But a city of men wast thou from of old
　Brave hearts were aye to thee more than gold
And he was brave that has now gone under,
He that was brave, is worth thy tears.

IV.

Twenty years in the breach he stood
　Watchful, keeping the foe at bay
Fighting the death which was in his blood
　Knowing still he had words to say
　That should lighten the hearts of his fellow-men,
　Twenty years with the fighting pen
He strove to make that knowledge good,
Made it; then let the doom have way.

V.

O loyal-hearted, O comrade dear
　What words shall serve for our grief or ruth
Soul found flawless from fleck of fear
　Lover of Art and Nature and Youth,
　You that have lifted the world's heart higher
　Drawing the hearts of us nigher and nigher,
" Let men be lovers; " your voice rang clear,
" Let men be lovers, and Truth be Truth."

VI.

" What shall be counted, what shall avail,
　O friends and lovers, when night is nigh
When the breath is caught and the pulses fail
　When the blood no more runs fervently,
　What shall learning or treasure be
　To the wearied eyes that turn and see
No loved face watching the face grown pale
No loved lips framing heart's love's reply ? "

VII.

O pleasant singing of lovely lovers
　O happy holding of young warm hands
O brotherhood of bright hearted rovers
　Companions happy in many lands
　Ye things found fair and of good report
　In the Royal House of this dead man's Court
What are ye now that the brown earth covers,
The friend, we would say, " who understands."

VIII.

Nay, but now that each turns and goes,
　Since the boat is waiting, the sail is spread,
Let each lay here in this grave a rose
　And breathe a prayer for England's dead,
　Keats and Shelley and Symonds, sleeping
　Here in the ancient city's keeping
Servants true of the Lord Eros
And living lights of the fair times fled

ATQUE. IN. PERPETUOM. FRATER. AVE. ATQUE. VALE.

Figure 8.1　Memorial Poem for J.A. Symonds, *The Artist*, 1 May 1893
Reproduced with permission of Laurel Brake

Symonds may not have been so credulous or so well disposed as those of the readership of *The Artist*.

A year later, in April 1894, Kains-Jackson again decides to override his usual strategies of embedded copy and use *The Artist* to enter into debate with Grant Allen in the mainstream press about the New Hedonism. His prose piece, 'The New Chivalry' might be regarded as within the tradition of Symonds's attempts at privately printed treatises on 'modern ethics'. But, lacking Symonds's independent status and residence abroad, and possessing a vulnerability in his post as editor, Kains-Jackson lost his job and his platform as a result of publishing the article. *The Artist*, as I have discussed elsewhere,[28] made a shift, in the face of competition from the illustrated *Studio*, to illustration and a new life of repentance and full-voiced reaction to its former self. Pater's death at the end of July found *The Artist* under new direction and publisher, but a paragraph on Pater's death appeared in a stop press position on the last page of the August number. The writer's plan to pay 'some small tribute' in the next issue was disallowed, and this marginal remnant of *The Artist* that was, is not re-enforced and hardly accommodated in the next issues, its homosexual and homosocial readers and subjects largely repudiated. So Pater, who continued to be reviewed and treated as a cultural icon of aestheticism in the alternative press after his death, is a causality of the lurching fortunes of *The Artist* between May and October 1894. He remains, characteristically it might be thought, without a discursive place in that periodical, which had managed to sustain itself and a reading community for over five years.

If Kains-Jackson had not acted so quickly to include the Pater paragraph in the August number, it would probably never have appeared at all. Most of the Pater obituaries in the monthlies appeared from September onwards, and it was unexpectedly one of these, *The Bookman* of September 1894, which located Pater as Kains-Jackson's *Artist* might have done, without demur within a homosexual tradition. 'A Note on Walter Pater. By one who knew him' (an anonymity still not cracked) ends, '"Philosophy without effeminacy" was the boast of Pericles concerning his native city. "Philosophy but through a love of youth," was the reply and corollary of Plato, and this or something very near thereto was the conclusion of his loving interpreter of our own day, Walter Pater.'[29]

A bid for the abandoned readership of *The Artist* and the *Spirit Lamp* was made in the autumn of 1894 by an Oxford undergraduate friend of Douglas's, J.F. Bloxam, who edited the first (and only) number of *The Chameleon*, which appeared in December 1894. Most of its contributors stemmed from its predecessors – Douglas, J.G. Nicholson, Kains-Jackson, Beerbohm and Wilde – who were spectacularly gathered for a single number whose allegiance to the 'new culture' and 'the new chivalry' was evident and reiterated. But this was a different market niche than either the 6d trade monthly of *The Artist* or the modest under-graduate termly magazine, the *Spirit Lamp*. Made up like *The Studio* or *The Dial* (though without illustration), Gay and Bird's *Chameleon* was expensive, quarto in size, with a dark green art-paper cover, heavy paper with deckled edges, with the letterpress set within generous margins. It contained a manifesto/story 'The Priest and the Acolyte' (pseudo-anonymous, but by Bloxam) which represented male–male love between two best-case lovers, a priest who serves also to make the intellectual arguments, and a young child whose innocence and devotion are demonstrated dramatically, and strenuously alleged by the priest. This story is in the didactic mode of Douglas's 'Two Loves' and Kains-Jackson's 'New Chivalry'. This was a venture that aimed at a commercial niche market, but Wilde's contribution was deployed in the trials to link him damagingly (and misleadingly) with the anonymous story, the publishers withdrew from the enterprise and the journal foundered. As mentioned earlier, the disappearance of these three journals and of other little magazines and the transformation of the *New Review* into the *Outlook,* go some way to explaining the eloquent scarcity of Wilde obituaries in the UK, all of which appeared in mainstream press titles, there being a decided dearth in late 1900 of suitable alternatives.

Turning to the press obituaries and *DNB* entry following Wilde's death in 1900, in the wake of the trials, the issues and treatment are notably transformed. The most salient difference between the treatment of Wilde's death and those of Pater and Symonds is the eerie silence in titles which had a tradition of obituaries of record for public figures, such as the *Bookman,* in journals for which Wilde had written, such as *Blackwood's* and the *Fortnightly* and *Westminster* Reviews, and in papers perceived as having a literary element, such as the *Nineteenth Century*, the *Contemporary Review* and the *Spectator*.[30] The absence of dedicated eulogies, obituaries or even notices about Wilde's death in these journals extends to the absence of any reference to his achievements in review articles in the *Quarterly Review* (Jan. 1901) and *Blackwood's* (Jan. 1900) on 'The Victorian Drama'. The silence is under-lined, for retrospective as well as contemporary readers by comparison with numerous memorial articles on John Ruskin, for example, and a generous piece, one among several notices on Max Müller, in the *Contemporary Review*.[31] Both men had died, like Wilde, late in the year 1900.

Of the dailies in Britain that noticed Wilde's death, *The Times*, which saw itself as a newspaper of record, was prompt in publishing a paragraph in its 1 December 1900 issue on page 8. Magisterial and authoritative, it was triumphalist, taking care to bury his reputation as a writer 'for ever' as well as recording the time and place of his death. In its only note of praise, Wilde's work was 'paradoxical', witty and humorous, but also 'perverted'. While it allowed Wilde to have gained 'a position in the dramatic world', it deployed overdetermined rhetoric to allege Wilde's '*disappearance* from English life'. Claiming on Wilde's behalf that he regretted the past, it assured the reader, this was to no avail: the alleged disappearance of his work was inevitable, and natural. In its condemnation of Wilde to 'ignoble obscurity' it functioned as a lurid gloss on the implications of the jury's verdict. This is a piece that in the main sought to achieve the eradication of Wilde's place in English cultural memory. Curiously it allowed, in its last sentence, an alternative to its harsh relegation of Wilde to the forgotten. Feeling perhaps journalistically obliged to record, as an afterthought, that one of Wilde's plays was currently being revived, it immediately curtailed any suggestion of Wilde's reinstatement by the respectable classes with the reassurance that it 'is not at a West End theatre'. No friend of Wilde's, or of his cause, could derive comfort or pleasure from this brief, grudging, judgmental notice.

Among the other dailies, the *Pall Mall Gazette* on the same date, but more prominently on page 2, published among its Occasional Notes two short irascible paragraphs pervaded by a personal animus that distinguishes this notice as the most hostile among those papers that published an obit at all.[32] A triumphalism similar to that of *The Times* is detectable in its opening lines: 'The tragedy of Mr. Oscar Wilde's life is ended. The labouring of moralities would be quite superfluous, but a word or two may be said upon the sum of his achievement.' However its estimate of the value of Wilde's work is even harsher than that of *The Times*, alleging its lack of originality, substance, dramatic craft and power to endure. On this last it is categorical, claiming recklessly that 'nothing that he ever wrote had strength to endure'. As a London evening paper attentive to clubland readers and the leisure activities of the governing classes, the *PMG* could be expected to report Wilde's death, but the imbalance here between the critical acumen and moralising is less predictable.[33]

Of the London dailies, the liberal *Daily Chronicle* devoted the most attention to the death of the author on the day of his funeral. Given its unique degree of coverage by this date, the *Chronicle* piece is copied the following day for example by the *Dublin Evening Mail*,[34] which publishes two items relating to Wilde at the tail end of its column on 'The Theatre', a short description of the funeral under the headline 'The Late Oscar Wilde' and the longer story from the *Chronicle* novelistically headed 'The Last Interview'. The former testifies obliquely to Wilde's surviving stature and fame: 'Many beautiful wreaths were sent', and reports as well the attendance of 'many' French 'literary and artistic' celebrities. The sympathetic note is unmistakable, and it is repeated below in the story the Dublin paper reprints, which provides an account of a recent interview with Wilde who was already ailing and bed-ridden, but apparently hopeful of recovery. It is a sentimental death bed story, unembarrassed about exposing Wilde's tears and the emotion of the Paris correspondent on seeing them, but also including a more clinical retrospective about the cause of death, those present, and Wilde's death-bed conversion to Roman Catholicism. This aspect of the report of the death scene is a continuation of the account of the interview, in which Wilde himself is reported as suggesting that, had he been allowed to convert as a child, his 'degeneration' would have been stemmed. Its yoking with religion may be read as a backdoor strategy of introducing the sensationalist notion of degeneracy, but the religious note might go down well with readers, generically, in London, and among Catholics in Ireland. Both could take comfort from the certitude that 'his death bed was one of repentance'.

Several points arise from the Dublin story. The position in the paper that the Wilde reports occupy is significant; what is a news story or with the obits in papers such as the *PMG* is relegated to a less conspicuous 'department' in others; in Wilde's case this is mainly 'Theatre' or 'Drama', as in the Dublin title, and in the two weeklies that publish full tributes. The meanness of English coverage is also revealed in comparison with the importance accorded Wilde's death abroad, and with the warmth of the coverage in the USA and France. In the *New York Times* the story is on page 1,[35] with a three-tier, new journalism headline, as Karl Beckson points out,[36] and occupies the length of an entire broadsheet column. As expected in the highly competitive news-paper climate in the USA at this date, it is as prompt as the London press, and dramatises this in its claim, 'Special cable to the New York Times' and its dateline, 30 Nov. Paris. The early part of the story, reporting the death, highlights its contemporaneity with the event, which took place 'today'. It spices up the story, in keeping with the 'yellow journalism' of the time, and includes in the headline the 'rumour' that Wilde 'committed suicide'. This is only one of many 'inaccuracies' – some ideologically driven, some sensationally – in the biography that follows which, in its more dour pronouncements, echoes the paragraphs in the London *Times* and *Pall Mall Gazette*.[37] However it is far more upbeat about Wilde's work than either of its London counterparts, insisting on the successful sales of *The Picture of Dorian Gray* (perhaps with its American periodical origins in mind), the respect for *Intentions* by 'literary people' and the recognition by 'a limited audience' of 'his wit, his pleasing literary facility, and his droll views of life' in the plays. While condemning Wilde's 'crime' as roundly as the London papers, the *New York Times* did not let this bridle either their recognition of his talent and achievements or Wilde's continued newsworthiness, reflecting his well-publicised visit to the USA and lecture tour, and his publication there. Wilde's twin national origins – both Irish and British – also endeared him to the Americans at the turn of the century, still culturally enthusiastic about the 'mother' culture, and at the same time host to large numbers of Irish Americans. Here, as in France, the 'local angle' on Wilde helped assure coverage, which in its distinctiveness helps us to understand that in Britain.

It is characteristic of weeklies that they do not usually make news, but follow it up. Nor do their production schedules allow for the rapid turnaround from event to page of dailies. Moreover those that carry the dateline of Saturday, in this case 1 Dec., the day that Wilde's death was reported in the London dailies, were probably issued early, on Fridays, to catch the newsstand sales of workers in town. Thus it is that most of the weeklies' obits of Wilde appeared a week later, on 8 Dec. This date has other implications for the weekly press. At the time of Wilde's death they are heavily committed to pre-Christmas numbers, bulging with adverts, full of bumper numbers with reviews of potential gift-books, and altogether geared up in mood and matter for the season of consumption. It is understandably difficult to find a comfortable space for obituaries among such copy. They could be said to be particularly indisposed to publish such material in December whereas, had the event occurred in January, July or August, it might well have received greater coverage. Of five weeklies I examined, coverage in two is perfunctory (the *Athenaeum* and the *Academy),* one (the *Speaker*) is short but fresh, while two (the *Saturday Review* and the *Sunday Special*) take the opportunity to contemplate Wilde's career and life, and to intervene positively in shaping his reputation at this crucial moment.

It is fascinating to see the strategies of inclusion of obituaries of Wilde among the weeklies. The perfunctory *Academy* notice is awkwardly included in the Bibliographical column by 'Bookworm' and thus manages to confine itself to a neutral description of Wilde's publica-tions.[38] Only the *Speaker*, which had published Wilde's review of Pater's *Appreciations* in 1890, includes the item in a general news position in its review of 'The Week', where it appears as the last paragraph in that department.[39] Although the items in this format are all paragraphs without headlines, the Wilde item begins atypically with Wilde's name in small caps, drawing readers' attention to it. The typography of the *Speaker* thus 'owns' the story, unlike weeklies such as the *Athenaeum* which bury it, if they cover it. The piece offers qualified praise to Wilde's writing, the 'undeniable talent' of the plays and the haunting 'Ballad of Reading Gaol', but the journalist in the *Speaker* also has a point to make about the implication of the press and publishers in Wilde's fate: 'Outrageously flattered by "smart" Society, the Press and the professional exploiters of whatever passes for genius, Oscar Wilde lost his literary with his personal reputation: but the *cowardly avarice which suppressed his name* [ed. emphasis] and still made money by his writings remains a signal illustration of the homage paid to vice by virtue.' While it is implied that the withdrawal of the flattery of the press among others seems to have caused the (unwarranted) loss of Wilde's literary as well as his personal reputation, the journalist's main attack is on publishers such as Leonard Smithers who published Wilde's work between 1895 and his death, without risking his name on the title page. In this, and various other critical aspects of the *Speaker*'s paragraph, the journal may be counted among supporters of Wilde's literary reputation.

Sixty per cent of the weekly coverage involves drama critics and drama space and culture, all of which retain a more bohemian and less Philistine character perhaps than other departments of journalism. If the *Athenaeum* takes cover in 'Dramatic Gossip' for its minimal if mainly positive lines on Wilde's work,[40] both the young aesthete Max Beerbohm, who was at the time employed as the drama critic of the *Saturday Review*, and J.T. Grein, founder of the Independent Theatre in London in 1891 who writes in the *Sunday Special*, produce signed obituaries in drama space which, in their positive celebration of Wilde's life, are unique at the time, not only in their sentiments but in their combination of praise with signature.[41] But we should not forget the journals themselves in the case of these signed contributions. The track record of the *Saturday Review* with respect to Wilde shows it (surprisingly) to stand honourably among publishers of Wilde's defenders after 1895. In addition to carrying Max's piece in 1900, in 1898 it published an important review of 'The Ballad of Reading Gaol' by a sympathetic Arthur Symons, who had written to Smithers offering help of any kind to Wilde after his release from prison;[42] and in 1905 the *Saturday* published a substantial and sympathetic review of 'De Profundis' by Cunninghame Graham who called it 'a scripture for our learning'.[43]

Beerbohm's *Saturday Review* piece appears in his weekly column which is headed in a manner ('A Satire on Romantic Drama') that gives no hint that nearly half of this two and a half column piece is devoted to Wilde.[44] Beerbohm immediately indicates both the greatness of Wilde's achievement and the effects of imprisonment on the writing and the artist. The first sentences pertaining to Wilde's death in the column are arresting and grave:

> The death of Mr. Oscar Wilde extinguishes a hope that the broken series of his plays might be resumed. The hope was never, indeed very strong ... not ... a born writer ... He experimented in all forms, his natural genius winning for him, lightly, in every one of them, the success which for most men is won only by a reverent concentration. His native energy having been sapped by a long term of imprisonment, the chance that he would write again was very small. His death is, in a lesser degree than his downfall, a great loss to the drama of our day. (720)

Beerbohm parenthetically here laments not only Wilde's death but his downfall on the basis of the loss to English drama, and he goes on to assert Wilde's character as a thinker, a wit and a stylist as manifest in his plays. He links him with the high dramatic quality of Pinero and the style (and by implication, the homosexual discourse) of Pater. He explicitly takes issue with the anonymous writer of the obit in the *Pall Mall Gazette*, making the counterclaim, 'Theatrical construction, sense of theatrical effects, were his by instinct,' while taunting that '"the dull ass's hoof" [of the *PMG* critic] must have its backward fling.' In winding up, Beerbohm charts the trajectory of public sentiment towards Wilde, from 1895 onwards: repulsion, satisfaction on release that he had 'suffered the full penalty', and the 'lamentable ... loss to dramatic literature' upon his death. The unstinting analysis is suffused with regret, a contained grief that pervades the piece, with no effort to disguise it. It is this insistence on praise, defence and personal witness, in the face of disapproval and danger,[45] that continues the tradition of defenders of homosexual icons such as Pater and Symonds by Kains-Jackson, Douglas and Bloxham in the early 1890s.

Grein has the strength of being an outsider, in that he is Dutch by birth and a producer of avant-garde drama by Ibsen, Shaw and others in a private theatre in London, the Independent, which he based on the Théâtre Libre in Paris. His piece in the *Sunday Special* on 9 Dec. 1900 takes up the whole of his drama column that week, and it is outspoken. Dismissing the moral question, he turns immediately to 'the artist who has gone', who 'not so very long ago [was] one of the finest intellects the contemporaneous English world could boast of'. Both at the beginning and at the end of this two-part piece, the critic makes a point of mentioning the reduction of Wilde's camp to 'a few stray devotees' who have not 'shunned the artist because the man had gone under'. At the end he insists on his pleasure in testifying for Wilde ('it behoves us to remember the man upon whom the friends of our drama once built their rosiest hopes'). Admitting sadly what others salaciously suggest, that Wilde 'has died almost in oblivion', he too, like the *Saturday Review* and the *Speaker*, comments on journalistic practice at the moment, and laments that 'the Press, which derived so much inspiration and so much amusement from him, dismisses his work and his existence with a couple of small printed lines, or none at all' (p.2d).

Grein has much to say of interest about his personal interaction with Wilde regarding his allegation of Wilde's debt to Sardou, which Wilde strenuously denied, but Grein is also lavish in his praise, noting the 'Aristophanic vein' of Wilde's 'last English play' which is 'the wittiest comedy of the nineties'. Like 'Max', Grein is convinced about the loss to English drama, inviting us to imagine how Wilde might have developed: 'Oscar Wilde has had no time to enjoy the ripening of his talent – he has seen followers but no disciples'. Grein is perhaps most admiring and informative about *Salome*, identifying it as responsible for opening to Wilde 'the gates of the literary stronghold of the "Mercure de France"', while noting sourly that, 'if Sarah Bernhardt had shown more courage, she might, by the production of *Salome*, have paved the way towards a rehabilitation of the author. But after the scandal the actress was ashamed to be associated with the fallen star' (p.2e). Grein, like 'Max', uses 'Drama' – the journalistic space and subject – to stage discussion of Oscar Wilde at the moment of his death. Such space, usually allocated for public figures in the journalistic formations of obits or eulogies, is in this case largely withheld, by timid editors and contributors alert to (and perhaps internalising) the public discourse of 'morality'. The gap between private and public discourse with respect to homosexuality, represented in the various deferral mechanisms of the press and public discourse described by Cohen during the trials, is in evidence again in 1900. But, as the articles that were published point out, the press was not unique; publishers and even powerful, celebrity actresses were implicated.

The silence of figures close to Wilde who might be implicated by association, and whose knowledge of Wilde's life might expose others associated with him, is striking in the signed obits (where are Ross, Turner, Douglas, Symons?) and regrettable if understandable. One tactic used by those in this position was to intervene in other, less exposed ways. Ross, for example, as literary executor, arranged with publishers for the re-issue of Wilde's work, most impressively in the Collected Edition, 1908ff. He also continued, as did others like Symons, to use the occasion of publications involving homosocial discourse for writing review articles. Thus Ross and Symons between them *review* work on or by Pater, Symonds, Wilde and Beardsley, including biographies. Symons publishes a long retrospective on Pater's work in the *Savoy* in 1896, which draws on his earlier reviews. Both men recirculate this material in volume form subsequently, keeping the discourse alive and constantly open to new readers.[46] With respect to Symonds and Wilde, the biographies by friends begin to appear, and relatively soon after death.

I want to finish by looking at the *DNB* entry on Wilde, which appeared so soon after his death that it might well be counted an obituary. Wilde's date of death, late in the year, just missed the publication of the first edition of the 'W' volume in 1900, in which his father's death (in 1876) appeared. In other words, the *DNB,* rolled out over fifteen years, was just coming to completion. Wilde's death was in time for the first Supplement which 'caught up' with all of those deaths occurring in 1900, and some other lives which had not for various reasons made the deadlines for their respective volumes. The Wilde entry was written by Thomas Seccombe (1866–1923), editorial assistant at the *DNB* from the beginning of the tenure of the new editor Sidney Lee, who took over from Leslie Stephen in 1891. By 1901, Seccombe was free-lancing for the *DNB,* the initial sequence of the *Dictionary* having ended in December 1900. Wilde dies, just, on Seccombe's watch.

In the employ of *The Bookman* from 1901, Seccombe was to coedit with its editor (Robertson Nicoll) a history of English literature to be issued in twelve monthly parts in 1905–6, into which he inserted sympathetic entries on Symonds, Pater and Wilde.[47] They represent an intriguing afterlife of the *DNB* lives, all of which appeared in the first nineteenth-century sequence of the *DNB,* and were written soon after their subjects' deaths. Seccombe's inclusion of Wilde, Pater and Symonds in the *Bookman Illustrated History of English Literature* was another important mechanism for keeping these writers of homosocial discourse in public circulation. Given the serial publication of the project, the teaching of English literature in the Board Schools, and the developing higher education of women, some of whom studied English literature rather than the classics, we may surmise that the serial parts of the *Bookman Illustrated History* were aimed at old and new readers of English literature, and that they circulated beyond the boundaries of the *Bookman,* its parent publication.

Seccombe was a graduate of Balliol, having taken a first in Modern History in 1889. Having served a literary and biographical apprenticeship on the *DNB* (he wrote over 700 entries), he was both academically and professionally appropriate to produce a workmanlike life of Wilde. The first thing to say about the *DNB* entry[48] is that it is to Sidney Lee's credit that he includes Wilde in the sequence of great English subjects, just after his death and in the long shadow of the trials. The *DNB* entry is certainly, in 1901, when it first appeared, the first full estimate of Wilde's life in English and in the public sphere. It is substantial, some four and a half columns in length, and does not reflect the recent discomfort about media attention to its subject. It treats Wilde routinely, in keeping with other *DNB* lives. Thus Oscar's entry hosts a few sentences about his less famous, journalist brother, Willie, who pre-deceased Oscar by a year.

Seccombe describes Wilde as a 'wit and dramatist', and the entry is explicit and unapologetic about Wilde's aestheticism and dandified ways. It is confident enough to deploy wit itself, and to take pleasure in Wilde's singularities: his 'precocity' at Oxford, the 'exotic splendour' of his rooms, and his cultivation of a 'reputation (not wholly deserved) of being a complete idler' (p.513). It hints at his bisexuality, referring to his 'natural aptitude for classical studies', his poems 'marked by strange affectations, but with a classical finish' and the 'notoriety' and 'undercurrent of very disagreeable suggestion' of *The Picture of Dorian Gray*. The trials *are* alluded to 'as the collapse of his career', but this does not preclude the biographer's approval of *The Importance of Being Earnest*, which is both 'irresistible' and 'at once insolent in its levity and exquisite in its finish' (p.514). He is quite willing to evaluate Wilde's theatrical work in superlative, if slightly defensive, terms ('The Victorian era, *it may fairly be said*, knew not light comedies which for brilliant wit, literary finish, or theatrical dexterity were comparable with Wilde's handiwork' (p.514; my emphases), while 'The Ballad of Reading Gaol' is 'powerful'. But Seccombe also reports the accusations against Wilde: the Hichens book, Wilde's 'fatal insolence' in charging Queensberry with criminal libel, and his own alleged violation of the Criminal Law Amendment Act. The only act of evident tact is the single reference to Douglas, as 'Wilde's friend' who undertook the translation of *Salome*. He ends by letting Wilde speak for himself, in a passage from the *Daily Chronicle* 'Last Interview', in which Wilde admits to '"moral obliquity"' and '"degeneracies"'. However, in quoting Wilde, Seccombe mischievously opens the reader to the seductions of Wilde's prose and wit, in which Wilde promulgates the blasphemous/moral and witty contention that '"the artistic side of the church and the fragrance of its teaching would have curbed my degeneracies"' (p.513). Although it may be argued that the quotation brings both the narrative and Wilde's life to an orthodox end of repentance, the last lines of the life also insist on Wilde's conversion to Roman Catholicism and remind us of the efficacy of forgiveness vouchsafed by that religion.

Although Seccombe and Nicoll's illustrated history of English literature was issued in twelve parts, it is divided intellectually into seven books, the last of which is given over to the Victorian era. As a retrospective assessment at the turn of the century, its observations are both of interest as a Victorian assessment of a period seen to be passing and analogous to our own perspective on the twentieth century:

> Our Seventh and last book is devoted to the literature of the era 1837–1900, which will probably be known as the Victorian.

> Although in inspiration, in intensity, and in sunny humour the
> Victorian age may have been surpassed, in fundamental brain power
> and in intellectual variety it is probably without a rival in our
> literary annals. It is the age of Carlyle, Newman, Mill, Emerson,
> Froude, Ruskin, and Spencer; of Tennyson, Arnold, Browning, and
> Swinburne; of Macaulay; of Dickens, Thackeray, George Eliot,
> George Meredith, and Thomas Hardy. To this age we give the title
> 'The Ascendancy of the Novel'. (I.vii–viii)

When defining this period, none of the three gay icons is named in the
indicative list, and although the novel is identified as the period's
characteristic genre, *The Picture of Dorian Gray* is never mentioned.

Of the three men I have been discussing, Wilde is the most tersely
treated in the *Bookman Illustrated History of English Literature*. But all
three authors are maginalised; none have illustrative portraits attached
to them, and they are either included *very* briefly in small type and only
under a single constraining category (Wilde), or briefly in small type (a
paragraph on Symonds) or, in the case of Pater, at greater length, but in
small type.

They are not considered together, but separately. Symonds is wedged
into a discussion of Pre-Raphaelitism, and follows on from a discussion
of the craftwork of William Morris. He is located in the subcategory of
'the lesser disciples of the aesthetic gospel in prose', being one of two
'brilliant essayists'. In a paragraph redolent with keywords ('classical
hothouse system', 'precocious', 'premature culture', 'curious', 'morbidly
introspective personality') Symonds is subtly identified as singular, and
the investigative reader is actually referred on to Brown's edition of
Symonds's 'interesting autobiography' should s/he wish to know more.
Seccombe and Nicoll finally identify Symonds as at his best an
'incomparable translator' (!), again alluding neutrally to his translations
of 'M. Angelo' among others, a nod to the writing.

The coverage of Wilde too is overdetermined. It is included in the
tailpiece to a chapter on English Drama called [Sheridan's] '"The
Critic", and After', which consists of a single long paragraph in small
type that covers the period 'after' Sheridan. Wilde is identified as the *first*
nineteenth-century dramatist since Sheridan who combines 'literary
excellence with stage efficiency'. In the authors' view, he is second only
to Pinero in the period. His English plays are highly praised, and judged
'almost as successful as "Sherry" himself'. Reference *is* made to Wilde's
'depraved' private life, but it is linked to an identification of 'intense but
insincere aesthetic products' such as *Salome,* which are in turn associated
with *continental* overvaluation of Wilde's 'Art for Art' theories. Here
subliminally Wilde's Englishness (!) is invoked to harbour his positive
characteristics, while the Continent accounts for his dubious ideas.

Otherwise, with respect to the man, we are assured that Wilde's cynicism was 'probably not much more than skin deep', and he was 'most humane and kindly dispositioned'. Given the context of drama for the Wilde element of the 'history', no mention need be made of his short stories, his poetry or his novel. Perhaps this was the price of including Wilde at all at this juncture.

Pater appears in the penultimate chapter and the penultimate part of the *Bookman Illustrated History*, as that of a mainstream critic with Matthew Arnold, the featured author, who is discussed at length, with a portrait. With respect to the juncture of life writing and sexuality, the treatment of Pater in two long paragraphs (p.508) is most interesting. A.C. Benson's life of Pater in the English Men of Letters series had just appeared in May 1906, and part XI of the *Illustrated History* appeared the following September.[49] The authors adopt Benson's simplifying view of Pater's life, a construction that reflects Benson's 'official' life, published by Pater's publisher with the blessing and oversight of Pater's sisters. The second paragraph in the *Bookman Illustrated History*, in which Pater's life is limned, begins: 'In the few words proclaiming him a college don of Oxford from 1864 to 1894, who wrote two or three essays annually in the leading reviews, travelled largely on foot in South-west Europe, spent a winter in Rome, lectured on Plato and published a novel of culture dealing with the psychology of an epicurean under the late Empire, Pater's biography is told, well-nigh exhaustively.' So the 'life' paragraph (which contains various errors) is largely occupied by a list of the titles with dates of his publications, and it ends with an encomium to his 'remarkable power of divination as to the crevices and joints in other artists' works'. But this 'faculty [which] is capable of suggesting the most elusive and advanced elements in criticism as a fine art' is shadowed by its binary other: 'a dangerous Grand Lamaism in criticism which expresses itself oracularly and hermetically, engendering a novel type of euphuism'. This vocabulary of danger is picked up from a first paragraph, in which significant keywords are deployed to mute any possible accusation of danger being attached to Pater.

Although in the first paragraph he is identified as 'a bachelor and also, in a very mild way eccentric', his 'oddity' is attributed largely to the way the outside world perceives him; it is clearly *not* located by the authors in Pater's intentions. He is compared explicitly and positively with Wilde: '*he* did not make his pose of Art for Art ridiculous by extravagance. He did not read the lessons in chapel holding a lily in his hand; nor did he profess his despair at his inability to live up to his blue china' (my emphasis), and any 'peculiarity' of Pater's – for example, his elaborate style – is seen as belonging to a *type* with which Pater is associated: the don. This donnishness is a vehicle of an attempt twice over to associate him with innocence: his 'unworldly isolation' and alliance with dons of 'the *sweet simplicity* of the eighteen-seventies'. This is all part of occluding any mention of the disquiet and notoriety with which Pater's *Renaissance* essays were greeted in Oxford in 1873, essays here that are described only as 'mainly gleanings from previous essays'. So anodyne is Pater supposed to be that his 'celebrity' is not attached to the 'danger' or meanings of his work, but to a construct of modern criticism, which used 'Pater' to fill a gap, and which, crucially, begins long after the furore around *Studies in the History of the Renaissance*. This is how the entry opens 'The literary celebrity of Walter Pater is a creation of the modern critic. Looking around the field of our literature after the deaths of Newman [1890], Matthew Arnold [1888], and Mark Pattison [1884], the purveyors of picturesque criticism became sensible of the fact that there was a highly eligible vacancy for a cloistered, exquisite, and if possible pre-Raphaelite Oxford don. The result was the discovery of Walter Pater.'

According to Seccombe and Nicoll, the vehicle of Pater's fame is not his work at all, but W.H. Mallock's caricature of Pater, Mr Rose, to whom alone the word 'pagan' is attached! So, while the work of Pater is re-viewed a dozen years after his death and reinstalled in the English literary canon,[50] it is a Pater associated with perfection, otherworldliness and the cloister, rather than those qualities of 'his best work' to be found in *Imaginary Portraits* and in *Greek Studies*. These last, to Seccombe and Nicoll's credit, are named to give a flavour of Pater's subjects: Dionysius, the Bacchanals of Euripides, Demeter and Persephone, Hippolytus among others. By opening out the cornucopia, the authors produce their reverse discourse: women and children beware. This reading is made explicit in the transitional sentence the authors use to move to their next subjects, Walter Bagehot and Leslie Stephen. Here is the spectrum, and Pater's position on it spelt out rather more clearly: 'At the other extreme of the critical range to Pater are the two critics, *par excellence*, of common sense and cold masculinity, as opposed to aesthetic enthusiasm' (p.509). My case rests.

I have demonstrated here the continuities between, on the one hand, the persistent and multivalent representations of homosocial, homo-sexual and homoerotic love accommodated in the serials of the early 1890s, at diverse levels of price, frequency, notoriety and articulation, and, on the other, the greatly expanded press and personal space that the subject 'Wilde' filled in 1895, which took place in the wake of a press actively exploring its limits and its articulation of 'the homosexual'. Together the press constructions and displacements of Cleveland Street, the discourses of *The Artist, The Spirit Lamp*, the *Chameleon*, the exploratory manifestos of Symonds and Kains-Jackson, and the dialogic, ambivalent obituaries and lives of Symonds and Pater, as well as the rare celebrations helped to define a community of readers and an identity. This cluster of print also exemplified the possibility that press space could be made for such discourse, and helped establish strategies for its publication. It pushed at the limits of public discourse for language to express alternative models of sexual orientation.

The similarly fractured representations and performance of his and his fellows' alternative sexual traditions that Wilde attempted in court in the spring of 1895 was to extend the limits of representation and the writable in the mainstream press and in the nascent mass newspaper market. The appetite for headlines (a burgeoning design feature of the press in the period), the huge space afforded court and police 'reports' which mixed documentation and drama, the competition for an expanded readership steeped in melodrama, and the enhanced regulation of sexuality are mid-1890s conditions which produce 'scandal' as a form of mass dissemination, as Ed Cohen[51] shows.

This opening out of public discourse of the homosocial was stemmed by the verdict of May 1895. By the time of Wilde's death in 1900, many of the titles which had circulated homosocial material before 1895 had disappeared, propelled into oblivion by the aftermath of the scourge; the opportunity for unalloyed celebration of the lives of men such as Pater, Symonds and Wilde was gone. The obituaries of Wilde are largely main-stream, and riven by the tolerances of their readers, writers and editors.

What we have lost by 1900 is put into a useful perspective by the writer of 'A Literary Appreciation' of Wilde, which was penned *during the trials* and published *contemporaneously with the verdict*.[52] His use of the Paterian term 'appreciation' signals the gist of the piece. It is a signed defence of Wilde's right to be different and it appeared in the *Free Review* in its June 1895 number. It is written by Ernest Newman, who was later to emerge as a well-known music critic. At this point he was a young critic, born William Roberts, who had adopted the pseudonym with which he signed this article for ideological reasons, to reconstruct himself as a new man; he later adopted this pseudonym as his identity in his private life as well.

Newman begins his 'appreciation' lightly by invoking the present climate in which he is writing his Wilde piece, and calling attention to the pleasure he gets from writing against the grain: 'subtly virtuous satisfaction that comes from writing up a man whom everybody else is crying down' (p.193). His organising trope for Wilde's work is paradox, and he analyses the way the rhetorical figure works to assess the effect of Wilde's discourses: 'we rise from the perusal of them with a self-conscious wisdom that we had not before' (p.197). Newman's object is to acknowledge Wilde's sexuality while defending his ideas and intellect.

He is one of the rare few willing to go on record as not only assessing Wilde's artistic achievement but also linking its accomplishments with that of his character and personal persona. Thus

> My object in this article is rather to call attention to less-known qualities of Mr. Wilde's genius, and to show my readers, if I can, that he is not the lackadaisical dandy they have always imagined him to be, but one of the best of contemporary critics and poets, with a style like polished agate, and a mind that combines most curiously extreme sensuousness with extreme virility of grasp and penetration. That he is a wit nobody requires to be told. (p.198)

The insistence on the combination of sexual vocabulary ('virility', 'grasp', 'penetration') with critical ('genius', 'style', 'wit') is pursued in other parts of the essay. For Newman, Wilde combines sweetness (here 'voluptuousness') with strength (p.201), as Pater claims for Michelangelo in *Studies*, and Wilde's style is soon contrasted favourably by Newman with Pater's, in which is found 'bad punctuation' and looseness of thought (p.201). Newman readily admits Wilde's hedonism and, like his subject, insists that its opposite is the truly blameable ('Mr Wilde, holding ideas like these on art, is a Hedonist in the fullest sense of the word ... It is not the philosophy of pleasure that is truly selfish, but the philosophy of sacrifice' (pp.203–4)).

This is a rare outright and public defence of Wilde's life and work in English from the trial period and immediately afterwards. Its provenance is overdetermined, in its ability to find a publisher in the *Free Review*, a title not available by 1900. But it is in the clear tradition of work by Kains-Jackson and others in journals of the 1880s and early 1890s, in which the work and life of Symonds and Pater were celebrated and expression of gay discourse was explored, by readers and writers who themselves were thinking hard about 'the new culture' and identity.

Notes

1. H.R.F. Brown, *John Addington Symonds. A Biography*, 2 vols (London: J.C. Nimmo, 1895).
2. Arthur Symons, rev. of H.F. Brown, 'John Addington Symonds. A Biography', *Saturday Review*, 78 (29 Dec. 1894), 709–10; reprinted in *Studies in Prose and Verse* (1904), p.83.
3. 'Both Sides of the Wall', *Spirit Lamp*, iv (27 May 1892), 53.
4. The editor of *The Artist* was practised in ingenious strategies to include gay discourse. To this end, he created a department of 'Art Literature', and its review of *Dorian Gray* in August 1890 begins in a manner that shows the strain of linking the novel to the specialist journal: 'The tales and stories which deal with pictures, treasures, and works of art have always had a

special popularity, and this still seems to be the case' (*The Artist*, August 1890, 245).

5. Two 'police' weeklies significant in 1890s 'coverage' of material adjudged unprintable and unrespectable were newcomers, the *Police Gazette* founded in March 1889, and the *Illustrated Police Budget* dating from June 1893.

6. On the issue of coverage, see my 'Government by Journalism and the Silence of the Star', in Laurel Brake and Julie Codell (eds), *Victorian Encounters* (Palgrave, 2004), pp. 213–35.

7. William A. Cohen, *Sex Scandal* (Durham, NC: Duke University Press, 1996), p.131; my emphases.

8. In the distinction between 'homosexual' and 'homosocial' I am following E.K. Sedgwick, with the former referring to both sexual identity and practice, and the latter to same sex orientation and social mores but excluding sexual practice.

9. *Times* (17 Jan. 1890), p.6c.

10. *North London Press* (16 Nov. 1889).

11. *Star* (30 Nov. 1889), p.2.

12. A, 'James Anthony Froude', *Chameleon*, 1 (Dec.1894), p.19.

13. *Times* (20 April 1893), p.10e.

14. Anon., 'Mr. J.A. Symonds', *Athenaeum* (22 April 1893), p.506.

15. For more on this biography, see Phyllis Grosskurth's informative life of Symonds (*Symonds: a Biography*, 1964) and her edition of Symonds's *Memoirs* (1984).

16. R[ichard] G[arnett], 'John Addington Symonds', *DNB* (London: Smith, Elder, & Co, 1898), p.274.

17. Charles Lefroy was a young poet of homosocial verse singled out for discussion by Symonds in an essay included in a collection, *In the Key of Blue*. He was also patronised by Kains Jackson, editor of *The Artist*, which published four of his poems in conjunction with a review of Symonds's volume in April 1892.

18. In a review of A.C. Benson's life of Pater, Robert Ross, Wilde's canny literary executor and friend, expresses surprise at the early inclusion of Pater in this series: 'His inclusion in the English Men of Letters Series, so soon after his death, somewhat dazzled the reviewers. Mr Benson was complimented on a daring which, if grudgingly endorsed, is treated as just the sort of innovation you would expect from the brother of the author of Dodo' (Robert Ross, *Masques and Phases*, London: Arthur L. Humphreys, 1909, p.126). Ross's elegant irony at Benson's expense is re-enforced for the reader by the title of this piece that appeared on the Contents page when the review was republished in book Masques and Phases. 'Mr. Benson's "Pater" (an imaginary portrait)', and by the blunt unmasking of some of Benson's fudges about Pater's sexual orientation later in the review.

19. Anon. [James R. Thursfield], 'Walter Pater', *The Times* (31 July 1894), 10c.

20. Walter Pater, *Appreciations* (London: Macmillan, 1889), p.8.

21. T.B.S[cannell], 'Mr. Walter Pater', *Athenaeum* (4 August 1894), 61–2.

22. Edmund Gosse, 'Walter Pater: a Portrait', *Contemporary Review*, 66 (September, 1894), 795–810.

23. Pater died just in time for the publication of the Ps in the original serial publication of the *DNB*.

24. Laurel Brake, *Subjugated Knowledges* (London: Macmillan, 1994) pp.169–97.

25. Symonds had died conveniently just before the deadline, the twentieth of the month.

26. Anon., 'In Memoriam. John Addington Symonds', *The Artist* (May 1893), 131.

27. Alfred Douglas, 'John Addington Symonds', *Spirit Lamp*, 4(1) (May 1893), 45.

28. Laurel Brake, *Print in Transition* (Basingstoke: Palgrave, 2001) pp.127–9.

29. Anon., 'A Note on Walter Pater. By one who knew him', *Bookman*, 6 (Sept. 1894), 173–5.This obituary intriguingly could be by Kains-Jackson.

30. It is surprising that there is no mention of Wilde in any of the December numbers of the *Spectator*, but the explanation is in part, interestingly, structural. That is, the 'News of the Week' section (a series of Occasional Note style paragraphs) with which each number opens is situated in the (front) political half of the weekly numbers, and all its news is strictly political. The literary half (the back) consists of reviews, and does not have a corresponding news section. The silence of another weekly, *The World. A Journal for Men and Women* (5 Dec. 1900) is more clearly the result of policy that amounts to censorship. One of the new 6d gossip papers, *The World* had employed Wilde's brother, Willie, until his death the year before. Moreover its staff and structure seem tailored to the inclusion of a Wilde obit. For example, in the 5 Dec. issue, the subject of the 'Celebrities at Home' column (pp.8–9) is Max Beerbohm, who is interviewed and identified as the new organizer of their illustrations; William Archer is their theatre critic, but he makes no mention of Wilde in his column (p.12), nor do either of the lengthy gossip columns, 'What the World Knows', on 5 and 12 Dec., refer to Wilde's death or funeral, although the deaths of others are noticed.

31. This piece on Max Müller is signed by Andrew Lang, who confesses that he has been requested by the editor to write the piece. This fuels my surmise that the widespread neglect of Wilde's death is editor-led.

32. Anon., 'Occasional Notes', *Pall Mall Gazette* (1 Dec. 1900), p.2.

33. At this date Sir Douglas Straight, former editor of the *Pall Mall Magazine*, edits the *PMG*. Replacing the aesthete Cust in 1896, Straight is described by T.P. O'Connor as a child of the previous century, 'with his lightheartedness, knowledge of the world in all its phases, a certain light cynicism and an eighteenth century hatred of all enthusiasms. ... He conducted the paper on the lines which might have been expected from such a temperament; it was decorous, reasonable and also a little dull'. John Morley writes of 'the smart-coloured waistcoat of the man of many, many friends, the diner-out, the best of after-dinner speakers, the man who can cap story with story, the connoisseur of the haute cuisine, of the drama' (quoted by Robertson Scott, *The Life and Death of a Newspaper*, London: Methuen, 1952), p.391.

34. 'The Theatre', *Dublin Evening* Mail (4 Dec. 1900), p.2g.

35. Anon., 'Death of Oscar Wilde', *New York Times* (1 Dec. 1900), p.1e.

36. Karl Beckson, (ed.), *Oscar Wilde: the Critical Heritage* (London: Routledge, 1970), p.19.

37. Because New York is five hours 'behind' London, the American paper may

have borrowed from its British counterparts via cable, or they may have had the same Paris correspondent.

38. *The Bookworm*, 'Bibliographical', *Academy* (8 Dec. 1900), 542.

39. 'The Week', *Speaker. The Liberal Review* (8 Dec. 1900), 257.

40. Anon., 'Dramatic Gossip', *Athenaeum* (8 Dec. 1900), 768.

41. [Beerbohm] Max, 'A Satire on Romantic Drama', *Saturday Review*, xc (8 Dec. 1900), 719–20, and J.T. Grein, 'Drama', *The Sunday Special* (9 Dec. 1900), 2d–e.

42. Beckson, *Oscar Wilde*, p.218.

43. R.B. Cuninghame Graham, 'Vox Clamantis', *Saturday Review*, 99 (4 March 1905), 266.

44. Because Wilde's name is not in the heading, this notice would not appear necessarily in an index, although it is the one entry in Stead's *Periodical Index* for 1900 under Wilde.

45. It should be noted that, because Beerbohm was a heterosexual dandy, he was not threatened at these nodes of time (1895 and 1900) when others of Wilde's friends were more exposed.

46. Robert Ross, for example, promulgates the issue of various pieces of Wilde's writing, both while Wilde is in prison ('Reading Gaol', 1898) and after his death ('De Profundis', 1905, and the Collected Edition); Ross also publishes journalism and lectures, both of which circulate homosocial discourses, traditions and values. He writes an obit of Simeon Solomon for the *Westminster Gazette* (1905); reviews A.C. Benson's life of Pater and also a reissue of Symons essay on Beardsley (1906), lectures to the Blue Coat School on decay (1908), and then republishes/recirculates this material in *Masques and Phases* in 1909.

47. Thomas Seccombe, and W. Robertson Nicoll, *The Bookman Illustrated History of English Literature*, 2 vols (London: Hodder and Stoughton, 1906), II, pp.501, 508, 329, respectively.

48. S[eccombe], T[homas], 'Oscar Wilde', *DNB Supplement*, ed. Sidney Lee (Oxford: OUP, 1901), III, pp.513–15.

49. Although the parts are bound into volumes in the British Library (BL) copy, they are dated by British Museum (BM) stamps of receipt; part xi carries the date of 25 September 1906. For more about Benson's life of Pater, see Brake, *Subjugated Knowledges*, pp.188–215 and *Print in Transition*, pp.52–66.

50. Pater's publisher and friends, like Wilde's, did not remain inactive during the dozen years since his death in 1894. C. Lancelot Shadwell, Pater's literary executor, edited two volumes immediately following his death, in 1895; Gosse oversaw another collection of critical essays from the *Church Guardian*; these volumes were all published by Macmillan, Pater's publisher, who issued a Deluxe edition of the works in 1900–1901.

51. Ed Cohen, *Talk on the Wilde Side* (London: Routledge, 1993).

52. Ernest Newman, 'Oscar Wilde: A Literary Appreciation', *Free Review* (June 1895), 193–206. The British Museum stamp of this issue of the *Free Review* shows that it had received the issue on 27 May. Circulation before its stated publication date was standard procedure for magazines of the day.

CHAPTER NINE

Sex Lives and Diary Writing
The Journals of George Ives

Matt Cook

George Ives, the early campaigner for homosexual law reform, is reticent about his sex life in his diary for the 1890s and early 1900s. Sex, Margaretta Jolly observes, is 'a classic literary challenge'. 'It is an experience that tests the limits of representation not for its bliss or indeed its trauma, but because it most expresses the gap between the body and language'.[1] For Ives this difficulty of rendering bodily experience and sensation in words was made all the more problematic because the sexual acts and relationships he was involved in were outlawed and stigmatised. A pragmatic need to evade prosecution and a desire to legitimise sex and relationships between men thus stood as further barriers between Ives's experiences and his ability to articulate them in his diary for these years. He tended to avoid a language of intimacy and interiority and instead couched his desires and also his campaign for the homosexual 'cause' in sexology and Hellenism, which he used to formulate his radical agenda and his sense of himself as a pioneer.

The 'homosexual' type he produced was 'serious', earnest and ethical, a figure quite different from the one emerging through the newspaper press. He evoked the ideal of an exemplary elite and introduced a gallery of heroes, Walt Whitman, John Addington Symonds, Edward Carpenter and Oscar Wilde amongst them (the 'four leaders of Hellas' as he called them).[2] In this he tapped into models of social and cultural renewal expounded earlier and variously by Thomas Carlyle, Matthew Arnold, John Ruskin and Benjamin Jowett at Oxford. Ives self-consciously wrote within this wider cultural framework and in relation to these different figures, and there is consequently a sense of his diary being in some ways a public rather than a private work. Indeed, as Martin Hewitt argues in his chapter in this volume, this was the way in which many nineteenth century diarists viewed their journals. 'By the 1830s,' writes Hewitt, 'it was impossible to write without a degree of self-conscious positioning within a published tradition, and without being fully aware of the ambiguous status of the diary's claim to privacy.' Ives anticipates publication, addresses his reader directly, and partly models his writing on published life writing. The pressing need for caution, however, meant that he felt unable actually to take his diary to a publisher or to draw his ideals into a public forum. These ideals are instead woven into the fabric of a diary which remained private until well after his death, and into a concept (and experience) of identity and community which was both secretive and exclusive. Ives thus clung to the safety of the closet and the comfort of a quasi-masonic elite inspired and 'enlightened' by Uranianism (one of the newly coined epithets for homosexuality) even as he sought wider legitimacy and legal reform.

Ives's transcendent tale of a Uranian 'faith' and homosexual ascendancy gave him a *modus operandi* in his life and his writing, but it was also stifling, limiting his ability to describe – and, he later claimed, to experience – everyday intimacies. Verso notes added largely after 1918, and constituting a kind of fragmented autobiography, indicate how Ives found it difficult to square his ideals with the pragmatics and minutiae of everyday life and sex in the early volumes of his diary in particular. He also repeatedly expresses regret at his earlier 'timidity'. In these later years there is a shift in Ives's sense of what it was possible and desirable to say, reflecting, I argue, changing cultural modes of sexual story telling which came with new published writing on sexual intimacy and homosexuality during and after the First World War. There is a language of pleasure, pain and emotional intensity which supplements the rhetoric of duty, responsibility and honour, of heroes and Utopias. This chapter explores the interplay of these different voices, modes of self understanding and methods of self narration in the diary, and shows how Ives's longing for cogency and coherence is mired by multiplicity and complexity, indicating a deeply conflicted sense of self.

George Ives was illegitimate; he never met his mother, the Baroness de Molarti of Spain ('the daughter of an English mother and a grandee of Spain') (v.63, 15.9.15, p.82) and had a fraught relationship with his father, Gordon Maynard Ives. He was raised mainly by his grandmother, the Hon. Emma Ives, in France, London and the family's country home at Bentworth, Hampshire. The limited information on his early life and parentage is indicative of the tone and content of the diary, where the personal is alluded to obliquely, especially in the early years. In adulthood Ives settled in London, lived on a modest private income, and dedicated his life to homosexual and penal reform.[3] He established the Order of the Chaerona, a secretive support and pressure group for 'homosexual' men, in the early 1890s. It was named after the final Battle of the Chaerona in 338BC, in which the Theban Bands (military units made up of men fighting alongside their male lovers) were finally defeated. These bands embodied for Ives the quintessential heroic elite, and were crucial to his sense of personal and cultural identity. Ives was also a founder member of the British Society for the Study of Sex

Psychology (1913), reflecting his commitment to the sexological project, and he was active in the Howard League for prison reform. He published three short volumes of poetry in the 1890s and in addition wrote a controversial justification of same-sex love, which appeared in *The Humanitarian* in 1894, and books on the penal system and ancient Greece.[4] His diary was his most substantial work, however, extending to 122 volumes and approximately 3 million words. He began it in 1886 as an earnest 19-year-old Cambridge undergraduate and his last entry was in 1950, the year of his death.

The first volume is prefaced with a verso note addressing the future reader: 'I would ask the future student to read further on. [...] For amidst a great deal that is purely personal and of no interest to anybody, there will be found a mine for the making of history' (v.1, p.1). The diary, he insisted later, is for 'important public work' (v.17, 14.10.93, p.119). Through such comments Ives established his journal as something to study and to 'make history' with, and they constitute a partial (and characteristically Victorian) denial of the necessary intersection between the private, the public and the political: the 'student' should ignore 'the purely personal' as insignificant to his fight and his 'cause'. Ives envisages his reader in the future; s/he is not his contemporary and he is in fact fearful of 'prying eyes' and of the diary becoming public property in the here and now. Instead this reader becomes a symbol of the more enlightened epoch Ives anticipates and which keeps him going through 'dark times'. 'I often think of the future,' he wrote in 1893, 'and how the great and the good will move about in the sunlight of truth, in the shade of true liberty' (v.17, 7.9.93, p.16). All diarists must envisage an outside reader at some level, but here the acute self-consciousness distinguishes Ives's work from the 'ordinary writing' Jennifer Sinor associates with much diary writing. The diary of Sinor's aunt, Annie Ray, for example, 'never adds up to even a fleeting whole but rather accumulates in a measured wealth of days'.[5] Ives's diary on the other hand is marked by extensive reflection and retrospection and has an explicit premise and so also a linking thread, all key characteristics of autobiography and also of the rather different tradition of diary writing discussed by Hewitt. There is often an evasion of the day-to-day and instead an overarching movement towards a homosexual Utopia (involving, it should be noted, not a whole society but rather 'the great and the good': despite his professed socialist and even anarchist sympathies Ives never felt able to democratise properly his vision).

Though Ives was certainly aware of, and in many ways wrote within, an established tradition of life writing, he had relatively little to go on in terms of writing about his own 'homosexual' subjectivity, not least because of the relative novelty of the idea of a distinctive and exclusive sexual persona at the time when he started to keep his diary. Sexological case studies, in which men 'spoke' of the genesis of their desires and sexual relations, certainly had some impact, as we will see, as did the more depersonalised arguments for homosexual legitimacy put forward by Symonds and Carpenter.[6] Extended individual accounts of sexual subjectivity and development, outside the medicalising sexological context, were more difficult to come by, however. If Ives had known of the existence of Symonds's 'Memoirs', compiled in the early 1890s, he certainly had no access to them. Horatio Brown's biography of Symonds, drawn in part from the 'Memoirs', skilfully evaded the issue of Symonds's intimate relations with men, and in this way further con-solidated the putative unspeakability of same-sex relations.[7] Ives' friend Carpenter did not publish *My Days and Dreams*, his autobiography in which he 'comes out' as a member of 'the intermediate sex', until 1916, and there is no evidence that Ives either read the manuscript or knew of its content before publication; its influence came later.[8] Diaries and personal notes were mentioned in various court cases involving male–male relations during this period, and Ives pasted newspaper reports of them in his scrapbook.[9] These highlighted the dangers rather than the advantages of personal revelation, however, and only the evidence of sexual misdeeds were drawn from this material by the courts and the press: the addresses of guardsmen or the mention of the notorious male brothel on Cleveland Street, for example. The judges and newspapers were not interested in the wider subcultural identifications or notions of selfhood these notes and diaries implicated.[10]

Finally, *Sins of the Cities of the Plain* (1881) and *Teleny* (1893), two homoerotic pornographic novels, used the personal record as a struc-turing device, but they also represented homosexual sex and dissident identities in ways which suited neither Ives nor his legitimising project. Sex was (unsurprisingly) the prime focus of these works and the figures involved tended to be frivolous, mercenary, amoral, abusive or – perhaps especially damaging – effeminate.[11] Ives wanted to delineate a homo-sexual subjectivity at one remove from what he saw as a generalised urban sexual dissipation and from an existing and highly sexualised homosexual subculture. He angrily rejected 'crudity', sexual frivolous-ness and pornography of whatever kind, describing, for example, his disgust with a pornographic postcard seller on a beach in Nice (v.28, 17.5.96, p.44). The catalogue of casual sex in Irish nationalist Roger Casement's diary of 1910 would have been incompatible with the model of identity Ives was developing, not so much because of the amount of sex Casement was having (though that was part of it) but because of the unreflective manner in which he entered into it. 'You tell me what was done with the body,' he wrote in 1900, 'but if you tell me not with what mind it was done you tell me nothing about the action' (v.38, 18.9.00, p.16).

The challenge for Ives was finding a voice which would allow him to come to terms with himself and bring a putative audience to terms with him. He did this partly by vigorously maintaining a conservatism and concern for respectability and propriety, for all his professed disdain for the mores and relationships of the Victorian middle class. He craved legitimacy on account of the felt marginalisation that came with his dissident desires and – I would suggest – his literal illegitimacy, and he sought it by acceding to social expectations, even as he campaigned against them. Unlike Carpenter, he kept a foot in London society and the gentlemen's clubs throughout the late Victorian and Edwardian period and had a keen sense of appropriate and inappropriate behaviour. His legitimacy at this level rested with conventions of upper middle and upper-class masculine deportment and it is thus hardly surprising that he also borrowed from a broader tradition of male literary life writing in which the public realm and the theoretical the intellectual and the historical subvert – but also stand in for – interiority, personal relations and the private sphere.

In her analysis of the *Mausoleum Book*, Trev Lynn Broughton shows Leslie Stephen constrained by his consciousness of possible publication and by a desire to secure the private realm from public view.[12] She shows how this relates to prevailing concepts of masculinity and their uneasy association in the later nineteenth century with ideas of domesticity and interiority.[13] Ives was attempting to investigate and legitimise sexual activity and a sexual subjectivity culturally cast as unmanly using a form which for some implicated a suspect and feminised self-obsession. In so doing he had to tread a very fine line. Mary Jane Moffatt has observed that women's diaries were and are often seen to be an analogue of women's lives: 'emotional, fragmented, interrupted, modest, not to be taken seriously, trivial, formless, concerned with self, and as endless as their tasks'.[14] For Ives to see and also project himself as a 'respectable' and 'masculine' 'homosexual', and to align himself and his writing with a 'progressive' and 'civilising' process, meant playing down the circularity, intimacy and ephemera associated with the diary form. His diary thus often resonates with a published and putatively more masculine tradition of life writing which downgraded the intimate and the everyday and sought to render a life and a life's work whole. The verso notes he added to the early entries are at one level an attempt to provide a unifying metanarrative. They reproduce a Victorian faith in the efficacy of close documentation and rigorous study in the pursuit of the 'truth' and, here, the 'true' Ives. Working under the influence of the sexologists he reflects back on himself as his own case study. Against his description in 1888 of the blending of the colours of his new cricket cap, for example, Ives observed in verso that this exemplified the pronounced aesthetic tendency of inverts (v.2, 21.7.88, p.87). The index he compiles to the volumes meanwhile provides a way into the manuscript which disrupts the diurnal form by directing the reader to the 'important' sections, those generally concerning published texts, and public figures and events. Despite these features, the everyday quality is inescapable and necessarily disrupts the quest for coherence, as do the verso notes which, while part of that quest, also suggest the inevitable partialness of Ives's earlier record.

Although Ives claims to want to include 'everything' in his diary he also seems to feel the need to justify the inclusion of day-to-day detail, often by relating it to the wider 'cause'. Many entries have little to do with the day in question and instead contain lengthy descriptions and précis of 'serious' theoretical work. Whilst Ives's fight was partly for rights within the putatively private realm, he tacitly aligns the private with the insignificant and the unimportant, as the verso note opening the diary (and cited earlier) indicates.[15] His mission becomes raising '[his] people' (Ives's term, and typical in its deployment of biblical rhetoric and the idea of an elite body) above the ordinary and everyday, and towards a higher purpose, a notion which resonates with other homophile writing of the second half of the nineteenth century (v.10, 22.4.91, p.98). Whitman, Symonds and Carpenter each saw a potential for social change through relations between men. Ives exploits the intense homosociality of Victorian middle and upper-class education and professional life but attempts to deflect the homosexual panic it also engendered by seeing homoeroticism as integral to the vision.[16] Ostensibly private relations are thus turned outwards and given a place and importance within the social realm, while retaining the exclusive and masculine tenor modelled in Victorian public life. This attention to the wider potential of the homosexual bond in particular and homosociality more broadly is especially important since, as I have argued elsewhere, marginalised groups were often associated with the here and now rather than the 'civilised' and 'civilising' movement into the future, a journey axiomatic to the self-definition of the Victorian middle class.[17]

This stasis and lack of productivity was another facet of emerging concepts of homosexual identity which, along with effeminacy and sexual dissipation, Ives was keen to counteract. He did this chiefly through study, analysis and writing, and we see clearly through his mammoth reading schedule and extensive output the importance Ives placed in rhetorical practice in shaping his sense of himself and furthering his 'cause'. Ives observed, for example, that 'all journals must be followed – and important articles copied down' (v.21, 10.8.94, p.33).

He built up an extensive personal library and was a member of the bibliographic subcommittee of the British Society for the Study of Sex Psychology. He laid especial stress on texts which had an obvious cultural purchase and an intellectual or academic standing: sexology, though marginalised in Britain in this period, reproduced a faith in the efficacy of science to produce 'the truth'; the Ancient Greeks had become a key reference point in the quest for national renewal,[18] and there was a cultural reverence for the Hellenic which Ives and other homophile writers shared and deployed in their arguments for the legitimacy of homosexual relations.

Both areas, sexology and Hellenism, will be discussed in more detail shortly, but it is worth taking a detour via the law and the press first. The legislative moves against sexual relations between men in the later nineteenth century (the 1885 Criminal Law Amendment Act and the 1898 Vagrancy Law Amendment Act) and the intensification of newspaper interest in, and sensationalisation of, male–male relations reminded Ives on a weekly basis of the urgency of his cause and also provided something tangible for him to pitch himself against. More importantly for this chapter, they gave Ives a further impetus to secrecy in his life and writing, a secrecy which disrupts the quest for a public role and status even as it reproduces the kind of exclusive homosociality associated with the gentlemen's clubs and public life more broadly.[19] The newspaper clippings detailing prosecutions for same-sex activity, which feature prominently in Ives's scrapbook, contribute powerfully to Ives's sense of himself and also structure his writing. He works to evade detection and the law, and to screen his personal life (his friendships and lovers) from view. Ives boasts that he had made his diary impenetrable, in contrast to Earl Russell's journal, which was used against him in his divorce case of 1896. 'What a task if they tried to get evidence out of this against me!', he wrote, 'how long would it take I wonder? And whatever would they find?'(v.29, 29.11.96, p.74). Ives throws down the gauntlet to 'prying eyes' and also teasingly suggests the potential for further scandalous revelation, a device also used in pornography of the period.[20] To this extent Ives enjoys what Oliver Buckton describes as 'the potent erotic and aesthetic pleasures of secrecy itself',[21] and the diary serves as only the most partial of confessionals and creates a secret space within the text which is part of Ives's self-conceptualisation: he builds a sense of distinction and distinctiveness by marking out areas of his life – and the parallel lives of others – as secretive and exclusive. There is, as H.G. Cocks suggests, a productiveness in the unspeakability of intimate relations between men,[22] and just as the diary was a means through which Ives sustained and constituted himself in the face of domineering and condemnatory rhetoric, so holding back material and rendering it secret served him in securing a sense of homosexual selfhood. This alternative means of configuring the self is represented for Ives by the secret and unrecorded proceedings of the Order of the Chaerona, which are indicated but not elaborated within the diary.

Whilst Cocks and others have shown the productive nature of secrecy we need, however, to be cautious about a nostalgia for the closet. Secretiveness and the bluff games of cat and mouse in the diary also suggest the more disturbing impact of the law and the press. Ives is extremely reticent about who he writes and speaks to. He refused to reply to a letter sent to him in the wake of his *Humanitarian* piece lest it be bait, for example, and is 'wary of common courtesy' because of his fear of blackmailers; 'the city is so dangerous that one must walk like a porcupine' (v.22, 14.1.95, p.96; v.42, 10.3.02, p.63; v.31, 15.2.98, p.64). There is rarely a sense of free flow and unself-consciousness in his prose, and he weighs and chooses his words with care. He also testifies to a horror of sleeping alone, of isolation and of claustrophobia; in the months after the Wilde trial he dreams of imprisonment (v.29, 17.8.95, p.16; v.29, 21.8.95, p.19). His love of night-time (v.39, 10.6.01, p.99), of the potential anonymity of the city, and the Masonic nature of the Order of the Chaerona also relate to the dangers associated with his homosexuality. 'I have had to be silent as to a multitude of things in which I yet glory', he observed (v.68, 13.9.17, p.123). The prosecutions, Ives was aware, strengthened his case and in many ways drove the movement for reform – 'I believe persecution really strengthens in the end'(v.45, 7.10.04, p.54) – but the weekly reports of further court cases and prosecutions also took their toll and fundamentally structured Ives's diary writing and life in London.

If the press cuttings underlined the need for change and fuelled Ives's battle against injustice, sexology provided some of the tools for a challenge to this domineering rhetoric. They gave Ives a *raison d'être* and an essentialist rationale for his desires and relationships. He followed the literature avidly and befriended, and corresponded with, key figures in the sexological debate, including Henry Havelock Ellis, Carpenter, Hirschfeld, Iwan Bloch and even the Italian criminologist and degeneration theorist Cesare Lombroso. Sexology offered Ives a language with which to describe himself: he used the term 'homosexual' in the 1910s and 1920s before it was in general use in the press and elsewhere, and appended the term in verso to earlier entries in which he had euphemistically refered to 'this question', 'the old question' and to Lord Leighton being 'Greek'. Ives measured himself and others against sexological criteria. In line with Havelock Ellis's assertion that the invert 'very frequently has hereditary relations that are markedly neurotic',[23] Ives noted the 'neurosis' of a member of the Order of the Chaerona in Berlin.

He had made Dr Roch (a name revealed only in the verso notes) 'scream with laughter'; homosexuals 'are moved up or down easily', he observed (v.56, 9.10.11, p.60). In his self-analysis Ives noted his soft muscle tone, and also that his wrists were 'smaller than most women's' (v.63, 4.6.15, p.24);[24] similar observations were made by continental sexologists Iwan Bloch, Charles Féré and August Forel.[25] Ives further claimed to have a 'keen aesthetic sense' ('like most of my species') and to be a 'mystic' ('a quality of our people'). Both characteristics accord with Edward Carpenter's claims for the 'intermediate sex' (v.3, 21.7.88, p.87; v.69, 23.12.17, p.95).[26]

Ives realised himself that he did not quite fit the model in some respects: he wrote to Ellis concerned about his desires for women (Ellis replied that it was unusual and that men tended 'to become more homosexual as they grew older') and he noted elsewhere that, contrary to type, he could 'play cricket, (real) tennis, shoot (revolver) and many other things' (v.39, 19.5.01, p.83; v.63, 4.6.15, p.24). Sexology provided an epistemological backbone to the diary and to his own sense of himself, and is part of his strong and enduring allegiance to a Victorian taxonomic imagination. But it also leads him to structure his record of himself carefully lest he accord too closely to the more 'negative' observations of the sexologists. He is especially vociferous in blocking any suggestion of effeminacy and urgently asserts his own masculinity, partly, as has been suggested, though his rhetoric and reticence.

Ives's enthusiasm for sexology also allowed him to position himself as part of the intellectual avant-garde during the period, and this sense is underscored by the verso notes which spell out his influential connections. When he decodes various initials he reveals Wilde, Lord Alfred Douglas, Carpenter, the architect and romantic socialist C.R. Ashbee, the sexologist Magnus Hirschfeld, the sociologist Edward Westermarck, Havelock Ellis and Radclyffe Hall (amongst others) to be his friends and associates. In this he tacitly offered up something akin to a literary life to the prospective reader or biographer. Ives claims legitimacy for himself partly though his association with figures who, and writing which, had a higher public profile (or notoriety) than his own.

In addition to the name dropping, the diary is littered with literary and especially Hellenic references, marking out clearly his class status, Cambridge education and masculine erudition, but also constituting a further prism through which to view and articulate his 'cause'. In the scrapbook there is an image of two naked youths embracing in the waves with the by-line 'the spirit of ancient Greece recreated for the camera',[27] and Ives attempts a similar recreation in his diary. Ancient Greece is never far away and he idealises the comradely bonds that empowered the ancient Theban Bands. The diary is significantly dated not only from the birth of Christ, but from the fateful battle of 338BC in which the bands were defeated; 1895 – the year of Wilde's prosecution ('that deed of blood' as Ives terms it) – is also registered as the 'Year of the Faith 2233'. This ancient Theban 'tragedy' is thus brought forcefully into Ives's daily record, providing an additional temporal structure to his work, and allowing him to imagine himself (and contemporary 'defeats' like Wilde's) existing in relation not only to the Christian epoch but to the ancient Greeks. 'I am,' he wrote in 1915, 'a normal Greek or Roman, I think, of the ancient cult. Paiderastia of course, but never effeminate' (v.24, 26.5.95, p.50).

The Thebans provided Ives with a martial rhetoric which inflected his demands for legitimacy (he talks of 'the battle', of 'the attack' and of 'traitors' to the cause) as well as a group of heroes to emulate. He evokes them with religious reverence and a florid style that characterises some of the nineteenth-century translations of the classics. 'Their shape is gone,' he wrote in 1892 (around the time he established the Order) 'but we shall hold their memory – their dust spread over that distant land; for each one grain will raise up life to speak of how they fell at Chaerona – and every life shall multiply until they fill the world and all the hearts of men to wake and see: all to swap the rotting bonds [...] that keep Art's truth stamped down to burn in secret' (v.12., 21.7.92, p.63). Comradely and homoerotic masculine bonds are revealed not only as a 'truth' of science, but a 'truth' of Art and, implicitly here, explicitly elsewhere, as an article of 'faith'. They are the epitome of 'true' beauty. In homoerotic comradeship, as Ives conceived it, lay a beauty which allowed for self and spiritual realisation and a reversal of the degenerating ('rotting') and repressive tendencies he saw in the late nineteenth-century organisation of affective relations. In this his language resonates with the likes of Cesare Lombroso and Max Nordau in their work on degeneracy, but he turns the tables, and it is a constrictive set of middle-class values that are cast as regressive (even though Ives in many ways abides by them himself).

Writing and studying were 'duties' Ives associated with the Order of the Chaerona, and the diary helps him to work through and enunciate the philosophical frame of reference for, and commitment to, the 'cause'. The Order, and his 'faith', enable him to embark on this work and to sustain his resolve. The tenor of the rhetoric associated with these portions of the diary, together with the pragmatic need to elude detection, give his writing a self-consciousness which in turns shapes our sense of Ives himself. While this tone and rhetoric are a repeated feature of the diary, other voices are also present, however. They indicate the fractures and limitations of this vision in relation to his everyday life and showing other ways of thinking about homosexuality, homosexual encounter and

domestic life. He wrote, following a visit to Cambridge, of the undergraduates on 'the beautiful sward' as 'the everlasting statues, the figures
of athletic shapes of youths, so fair: ah how many of them belong to
"Us"?'(the capitalised 'Us' is common throughout, suggesting again a
Uranian elect, a distinct and elevated grouping). His rhetorical question
gives way, though, to more gossipy conjecture: 'I have been trying to find
out from x [sic] who says very few – but does he know? I think not [...]
there must be a great many and in such surroundings – I like to think all
of them' (v.20, 26.6.93, p.91).

At moments like this we see the more immediate erotic import of such
heroic and aestheticised scenes and Ives's fantasies and desires emerge
more fully, marked out by a shift in tone. Similarly, although he wants to
'make' his friends 'Mog' (Charles Gee) and 'Cubby' (Harold Holt) 'live
according to the wisdom of the Order' when they move with him to
Adelaide Road, near Primrose Hill in 1905 (v.47, 31.5.05, p.13), he
employs a domestic language when he talks about them, rather than one
of heroic relations. He refers to them by their infantilising nicknames
and also as his 'children'. In 1901, Ives records going to a ball with the
men he lives with and so of 'the whole family' being present (indeed
he has more to say about this 'family of choice' than he has about his
blood relations) (v.39, 30.6.01, p.110).[28] In 1917, he gives an inventory
of his 'family' 'home': 'Kit [James Goddard] has been with me some 35
years. His wife over 20. Wappy [Charles Gee, also known as 'Mog'], Pug
[Harold Bloodworth] 9 or 10 [...] and the 2 Kit girls [Goddard's
daughters] all their lives.' 'That,' he concludes, 'is my little circle in the
world' (v.70, 21.5.17, p.118). There is a sense again of creating an
insulated realm separated from a contemptuous society. But it is quite a
different circle from either the Order, the Thebans or the elite he refers
to elsewhere, not least in including a women and her daughters (though
they are significantly not named and are listed as adjuncts to Kit).

Ives often ameliorates the triviality he attaches to daily life by
deploying a broader and, he suggests, timeless, Hellenic 'spirit' and
'faith' (note that the athletic undergraduates are 'everlasting'), but
this ideal also sometimes fails to capture adequately these day-to-day
experiences and what he wants to say about them – about his frustration
at missing egg cups, surprise at the frugal meal served up by Carpenter,
or his sadness and pleasure at receiving Cubby's latch keys back when
he marries (v.20, 30.6.94, p.100; v.30, 8.4.97; v.43, 20.8.03, p.45).
Conversely there is a perennial sense of disappointment that the everyday
fails to live up to his ideal. He expresses annoyance with Mog and Pug
for their late nights; with Wilde and his set for their extravagance; with
the 'silly' 'inverts' dancing on the streets of Paris on Bastille day; and
with a member of the Order who 'does nothing save amuse himself'

(v.69, 28.10.17, p.39; v.22, 1.1.95, p.84; v. 57, 14.7.12, p.100; v.60, 5.5.14, p.87). Homosexuality, he insists, must be approached 'earnestly, seriously' (v.45, 17.11.04, p.94), and he draws a line, as Paul Robinson notes of later gay autobiographers, between '[his] own legitimate brand of homosexuality and the disreputable brand of others'.[29]

Ives's disapproval often relates to sexual frivolousness and a lack of self-consciousness, as has already been observed. For him sex was a theoretical and moral 'problem' in the early years, something that required careful 'thought' (v.9, 15.10.90, p.18). He discusses a sexo-logical approach to homosexuality with a young Russian he meets on his way from Nice to London in 1889, but notes disappointedly that his companion was 'more raised in practice than theory, like so many' (v.3, 31.3.89, p.98). On another occasion he visited the Army and Navy Club with a 'distinguished, decorated, brave man who yet knew nothing what-ever of the philosophy of what he blindly does' (v.38, 30.9.00, p.30). Men he meets casually become interesting because of their potential usefulness to the 'cause', or because, as in the case of a young sailor he meets in Nice, of 'their natural history' (v.18, 27.12.93, p.90; v.6, 13.12.89, p.66). He talks of being 'on duty' for the Order, and the need to abstain in those periods. 'I must be disciplined,' he wrote in 1894, 'or I would much injure the work' (v.21, 28.8.94, p.48). In the same year Ives writes of 'the little minority who have kept their faith in Hellas, we who work at night when the rabble revels in its orgies, we who dream of love when the philistine soaks in the sticky bed of lust' (v.31, 20.6.94, p.38). Ives, echoing Arnold and also Carlyle, divides the elite from the rabble here. He implicitly figures himself as a hero, pursuing and articulating the 'truth' in the face of the ignorant and the uncommitted. Like a railing puritan minister, his fervour for the 'cause' stands in for the homosexual passion he works so hard to defend but somehow finds difficult to countenance.

What I have suggested thus far is that the revelations of the news-papers, the pathologising tendency of sexology and the highly structured and idealised male–male relations of ancient Greece limited Ives's self-description and his depiction of his intimate relations, even as they also provoked and allowed him to speak about homosexuality and the homo-sexual cause. These compounded the restrictions inherent in prevailing models of male life writing. Ives was in a double bind between the desire to reveal and the injunction to keep quiet, an injunction which operated at a number of levels, relating to prevailing notions of masculinity and respectability, to the 'civilised' pursuit of truth and knowledge, and to a more pragmatic need to evade detection and the law. Ives is scathing about the 'conspiracy of silence' surrounding the issue of homosexuality but he also replicates this in some ways within his diary (v.52, 15.1.09, p.101). Ives's emotional and physical intimacy are masked by his attempts to invoke a grand future, to connect with a heroic past, and to pursue a scientific 'truth'. There is little space in the early entries for himself in the present, and this exasperates him at times. 'I have learned to crush everything,' he observes in an undated note added to an entry of 1893, 'it is the discipline of the miserable times in which we live not to be led by impulses but by cold methodical calculation.' In a further note added to the same entry in 1925 he writes: 'I wish I had more pluck, more erotic enterprise, but I was slow and timid long ago' (v.17, 26.7.93, p.16). When he observed some sort of erotic encounter (probably on Clapham Common in 1901 – as ever it is unclear what), he wrote: 'I was rather interested and pleased. It was such a piece of private animalism – ah yes these happy, natural, passionate, gloriously "immoral" or rather non moral people have a better time than a morbid, reflecting being like myself who is forever wondering why, instead of stretching out both hands with simple ecstasy at the wondrous emotions that are here' (v.39, 1.5.01, p.73). 'You have passed your life saying no,' Wilde reportedly told Ives (v.50, 16.8.07, p.75).

There is a parallel account, however. The verso notes, which provide a more clearly retrospective account, reveal a shift in what Ives felt it was possible to say, and he explicitly conceives of them as notes for a student or even a biographer. They weave a more overt emotional and erotic thread through the volumes, validating some of the intimacy he had had with other men. His attachment to Wilde and his passion for Lord Alfred Douglas, for example, emerge more clearly in the comments added to the original entries. Against the fact of dining with Oscar Wilde in 1893, for example, he notes that such an event was a 'privilege one does not forget' (v.17, 15.10.93, p.119). Later in the same year he mentions matter-of-factly (and evasively) that 'O came to the NTC to say goodbye.' An undated verso note signals that 'O' was indeed 'Oscar Wilde'. He had visited Ives at the New Traveller's Club, where he 'kissed me passionately before we parted – having asked my permission for I was very shy in those days' (v.18, 23.12.93, p.78). Beyond the prosaic initial entry is a potent memory of a passionate kiss, recorded only in verso and over twenty years after the event. It is also in the verso notes that we find Ives's 'fascination' with Lord Alfred Douglas's 'beauty' and discover that the two men slept together (v. 21, 28.8.94, p.48). Other notes indicate how his opinion of Douglas changed with Wilde's trials. Most entries dealing with him are appended with the words 'traitor', and in the early 1930s Ives reports, apparently with some glee, Radclyffe Hall's observation over tea that Douglas was 'now ugly' (v.98, 5.12.33, p.158).

Other affairs are also fleshed out in verso. In 1900, a liaison in Nice is remotely suggested in the original entry: 'I met him in the sea swimming the other day, so I suppose he must be a respectable person.' His concern with respectability is to the fore in this first elusive mention of the affair, but later, and more romantically, he notes that they were lovers and regrets it was not taken further. 'We could have travelled together: what I missed! But we were perfect lovers before we parted: all fulfilled.' A further verso note explains that he tried to trace this man to Paris but failed: 'at least links were forged and I have not forgotten them' (v.37, 28.4.00, p.38). In the same year Ives had a fleeting encounter with a man on the street in London, and again the verso notes give an insight into the potent experiences which underpinned Ives's abstracted discussions of spiritual unions and of a faith in Uranianism. He wrote in verso: 'I think this alludes to a very strange experience of mine which never occurred again. I felt once a sudden sense almost of worship for a youth, we met, we passed, and a gleam from heaven went with him.' In a further note of 1927, 28 years after the encounter itself, he wrote: 'I believe that on that wonderful occasion mentioned above, the mysterious one may not even have spoken to me [...] to exchange a look of admiration and desire is not uncommon. But the sense of almost hero worship [...] came to me openly once and is inexplicable to me still' (v.36, 3.3.99, p.108). What was rare for Ives here, and what stays with him, is finding his hero in the everyday, his Utopia on the streets of London.

These notes show Ives remembering, revisiting and remaking his former self, and also self-consciously providing additional information and analysis for the future reader. They constitute a parallel text which gives a retrospectively constituted sense of his earlier self – as overly serious and timid, for example – and beautifully illustrates changing priorities and perceptions, most notably in the way he draws the intimate and erotic into his record. This does not make him any more 'honest' in these later years; the verso notes do not represent the 'true' Ives somehow occluded in the original entries. Rather they mark a shifting sense of self and possibility, which in turn reflected a changing cultural climate.

The notes were added after the foundation of the British Society for the Study of Sex Psychology in 1913 and as Ives was attending, meeting and working as treasurer and as a member of the bibliographic sub-committee. The explicit mission of the organisation was open and dispassionate discussion and study of the 'sex question'. The society drew of course on the 'wisdom' of sexology, and attracted a substantial (and registered) membership to frequent meetings. It provided a model of open, serious and radical (though again largely depersonalised) discussion of human relationships and Ives reports being buoyed up by various papers and discussions. Edward Carpenter's 'coming out' in *My Day and*

Dreams (1916) provided a more immediate consideration of homo-sexuality and is symptomatic of a greater willingness during and after the war years to open out sexual questions more fully in print. A.T.Fitzroy's novel, *Despised and Rejected*, which dealt with male homosexuality and lesbianism, and Marie Stoppes's, *Married Love*, appeared in 1918, for example. Though both were controversial, they indicate a new thirst for a less euphemistic exploration of sexual identification, pleasure, guilt and pain than had hitherto seemed possible. They are certainly cautious but they also carve out a more substantial public space for discussion of sexual subjectivity: 'What was there written about inversion 30 years ago?' Ives wrote in 1917: 'some privately printed essays by John Addington Symonds; that is all I can think of in English. Now there are some half dozen writers' (67, 1.2.17, p.47). This tendency, I would suggest, allowed Ives to acknowledge more clearly, even if still only in outline, parts of his own sexual and erotic history in the verso notes added after the war. He also begins to acknowledge their importance more fully. Ives wrote a year before the end of the war (shortly after Pug had come back from the trenches): 'nothing is more contemptible in a diary than to chronicle one's dealings with the great [...] and to leave out all ones intimacies with people who constituted one's life' (v.68, 13.9.17, p.123). There is a marked shift here (which he does not fully sustain) from his hero worship and keen interest in 'the great and the good' to the more immediate relationships which structure his everyday life and – he confesses explicitly for the first time – 'constitute' that life. His earlier rhetoric is here played down in favour of a validation of the intimate in the record of and formulation of a life.

This was clearly no panacea: reactions to the published texts also demonstrated the continued dangers of revelation. *Married Love* was widely condemned and Fitzroy's book was banned (Ives met Fitzroy – the pseudonym for Rose Allatini – to discuss the case and what he could do to help). In the same year the dancer Maude Allen sued Noel Pemberton Billing for suggesting she was a lesbian. At the heart of the case was a supposed 'black book' listing the names of those men and women the Germans would be able to blackmail on account of their sexual deviancy.[30] The dangers associated with private records and with sexual secrets were manifest, and Ives's diary and scrapbook continued to catalogue the arrests and prosecutions of men having sex with each other: he was certainly not ignorant of the continued persecution of homosexuality in these later years and indeed the Utopian optimism of the early 1890s fades. And yet Ives's own prose does become less self-conscious, reflecting perhaps a greater ease with himself and others in middle and old age and also signalling a broader shift in sexual discourse. The importance of Hellenism and sexology remain and large portions of the verso notes refer to work for the 'cause' and the wider vision, but these aspects also become more integrated into Ives's daily record of the 1910s and 1920s rather than being a means of reaching beyond it. The tenor and content of the later entries and verso notes mark a validation of the intimate and the daily, and these become part of the 'Ives' he wants to leave to his future reader. In the light of broader public debate and in an era when psychoanalysis was beginning to gain some cultural purchase in Britain (partly in fact through the British Society for the Study of Sex Psychology), what it felt important to say about sexual and emotional intimacy was changing, in particular by suggesting more strongly than before that the fantasies, dreams and yearnings of the individual were themselves highly significant. Though Ives remained wedded to the theories of Ellis rather than Freud, this is partly I believe what lay behind his attempts to reinflect the early story he told about himself. Gayatri Spivak has argued in a different context that one story necessarily occludes another.[31] By reflecting back and commenting on his late Victorian and Edwardian former self, however, Ives begins to signpost some of the other ways he might, in hindsight, have told his own tale, and introduces further (and frequently conflicting) voices to speak to that much anticipated future reader.

What this working and reworking, this careful putting together of a life, indicates is the crucial importance of life writing to Ives: of the diary form in the first place and the more overtly reflective verso notes in the second. Both were a means of self and group affirmation, and of bearing witness to a long, frustrated and frustrating fight for legitimacy. For all his desire for certainty and drive towards a hopeful future, Ives veers in his diary between optimism and despair (see, for example: v.18, 1.2.94, p.154) and figures vividly the pressures and tensions which structured his writing and his life. As readers, we see the importance to Ives of the abstract hero, of the hero in the everyday, and of himself as a hero, but also the significance of the more prosaic intimacies associated with his domestic and daily life; we follow the Arnoldian construction of an exclusive elite and his denigration of the 'rabble' but also his commitment to the less exclusive visions of Whitman and Carpenter; we observe the Utopia he holds up but also the ways in which the everyday fractures and compromises this vision. We hear, finally, the high-flown rhetoric, the pseudoscientific language of sexology, the poetic and the literary, but also other voices – gossipy, judgmental, conspiratorial, intimate – which allow us to build up a more complex picture of Ives and get behind his Victorian impulse to construct a cohesive and conclusive account of his life and work.

His sense of himself and his desires are not as easily summed up as the brief autobiographical sexological case studies might have suggested was possible. The putative Hellenic social and cultural system, moreover, was not easily applied in its totality either to his understanding of himself or to his community of friends in London. While we might point to the crucial importance of these discourses in shaping ideas about and experiences of homosexuality, the multiple and sometimes conflicting voices in Ives's diary show us that they cannot be applied formulaically and are only a part of a complex matrix of ideas, experiences and influences which shape his sense of who he was. This sense of course shifts over time, marking out within one lifespan the ruptures as well as the continuities in understandings and experiences of homosexuality and of the self and identity. This is important since, in the rush to reclaim the gay past of the late nineteenth and early twentieth century there has often been an understandable tendency to look for sameness rather than difference, rather as Ives does in his approach to the ancient Greeks. Where there is a deep resonance between Ives's work and that of many gay men writing more recently, however, is in this impulse to bear witness, to use the diary to mark out a marginalised and dissident experience. The filmmaker Derek Jarman, who was eight when Ives died and later kept his own diary during the first decade of the AIDS crisis, wrote of the personal need and wider responsibility 'to write of sad times as a witness'.[32] Ives's remarkable diary and his appeal to the future student and biographer show a similar self-consciousness in his formulation and record of himself and a largely invisible early fight against sexual injustice.

Notes

1. Margaretta Jolly, 'Sex Lives and Life Writing: the challenge of queer'; paper delivered at the Queer Lives Symposium, Kings College, London, 31.01.04. I am grateful to Dr Jolly for allowing me to read and cite her paper. See also Jolly, 'Lesbian and Gay Life Writing', in *The Encyclopedia of Life Writing*, ed. Margaretta Jolly (London: Fitzroy Dearborn, 2001), pp.547–50.

2. George Ives, 'Diary', vol.19, 31 March, 1894, p.67; George Ives's papers, Harry Ransom Humanities Research Center, University of Texas at Austin. Further references in the text.

3. Short accounts of Ives's life and reform work, his involvement in the British Society for the Study of Sex Psychology, his friendship with Wilde, and his poetry appear in, respectively, Jeffrey Weeks, *Coming Out: Homosexual Politics from the Nineteenth Century to the Present* (London: Quartet, 1979), pp.118–24, 130–36; Lesley Hall, '"Disinterested Enthusiasm for Sexual Misconduct": The British Society for the Study of Sex Psychology, 1913–47', *Journal of Contemporary History*, 30 (1995), 665–86; John Stokes, 'Wilde at Bay: the Diaries of George Ives', *English Literature in Transition, 1880–1920*, 26 (3) (1983), 175–84; Timothy d'Arch Smith,

Love in Earnest: Some Notes on the Lives and Writing of English Uranian Poets from 1889–1930 (London: Routledge and Kegan Paul, 1970), pp.110–14. See also Matt Cook, *London and the Culture of Homosexuality, 1885–1914* (Cambridge: Cambridge University Press, 2003), ch.5 and epilogue.

4.   George Ives, 'The New Hedonism Controversy', *The Humanitarian*, vol.v, no.4 (Oct. 1894), 292–7. Ives's piece was attacked in *The Review of Reviews*: 'In Praise of Two Crimes', *The Review of Reviews*, vol.x, no.4 (October 1894), 356. See also 'Diary', vol.22, 6 Oct. 1894–15 Oct. 1894, 2–14. Other works: C. Branco (pseud.), *Lifting of the Veil* (London: Swann Sonnenschein, 1892); anon., *Book of Chains* (London: Garland, 1897); Ives, *Eros Throne* (London: Garland, 1900); Ives, *History of Penal Methods: Criminals, Witches, Lunatics* (London: Stanley Paul, 1914); Ives, *The Sexes, Structure and Extra-Organic Habits of Certain Animals* (London: Unwin, 1918); Ives, *The Continued Extension of the Criminal Law* (London, 1922); Ives, *The Graeco-Roman View of Youth* (London: Cayme Press, 1926); Ives, *Obstacles to Human Progress* (London: Allen and Unwin, 1939).

5.   Jennifer Sinor, *The Extraordinary Work of Ordinary Writing: Annie Ray's diary* (Iowa City: University of Iowa Press, 2002), p.56.

6.   See, for example, Richard von Krafft-Ebing, *Psychopathia Sexualis*, trans. Charles Chaddock (London: Davis, 1892); H. Havelock Ellis, *Studies in the Psychology of Sex*, vol.1, *Sexual Inversion* (London: Wilson and Macmillan, April 1897); John Addington Symonds, *A Problem in Modern Ethics: An Inquiry into the Phenomenon of Sexual Inversion* (1891; London: privately printed, 1896); Edward Carpenter, *Homogenic Love and its Place in a Free Society* (Manchester: Labour Press Society, 1894).

7.   John Addington Symonds, *The Memoirs of John Addington Symonds*, ed. Phyllis Grosskurth (London: Hutchinson, 1984); Horatio Brown, *John Addington Symonds* (London: J.C. Nimmo, 1895). On this point see also Trev Lynn Broughton, *Men of Letters, Writing Lives: Masculinity and Literary Auto/Biography in the Late Victorian Period* (London: Routledge, 1999), pp.15–20.

8.   Edward Carpenter, *My Days and Dreams* (London: Allen and Unwin, 1916).

9.   The scrapbook is a vast 45-volume compendium of published work and, to a lesser extent, personal memorabilia, and itself illustrates the ways in which Ives constructed and understood himself and his relation to society. I am extremely grateful to Maggs & Co. Booksellers, Berkeley Square, London, who gave me access to George Ives's scrapbooks before they were sold to the Beinecke Library, Yale University.

10. See, for example: 'West End Flat Scandal', *Reynolds*, 5 Apr. 1906, p.5; 'Other Serious Charges', *Reynolds*, 14 Apr., 1895, p.1; 'The Studio Crime', *Daily Graphic*, 1 Jun. 1906, p.3.

11. *Sins of the Cities of the Plain, or Recollections of a Mary-Ann* (London, 1881); *Teleny, or The Reverse of the Medal* (1893; Ware: Wordswoth, 1995).

12. Broughton, *Men of Letters, Writing Lives*, pp.3–7.

13. Oliver Buckton develops a similar argument. The 'confessional secret' in autobiography by 'homosexual' men during this period is 'produced in part by an unwillingness to jeopardize the cultural privilege and textual

authority of the Victorian male author': Oliver J. Buckton, *Secret Selves: confession and same-sex desire in Victorian autobiography* (Chapel Hill: University of North Carolina Press, 1998), p.14.

14. Mary Jane Moffat (ed.), *Revelations: Diaries of Women* (New York: 1974), p.5; cited by Sinor, *Extraordinary Work*, p.47.

15. On this point see also Sinor, *Extraordinary Work*, p.37.

16. On this point see, especially, Eve Segwick, *The Epistemology of the Closet* (Berkeley, 1990) and Elaine Showalter, *Sexual Anarchy: Gender and Culture at the Fin de Siècle* (London: Virago, 1990).

17. Cook, *London and the Culture of Homosexuality*, ch.3.

18. See Richard Jenkyns, *The Victorians and Ancient Greece* (Oxford: Blackwell, 1980); Jenkyns, *Dignity and Decadence: Victorian Art and the Classical Inheritance* (London: Harper Collins, 1991); Linda Dowling, *Hellenism and Homo-sexuality in Victorian Oxford* (Ithaca: Cornell University Press, 1994); Louis Crompton, *Byron and Greek Love: Homophobia in 19th-Century England* (London: Faber, 1985).

19. Ives's particular emphasis on the law and the press, sexology and Hellenism underscores claims made by Michel Foucault and subsequent historians and critics for the importance of these discourses in providing a framework for the understanding and experience of homosexual dissidence in the later nineteenth century and beyond. See Michel Foucault, *History of Sexuality*, vol.1, *An Introduction*, trans. Robert Hurley, 1976 (London: Penguin, 1990); and, for example: Jeffrey Weekes, *Sex, Politics and Society: The Regulation of Sexuality Since 1800* (London: Longman, 1981); David Greenberg, *The Construction of Homosexuality* (Chicago: University of Chicago Press, 1988); Ed Cohen, *Talk on the Wilde Side: Towards a Genealogy of a Discourse on Male Sexualities* (London: Routledge, 1993); Harry Oosterhuis, *Stepchildren of Nature: Krafft-Ebing, Psychiatry and the Making of Sexual Identity* (Chicago: University of Chicago Press, 2000); Linda Dowling, *Hellenism*; Alan Sinfield, *The Wilde Century: Effeminacy, Oscar Wilde and the Queer Moment* (London: Cassell, 1992).

20. The preface to *My Secret Life* reads: 'No names are mentioned in the book, though they were given freely in the margin of the original manuscript, and I alone know to whom they refer'; the narrator of *Teleny* refers at the end of the novel to 'another strange incident in my too-eventful life', but adds teasingly: 'perhaps I'll tell you some other time'. See 'Walter', *My Secret Life* (1888–92) (London: Arrow Books, 1994), p.5; *Teleny*, p.153.

21. Buckton, *Secret Selves*, p.15.

22. See H.G. Cocks, *Nameless Offences: Speaking of Male Homosexuality in 19th Century England* (London: I.B. Taurus, 2003); see also Buckton, *Secret Selves*.

23. H. Havelock Ellis and John Addington Symonds, *Studies in the Psychology of Sex*, vol.i, *Sexual Inversion* (London, April 1897), p.140.

24. Iwan Bloch, *The Sexual Life of Our Time in its Relation to Modern Civilisation*, trans. M. Eden Paul (London: Rebman, 1908).

25. Bloch, *Sexual Life of Our Time*, p.497. August Forel, *The Sexual Question: A Scientific, Psychological, Hygienic and Sociological Study for the Cultured Classes*, trans. C.F. Marshall (London: Rebman, 1908); Charles Féré, *The Evolution and Dissolution of the Sexual Instinct* (Paris: Charles Carrington, 1904).

26. Edward Carpenter, 'The Intermediate Sex', *Selected Writings: Sex* (1908; reprinted London: GMP, 1984).
27. 'The Spirit of Ancient Greece Recreated for the Camera', c.July 1905, in Ives, *Casebook*, vol.v, p.92 (magazine not cited).
28. For more on the concept and experience of 'families of choice', see Jeffrey Weeks, Brian Heaphy and Catherine Donovan, *Same Sex Intimacies: Families of choice and other life experiments* (London: Routledge, 2001).
29. Paul Robinson, *Gay Lives: Homosexual Autobiography from John Addington Symonds to Paul Monette* (Chicago: University of Chicago Press, 1999), p.xvii.
30. For more on this case, see Philip Hoare, *Wilde's Last Stand: Decadence, Conspiracy and the First World War* (London: Duckworth, 1997); Lucy Bland, 'Trial by Sexology?: Maude Allen, Salome and the Cult of the Clitoris Case', in Lucy Bland and Laura Doan (eds), *Sexology in Culture* (Cambridge: Polity Press, 1998).
31. Gayatri Spivak, 'Three Women's Texts and a Critique of Imperialism', in Robyn R. Warhol and Diane Price Herndl (eds), *Feminism: An Anthology of Literary Theory and Criticism* (New Brunswick: Rutgers University Press, 1997), pp.896–913; first published 1985.
32. Derek Jarman, *At Your Own Risk: A Saint's Testimony* (London: Random House, 1992), p.119.

CHAPTER TEN

'House of Disquiet'
The Benson Family Auto/biographies

Valerie Sanders

The Bensons were a Victorian family dedicated to telling and retelling the story of their lives. Though they also wrote about other lives, they returned time and again to a densely incestuous obsession with their own, explaining their upbringing to an outside readership, and inevitably to themselves in the process. All seemed driven by a need first to understand, and then to tell others, the peculiarities of their childhood and the effect it had had on their subsequent careers. As a family, they exemplify the mid-to-late Victorian, male-dominated literary culture, but were also atypical of the ideal middle-class family, riven as they were by religious differences, tragic deaths, mental instability and sexual failure. Georgina Battiscombe describes them as 'introspective, volatile, and highly articulate. Scorning the middle way, they rushed from the heights to the depths; charming they certainly were but it must be admitted that they were also a little second-rate'.[1] They were all fluent writers who found it easier to write about themselves than to form relationships outside the family. None of the children married: all adored their mother, and felt overwhelmed by their father's personality. As a group of life writers poised on the edge of the Victorian period in its interface with modernism, they exemplify the undermining of the heroic form of life writing, even as they struggled to uphold it.

The Bensons have recently attracted considerable interest from critics and historians working in the field of Victorian family relations and masculinity, especially the role of the father. Edward White Benson (1829–96) was Archbishop of Canterbury from 1883 until his death, and his two best-known sons, Arthur Christopher ('A.C.') and Edward Frederic ('E.F.') both followed literary careers. David Newsome, David Williams and Betty Askwith have explored their family relationships, and John Tosh, in his chapter on the Bensons for his book with Michael Roper, *Manful Assertions* (1991), has focused on the relationship between manliness and domesticity in Benson's household, especially during his time as headmaster of Wellington College.[2] Far from being the distant and autocratic paterfamilias that we (mistakenly) associate with Victorian fatherhood, Benson was an intensely involved father who dominated his children's domestic life. The collapse of 'separate spheres' within the home, especially where the home doubled as the man's place of work, is a key factor in understanding the Bensons, who were configuring their family life at a time when traditional middle-class models of fatherhood were giving way to a sense of confusion as to what a father's role should be. This was partly because fatherhood was never as publicly theorised as motherhood. 'Of all the qualifications for full masculine status,' John Tosh suggests, 'fatherhood was the least talked about by the Victorians.' Beneath the surface of family life, moreover, it 'held a decidedly ambiguous position.'[3] Those who did discuss it – periodical journalists, for instance – as Claudia Nelson has argued, 'found it difficult to reach any kind of consensus about what fatherhood meant.'[4]

For Edward White Benson it meant an unremitting earnestness about his children and their moral and educational achievements. According to his second son, Arthur Christopher, Benson was 'of a deeply affectionate and at the same time anxious disposition; he loved family life, but he had an almost tremulous sense of his parental responsibility'. His sensitivity was such that a careless word from one of his children 'might distress him out of all proportion.'[5] Benson's emotional intensity about his children peaked when his eldest son Martin died of meningitis while he was at school in Winchester in 1878. A note written at the time shows the complexity of the roles the Benson children seem to have performed for both their parents: 'To me he was more like a little daughter than a son, and to his mother he was more like a devoted brother,' Edward Benson explained, in a free jumbling of the sexes and generations.[6] Neither seems to have seen him straightforwardly as what he was, an eldest son away at school. Indeed John Tosh has recently referred to the presence of 'significant structural tensions' in the Victorian bourgeois marriage, where men especially would look to their wives as mother figures, while their children occupied other complicated roles. He cites the Bensons as an example, the various members becoming emotional substitutes for lost relationships with others.[7] Edward's wife, Mary, who was thirteen years his junior, looked to her husband as a kind of father figure, while he partly saw her as a mother, and partly as a replacement for a sister who had died young. The children too formed intricate patterns of allegiance with one another, which were subsequently explored in the brothers' autobiographical writings. As a family of auto/biographers, the Bensons have received considerably less attention than they have simply as family, and it is the dynamics of their mutual life writing that I wish to explore in this chapter, in the context of late nineteenth/early twentieth-century biographical writing. Their experiments with the genre, and their reconstruction of the 'silent' members of the family who were on the margins of the life writing industry (their mother, their sisters, and even their father) will be the focus of discussion.

Arthur Christopher (1862–1925) was the most active chronicler, not only of family affairs but of recent history (his publications included an edition of Queen Victoria's letters). Most of his career was dedicated to writing biography, largely of great men, beginning with a set of exemplary lives for boys, *Men of Might: Studies of Great Characters* (1892), but also of his father (1899), sister Maggie (1917) and brother Hugh (1915). In 1923, he returned to the family group once again, with a biographical study called *The Trefoil* (named after the trefoil leaf on the family coat of arms), which focuses on his father's career at Wellington College, Lincoln and Truro, before he went to Canterbury. This earlier period of his father's life he felt had 'an intensity and romantic quality infinitely more arresting and vivid than the later years'.[8] By this stage, Arthur is going back fifty to sixty years, to tell the story one more time, freely admitting the risk of repetition. Strangest of all his productions, however, was his fictitious autobiography, *The House of Quiet* (1904), which is an account of a life beset with limitations, a 'life of the obscure', though, unlike Virginia Woolf's interest in such lives, essentially a male life. Similarly his *Memoirs of Arthur Hamilton* (1886) is a fictitious biography, largely about himself, presented as an unknown and short-lived man, whose brief and hidden life passes in a world of school-mastering and Cambridge colleges, as did Benson's own. His brother Fred (1867–1940) (E.F.) meanwhile published *Our Family Affairs 1867–1896* (1920), *As We Were: A Victorian Peep-Show* (1930), *Mother* (1925) and *Final Edition* (1940), in the last of which, as Virginia Woolf commented rather acidly, 'he tried to rasp himself clean of his barnacles'.[9] There is a neat irony in the fact that several of Fred's memoirs were reissued by the Hogarth Press in 1985, with new critical introductions. The youngest brother R.H. (Hugh) (1871–1914), who converted to Catholicism and became a priest, added another perspective to the collective family history with *Confessions of a Convert* (1913).

What is notable about the Benson biographies, however, is the silence of the women, who avoided both biography and autobiography, though Maggie (1865–1916), described as 'priestly' by her brother Arthur, edited some of her father's work and helped him with the monumental two-volume *Life*. Their father and Arthur both prefaced works written by the other sister, Eleanor (Nellie) (1863–90) with memoirs of their own; but the sisters are essentially written *about*: they play a minimal part in the shared construction of the family image, yet Arthur recalls that, when they were children, even they 'began to tell each other stories, supposed to be biographies of their dolls', which actually moved them to tears.[10] Both, in their different ways, disturbed the family's image of itself: Nellie, by dying of diphtheria in her late twenties, and Maggie by suffering a series of mental breakdowns, which landed her permanently in a mental institution. Maggie claimed that 'this odd outburst of books, in an unmarrying family, is better than marriage'. Not only did it preserve the original blood ties: it also gave the brothers and sisters an opportunity to know each other, all over again, by reading each other's analyses of the family: 'one gets to know you in a double way, by a sort of second channel'.[11] Indeed their comments on each other suggest that what survived of each, in their memories, were scenes, words and sayings. Arthur recalled in his biography of Hugh: 'My brothers, Fred and Hugh, my sister and myself would sometimes be at home together, and all writing books.'[12]

What was problematic about this kind of life writing was the inevitable retelling of the same stories, the struggle to define oneself differently from the other brothers and sisters, and establish a distinct identity. As the two brothers, Arthur and Fred, repeatedly told the story of their melancholy and unfulfilled family, they each questioned what they meant by 'identity', a word that recurs with increasing urgency in Arthur's writing as he felt threatened by the fear of psychological disintegration. As Jenny Bourne Taylor and Sally Shuttleworth have shown, Victorian psychologists such as William Carpenter were fascinated by the issue of identity formation via the diverse influences working on it. Specifically they questioned whether the self was unified, divided or multiple, and asked how 'a sense of personal identity' was formed through different patterns of memory: for example 'the relationship between the individual's childhood and the collective, historical and organic past'. Taylor and Shuttleworth add that 'the stress on inheritance and transmission of acquired traits from parents to children contributed to the growing centrality of childhood in late nineteenth-century discussion of individual and social development'.[13] These were clearly central issues for the Bensons, who shared a collective familial past and many of the same memories. The one member who most successfully pulled herself free of the others – ironically in view of her marriage to an overwhelming personality – was their mother, the most flamboyant of them all. Selected as her husband's future bride when she was only twelve, she eventually found happiness in a same-sex relationship with Lucy Tait, daughter of the previous Archbishop of Canterbury. The account she wrote of her marriage in 1875 remains unpublished, in the Bodleian Library.

Though the circumstances were different, comparisons can be made with the serene individuality of Sir Leslie Stephen's second wife, Julia, commemorated in *The Mausoleum Book* (1895) by a husband who felt destroyed by her premature death. The Benson men were writing in the great age of male-dominated life writing, of which the best-known practitioner was indeed the founder of the *Dictionary of National Biography*. In her study of Stephen and Froude in the context of masculinity and literary auto/biography (1999), Trev Lynn Broughton has argued that, at the end of the nineteenth century, life writing was 'not just an inscription but a medium of gender relations, both at the level of the micropolitics of daily life for writers, and in terms of professional practices and aesthetic codes'. What was important about this period, according to Broughton, is that it witnessed 'a large-scale reassessment of domestic accountability, a reframing of what it meant to be married and a crystallization of gender identities around what we now think of as the hetero/homosexual divide'.[14] These, too, were crucial matters for the Benson life writers, who had to take account of their collective failure to live either emotionally satisfying private, or conventionally acceptable public lives in the wake of their father's 'domestic accountability'. In telling the story of any one member of the family, they inevitably told (and retold) the story of the rest, and tried to work out for themselves why they had all felt troubled by a father who clearly valued a full domestic life, and had tried his best for them as children.

Taken in conjunction with Martin Danahay's view, expressed in his study of masculine autobiography, *A Community of One* (1993) that nineteenth-century male autobiographers 'inscribe themselves within their texts as autonomous subjects free from the constraints of any social context', Broughton's argument suggests that individual male autobiographers need to be repositioned within the family context they tried to overlook. Danahay adds that the masculine subject of Victorian autobiography 'emphasizes the autonomy of self at the expense of family and community'.[15] He is thinking here primarily of Wordsworth, who of course belongs to a much earlier phase of the nineteenth century, but Wordsworth's effacement of the female in *The Prelude* he takes as a paradigm of this kind of male-authored self-writing. Similar claims could be made of the other famous nineteenth-century male autobiographers: John Stuart Mill, who omits his mother and sisters from his *Autobiography*, and focuses intently on his relationship with his father; John Henry Newman, who says virtually nothing about his family in his *Apologia*; or Ruskin, who omits his relationship with his wife Effie from *Praeterita* (though he does talk about his mother).

The Bensons were active participants in this new discourse of 'domestic accountability', of which the best-known examples are probably Leslie Stephen, in *The Mausoleum Book*, and Edmund Gosse in *Father and Son* (1907), which, like the Benson biographies, saw the two generations locked together in a state of unavoidable mutual dependency. Writing the lives of the Bensons presented distinctive challenges, but why did they need to recount their lives at all? And so often? Their claims to fame were modest in proportion to their biographical output: they were the children of an Archbishop of Canterbury, and three of them were, as Georgina Battiscombe indicates, capable, but 'second-rate' writers. Clearly they thought of themselves as in some way peculiar or special, people whose lives were worth close recuperation. As children they were clever, argumentative, critical and isolated. Something about them was wrong from the beginning. 'Nothing serious or tragic happened to us at Lincoln,' Arthur notes half way through *The Trefoil*; 'we grew up prosperous, innocent, and harmless, and everything went well; but there was no contact with realities.'[16] This isolation from the normal outside world is the crucial point. It remains a theme in all their writing, magnifying the intensity of their experiences, especially their knowledge of each other's psychological and emotional shortcomings. Throughout their lives, they observed the other family members and, as each died, the survivors scrutinised their interlocking roles one more time.

The family's problems, which all the children recognised, were their parents' complex relationship, especially their mother's early unhappiness in the marriage, her preference for same-sex relations, a religious crisis she suffered in the 1870s, their sister Maggie's complete mental breakdown and hostility to their mother from 1907 onwards, their brother Hugh's conversion to Catholicism and Arthur Christopher's own psychological collapses. A *fin-de-siècle* depressive illness, their collective inheritance, seemed to drive them into further introspection. Above all, the impact of their father's monumental personality was something Arthur and Fred needed to understand and explain, in relation to their mother, as well as to themselves.

Written as they were in the last ten years of the nineteenth, and first twenty-five years of the new century, the Benson auto/biographies coincide with a time when psychoanalysis was developing, and the writing of biography was freeing itself from Victorian constraints. After his siblings' deaths, Fred became particularly interested in the writing of biography, and saw himself as positioned somewhere between the Victorians and the 'belittling' tendency of the modernists and Bloomsbury.[17] The Bensons were about twenty years older than the Woolf circle, but collectively experiencing a variety of family secrets and traumas on a similar scale. There are moments in the Benson biographies when the parents sound like Woolf's Mr and Mrs Ramsay in *To The Lighthouse*: the high-tempered father, irritated by trifles, the loving mother adored by all her children. 'Never was anyone so like a flame as she,' claimed Fred: 'her light illuminated you, her ardour warmed and stimulated.'[18] The family itself was in many ways the source of its own traumas, but where no one married and friendships could not always be relied upon, the family was also the only long-term refuge. Their writing suggests they both needed it and needed to escape. They told the story of themselves in order to commemorate those who had died young, but also in order to understand their own role as survivors: hence the conflicting pulls of their autobiographical impulses. The two-volume *Life* of their father had to be a monumental tribute to a former Archbishop of Canterbury, yet he was seen by the children as the root cause of the family's collective unease with itself, while the *Life* of Maggie had to deal with the modest public achievements of an Archbishop's daughter who had ultimately gone mad. As a family emerging from the demands of Victorian reticence into a modern world of mental collapse and sexual experimentation, it was as if they needed someone to blame, and their father seemed the obvious choice: successful in his professional life, which necessarily invaded the lives of his wife and children, but innocently unaware of the emotional damage he had caused at home. John Tosh suggests, 'The modernist script required not only rebellion, but an oppressor who justified that rebellion'.[19] As generational conflict became more acceptable in literary culture towards the end of the nineteenth century, the Bensons bided their time: although their Victorian auto/biographies were mostly published during or after the First World War, they found ways of recounting their history by adapting the traditions of life writing to suit their needs.

One way – the simplest – was to return repeatedly to their childhood, and make anecdotal work of it. Another was to hide what they wrote under somewhat thin disguises. As historian and novelist, the Benson brothers were used to assessing the relationship between character and events, so in their experimental self writing they both fictionalised and historicised themselves and their family. Although A.C. Benson was largely a serious historian, unlike his brother Fred, who was mainly a society novelist, he continually plays games with veracity and trust in his life writing. In *The House of Quiet* (1904) he also plays down his own masculinity. Continually postponing the real beginning of his fictitious autobiography by writing a Preface, an Introduction, a Prefatory Note to the Original Edition, and finally an 'Introductory' (dated Christmas Eve 1898), he claims the work was 'from the first, meant as a message to the weak rather than as a challenge to the strong'. Moreover he rejects a 'theory of life ... that the whole duty of man is to dash into the throng, to eat and drink, to love and wed, to laugh and fight'. Instead, he imagines 'a temperament of a peaceful and gentle order, a temperament without robustness and *joie de vivre*, but with a sense of duty, a desire to help, an anxious wish not to shirk responsibility'. This person he then imagines to be somehow pushed into a 'backwater of life, made, by some failure of vitality, into an invalid'.[20]

Benson is playing with issues of identity here. Is this a book about himself or about someone else? Is this person real or imaginary? The book first came out anonymously, but its true authorship was soon revealed. In addressing the problem further in his 'Introduction', he 'comes out of the closet' in adding his name to the text, but only so far, in that he fudges the issue of historical truth: 'the subjective part of the book may well wear an air of veracity, for it is mostly true, while on the other hand, the intimate nature of it gives every excuse for my attempting to take refuge in anonymity' (p.xiii). The Prefatory Note to the Original Edition confuses the situation further by announcing that 'The writer of the following pages was a distant cousin of my own, and to a certain extent a friend' (p.xviii). Benson says it fell to him to administer his estate after the cousin's death in 1900, in the course of which he found the papers for this book. Fred's later comment that the key to Arthur's 'strangely self-contradictory character' was that he had 'a double personality, sharply divided', seems to align him with the Jekyll and Hyde ethos of the 1880s invoked by Robert Louis Stevenson. [21]

The House of Quiet indeed seems a product of the decadent culture of the *fin-de-siècle*: the story of an effete and exhausted man, whose only relationships, like Dr Jekyll's, are with eccentric bachelors. He describes himself at one point as 'a lonely, shabby man, bruised by contact with the world, dilatory, dumb, timid' (pp.186–7). In the early chapters, he says he was the only child of a father who died when he was six, leaving his mother 'the presiding deity of the scene'. Starting a new chapter, he writes with passion and enthusiasm of her many qualities:

> How shall I describe her? Seen through her son's eyes she has an extraordinary tranquillity and graciousness of mien ... She is intensely affectionate, and has the largest heart I have ever known, but at the same time is capable of taking almost whimsical prejudices against people ... Her sympathy and her geniality make her delightful company. (p.15)

The mother largely disappears from the rest of the text until right at the very end, when he is about to propose to a Miss Waring and instead suffers a collapse: 'there was a face at the door – and then a blackness closed round me and I knew no more' (p.223). The page heading calls it 'The Stroke of God'. Whatever it is, it restores him to a childlike state of dependence on his mother: 'Almost the only feeling left me is the old childlike trustfulness in mother and nurse' (p.227), 'this sense of unity with my mother – that inseparable, elemental tie that nothing can break.' This restoration to his mother he sees as giving pleasure to both of them: 'it gives her, though she could not describe it, a strange elation in the midst of her sorrow, the joy that a man is born into the world, and that

I am hers' (ibid.). For both son and mother, this is a moment of rebirth, as if Arthur (or his persona) is allowed a private rerun of his own nativity and his mother's pleasure in bringing a man into the world. The Bensons were also emotionally dependent on their old nurse, Beth, who as 'Susan' makes a welcome appearance in this return to childhood. Like the nanny in *Brideshead Revisited*, she still sees him as a child: 'I have become "Master Henry" again, and am told to "look slippy" about taking my medicine' (p.228). Though this is not quite the end of the text, it is certainly its emotional climax. The goal of Henry's life is a return to childhood, and perfect unity with his two mothers.

In a collection of essays titled *From a College Window* (1906), A.C. Benson comments on the difficulties of the father/son relationship, which he sees as seldom successful, especially in the area of camaraderie. 'A boy goes for sympathy and companionship to his mother and sisters, not often to his father.'[22] This is surprising in view of the companionship a boy would have enjoyed at school, and the emphasis at the time on a thriving cult of masculinity among young men growing up together, to the extent that, as John Tosh observes, 'The late Victorian upper middle class was significantly over-populated with men who were permanently disqualified from family life.'[23] Perhaps the problem with the Bensons' father was his excessive virility. 'His temper was high, he brooked no opposition, and he had little overt sympathy for the weak and erratic,' Arthur recalled in *The Trefoil*, remembering the dramatic sweep of his father into a room. His public appearances were nothing short of 'magnificent' (p.50). His brother Fred describes him in similar terms when he became Archbishop of Canterbury, but adds that his children had no real understanding of his professional life: 'Stupendous as my father had become, we knew but little of his work and of its national significance, and it was my mother who to us, far more than he, was exalted into the zenith' (*Our Family Affairs*, p.167). Moreover his father was a self-made man, who at the age of twenty-one had taken on responsibility for his orphaned brothers and sisters. Arthur recalls the shared pride felt by the Benson children in their father, but they were also 'profoundly convinced that he could do everything better than anyone else' (*The Trefoil*, p.51). Their very admiration for him was in itself a source of disquiet, disturbed as it was by their guilty sense of preferring their mother.

The Bensons repeatedly presented themselves as being taken over by the personalities of other members of the family, or as seeking intense one-to-one relationships with each other, instead of struggling with the wider group. When they write about their mother and sisters, the brothers suggest that the demands of this exceptionally demanding family obliterated the personalities of the women. Yet these personalities, especially those of Maggie and their mother, resist the language of restraint and overwhelm the sons' and brothers' attempts to contain them. This was a view shared by Arthur's younger brother, Fred, whose tributes to his mother and sisters are to be found throughout his autobiographical writing. Like Arthur, Fred was anxious to separate them from the looming presence of the Archbishop, and make them into something he could possess of his own accord. His father's dominant personality (in his own and Arthur's writing) is often presented as a direct threat to the distinctive individuality of the rest of his family, especially his wife and daughters. Hugh, the youngest child, remembered: 'My father's influence upon me was always so great that I despair of describing it,'[24] but for Maggie it was even worse. While she was working on his manuscript discussing the Revelation of St John, Fred recalls, it was not just his argument that took hold of her, but her father's whole mind and personality: 'she became markedly more like him in acts and attitudes', including his depressive tendencies.[25] Returning to Maggie's situation in his more outspoken *Final Edition* (1940), Fred alleges that, in assuming her father's personality, she claimed responsibility for her mother's actions: her father's works 'gripped her mind, with the effect that his very personality, dominating and masterful, and his sense of responsibility for the spiritual strenuousness of those round him began to take possession of her'. Instead of merely writing about him, she *became* him. Fred describes it as a 'strange psychical obsession' that would have been farcical to their mother 'were it not for the tragic undertone that anyone should interpret my father to her'.[26] In Maggie's case the complete absorption in reconstructing her father's life and mind seems to have contributed to her total breakdown in middle age, when, in trying to be her mother's keeper, she became so unfitted for life in the family home that the family removed her from it. In turn, writing about Maggie, Arthur succumbed to a neurasthenic fear that he might be attacked by the same malady.[27] Their collective self-writing made their hereditary depression in a sense contagious. It spread unease and self-doubt, as they realised that each other's problems had originated in a shared upbringing, the same difficulties in dealing with the world both inside and outside the home.

In remaining more detached from his siblings, all of whom he outlived, Fred becomes increasingly critical of their relations with each other, seeing his brothers as unfitted for normal affectionate companionship. Hugh, for example, 'never set much store on human relationships', while Arthur's fear of women led him to shun emotional experience altogether.[28] In *Final Edition*, Fred recounts an awkward evening's family entertainment when the three brothers decided to parody each other's work, which only their mother found amusing (p.102). Indeed their mother is the only member of the family, apart from the prematurely dead Martin and Nellie, who emerges from the family biographies unscathed by criticism, and she was also the one member of the family who never published anything. Yet, or perhaps because of this, her response to life is what her sons eagerly explore in their biographical writing, where their reconstruction of her enacts a battle between self-obliteration and flamboyant presence. In recording what his mother wrote of their honeymoon visits to French churches, when she noted the architectural details that she thought would please her husband, Fred comments: 'She obliterates herself altogether, and is concerned only with throwing her whole energy into appreciation of all that my father, not she, enjoyed' (p.19). As the wife of a high-ranking churchman, she seemed to her son to have no freedom to lead her own life: 'she had absolutely no life of her own' (p.2), in support of which he quotes her diary comments on her husband's death:

> There is nothing within, no power, no love, no desire, no initiative: he had it all, and his life entirely dominated mine. Good Lord, give me a personality, a scorn of small petty indulgences. (p.40)

Only five years earlier, in *Our Family Affairs* (1920), however, Fred describes their mother as being 'the most individual' of the family, living, so far as she could, 'entirely for pleasure' (p.22): 'She was, as far as concerns my memory of her at Wellington, a glorious sunlit figure, living a life that appeared to be the apotheosis of hedonism' (p.24). Intensifying the unreality of his mother's appearance, he recalls that she once dressed up as 'the fairy Abracadabra': 'a huge bedizened fairy standing in front of the fire-place' (p.12), in order to give her son a surprise present of a clockwork train. Having taken elaborate steps to fool him into thinking she was resting in her room when the fairy came, his mother 'blew a piercing trumpet at intervals, and made dance steps to the right and left'. Fred's interpretation of their mother suggests that, far from being swamped by the pressure to behave in a certain way as a headmaster's wife, she deliberately enjoyed herself: 'What a life was hers! She ordered lunch and dinner precisely as she chose.'

This is of course a child's eye view of his mother, where the parents loom large and incomprehensible, as at the beginning of Joyce's *Portrait of the Artist as a Young Man* (1916). At this early stage of his life, it is his mother, rather than his father, who makes the impression on Fred, whose opening chapter begins by introducing and then dismissing him: 'My father was headmaster of Wellington College, where and when I was born, but of him there, in spite of his extraordinarily forcible personality, I have no clear memory' (*Our Family Affairs*, p.9). Like the young Stephen Dedalus, all he initially recalls of his father is the texture of his face: 'my father's face was rough, not smooth like the face of my mother and of Beth' (p.10). Reduced to a rough surface, and a smell of books and soap, the headmaster shrinks in comparison with his bedizened fairy wife: another version of the 'presiding deity' Arthur described in *The House of Quiet*.

Yet the headmaster/archbishop, too, played a part in adjusting the perspective on his family: specifically in the case of his elder daughter Eleanor, or 'Nellie', the most shadowy of the Benson children, who, like her sister Maggie, went to Truro High School for Girls, and Lady Margaret Hall, Oxford, where she began studying mathematics, but, according to her father, switched to Modern Languages for health reasons. Two works by Nellie were prefaced by her father and brother Arthur. In his 'Brief Memoir' attached to her *Streets and Lanes of the City* (1891), her father recalls that 'Nearly every narrative in it has been told me in rides and walks, mostly in fragments as the facts occurred'; moreover the book was 'written at the suggestion and request of her Mother'.[29] In thus introducing the book, her father stresses the role of both parents in ensuring its publication, thereby reducing any sense of Nellie's ambitions for herself as a writer. The content of the book, in fact, is essentially talk between father and daughter on their leisurely walks. Ingenuously, as he describes her role in the family, he admits: 'she seemed to give each of us just what each wanted' (p.xii), very like Julia Stephen in her husband's account of her ceaseless activity in the family.

While her father's miniature biography of Nellie makes her seem only a part of everyone else, with no assertive identity of her own, the main body of the text is actually a series of essays about the social conditions of the poor, gathered from her experience of working for the Women's University Settlement in Southwark, and her teaching of classes of boys and girls. Though this could be seen as another way of expending herself on behalf of others, Nellie's writing is testimony to her energy in carving out a role in a family which otherwise revolved around the needs of its head.

As portrayed by her brother Arthur in his unsigned 'Memoir' of her included in her novel *At Sundry Times and in Divers Manners* (1891), Nellie in fact had 'a very strong individuality', which was what motivated him to publish her work (p.vi). Like her father, though, he recognises that she was all too easily dismissed as selfless: people were 'disposed to classify her as an active district visitor, and not to think that she had any particular life apart from that'. Nellie's particular skill within the family was to make everyone feel as if they had been singled out for a special relationship with her, whereas she was actually doing the same for everyone. According to Arthur, she was ambitious, especially about her writing, energetic and discontented with the kind of life she was leading. Because of her closeness to the eldest brother, Martin, to whom she wrote breathlessly adoring letters while he was away at school, Nellie had suffered from what Arthur called 'that overshadowing of the spirit which is so much harder to bear than physical pain' (p.xvi). His presentation of her takes more risks than their father's, so that she appears less saintly, more interested in herself and her own needs.

The hardest biographical challenge of all was presented by the other sister, Maggie, whose mental instability permanently clouded the brothers' image of her. Concerned, like his brother Arthur, with the core of self, or identity at the heart of each biographical episode, Fred recalls that 'It was still she, but you could not reach her' (*Our Family Affairs*, p.228). Unsurprisingly Maggie is written about most as a child, who had at various times a special bond with her brothers Fred and Arthur. Arthur, who wrote her *Life and Letters* (1917) immediately after her death, was aware, as he was with Nellie, of the impact of gender on her course in life. 'If she had been a man,' he writes of Maggie, 'she would, I do not doubt, have been a great student, and might have done valuable, philosophical work.'[30] As it was, she rarely talked about her work, but confessed to suffering from 'tyrannous fancies': 'such as seeing in the faces of people, whom she passed in the streets, underlying darknesses and vilenesses, old animal inheritances and evil taints of blood' (p.392). She too sounds like a product of the decadent culture of the 1890s, not unlike the young Virginia Stephen, another daughter overwhelmed by her father's personality, whose hallucinations took a similar bestial turn. In 'A Sketch of the Past', Woolf remembers lying awake in her room horrified one night by hearing, as she imagined, 'an obscene old man gasping and croaking and muttering senile indecencies'.[31]

In his reconstruction of the family story, Fred represents himself as the only one who was sane and well. His method of dealing with the family problems was to escape from them: corresponding exactly with John Tosh's description, cited earlier, of late Victorian men who were 'permanently disqualified from family life'. In *Mother*, he alternates chapters on the family's spiralling breakdowns with descriptions of the holidays he took in Italy, in a sense imitating his mother, who wanted her relationships with her children to be untroubled: 'she wanted to be without woes in her dealings with us' (p.267). When not escaping abroad, Fred wrote schoolboy stories, focusing on the romance of male adolescence: for him, it was easier to express himself emotionally as an androgynous boy than as a troubled adult son. Arthur meanwhile theorised that, however wholeheartedly one lives in events, causes and people, 'the victory consists in feeling it all deeply, and even morbid feeling is better than apathy or consent' (*The Leaves of the Tree: Studies in Biography*).[32] Together, these two outlooks seem to offer a clue to the Bensons' approach in tackling the challenges of life writing at a time when 'domestic accountability' and the reframing of gender identities were the key issues in auto/biography. They imply that the act of living was somehow less crucial than the subsequent analysis of it, and they preferred to feel sentimentally or morbidly rather than not at all.

With a father and husband who invaded his family's personalities, two daughters who might have suffered less as men, a wife who preferred women, and sons who longed to remain as schoolboys, the Bensons demonstrate a complete subversion of the ideal archbishop's family at a point in the literary history of life writing when the failure of the monumental Victorian husband and father was being exposed, and the children's neuroses becoming the new focus of modernist scientific and literary inquiry. Taken together, the Benson auto/biographies chronicle a collective obsession with life writing and introversion that hardened over the years into mutual criticism and distancing. Brother turned against brother, son against father; the sisters were seen as swamped by their father's powerful personality and the sons themselves felt fragmented, torn as they were between the all-absorbing demands of their family and their attempts to develop a life outside it. While Fred depicts himself as fleeing his mother's home, whose undiluted femininity stifled him, Arthur struggled to connect his literary refinement with his vehement personality and fear of total breakdown. For all his devotedness, Edward White Benson fails as a father in his children's many accounts of his life. In *The Trefoil*, Arthur even deals a final blow by suggesting his father should have declined the Primacy, which it was 'the great mistake' of his life to have accepted (p.281). Considering this was the peak of his career, Arthur's dismissal of it seems uncharitable, even perverse: 'He yielded perhaps to what had always been a temptation of his, the love of ruling.' In posthumously telling his father it was wrong to rule, Arthur sets the seal on his final act of subversion against the dead archbishop.

In writing and rewriting the same family stories, the Benson brothers were producing unresolved case histories that seemed stranger as time passed: relics of a bygone Victorianism whose legacy continued to dominate its Edwardian and Georgian afterlife. As sole survivor, Fred was left with piles of family papers to sift through and analyse, accompanied by a belated sense that it was a mistake to take oneself too seriously: 'No doubt it is an excellent thing to know oneself, but self-consciousness is a heavy price to pay for that knowledge. Indeed, perhaps the main reward for knowing oneself is the power to forget about oneself.'[33] Arthur, by contrast, had written that a 'sense of identity' was the only thing of which he was certain in the world: 'What matters,' he wrote in his introduction to *The Leaves of the Tree: Studies in*

Biography (1911) 'is that I should still be able to feel, under whatever change of scene and circumstance, that I am still myself.'[34] Throughout Fred and Arthur's writing, the words 'identity', 'personality' and 'individuality' are bandied about and interrogated, as they tried to solve the underlying problem of their lives: the fact that they were known as a group of their father's children, or as siblings damaged by a tragic inheritance, rather than for what they had achieved individually. While Arthur clung to a sense of identity in the face of threatened disintegration, Fred tried to transcend his altogether, seeking in social bachelorhood a nonchalant distance from himself and his all-pervasive family.

But the last word, perhaps, should go to the child-wife: the mother who achieved this self-forgetfulness, overcame her guilt, regained her lost faith, combined it with a secular hedonism and enjoyed a widowhood free of male sexual demands. Ultimately Mary Benson withstands the gendered limits of the theory of identity explored by her sons. Perhaps the fact that she stood alone, an emotionally robust widow, without any threats to her sense of selfhood, made her stronger than her troubled children. Fred admits in his biography of her that her sons' books gave her no joy, 'because she did not agree with the standpoint from which they were written'. She laughed irreverently at their parodies of each other's writing, but was not otherwise a great reader, preferring 'human beings themselves, not imagined ones but real ones.'[35] Unlike her children, she concentrated on living rather than writing. In her passion for friendship, freely admitted by her son, she was in effect transcending the limits of the traditional family; and in her passion for people, she was dismissing the books in which the Benson auto/biographers had done their best to console themselves for the loss and lingering trauma of their troubled existence as a family.

Notes

1. Georgina Battiscombe, *Reluctant Pioneer: A Life of Elizabeth Wordsworth* (London: Constable, 1978), p.30.
2. Betty Askwith, *Two Victorian Families* (London: Chatto and Windus, 1971); David Newsome, *On the Edge of Paradise: AC Benson, Diarist* (London: John Murray, 1980); David Williams, *Genesis and Exodus: A Portrait of the Benson Family* (London: Hamish Hamilton, 1979); John Tosh, 'Domesticity and Manliness in the Victorian Middle Class', in Michael Roper and John Tosh (eds), *Manful Assertions: Masculinities in Britain since 1800* (London and New York: Routledge, 1991).
3. John Tosh, *A Man's Place: Masculinity and the Middle-Class Home in Victorian England* (New Haven and London: Yale University Press, 1999), p.79.

4. Claudia Nelson, *Invisible Men: Fatherhood in Victorian Periodicals 1850–1910* (Athens and London: University of Georgia Press, 1995), p.204.

5. Arthur Christopher Benson, *Hugh: Memoirs of a Brother* (London: Smith, Elder & Co, 1915), p.32.

6. *The Life of Edward White Benson, by his son Arthur Christopher Benson*, 2 vols (London: Macmillan, 1899), I, p.466.

7. Tosh, *A Man's Place*, 1999, p.70.

8. A.C. Benson, *The Trefoil: Wellington College, Lincoln and Truro* (London: John Murray, 1923), p.v.

9. *The Diary of Virginia Woolf*, ed. Anne Olivier Bell and Andrew McNeillie, 5 vols (London; Hogarth Press, 1977–84), V, p.334.

10. Mary Eleanor Benson, *At Sundry Times and in Divers Manners*, 2 vols (London: Kegan Paul, Trench, Trübner & Co, 1891), p.viii.

11. Askwith, *Two Victorian Families*, 1971, p.202.

12. A.C. Benson, *Hugh*, p.169.

13. *Embodied Selves: An Anthology of Psychological Texts 1830–1890*, ed. Jenny Bourne Taylor and Sally Shuttleworth (Oxford: Clarendon Press, 1998), p.67; p.289.

14. Trev Lynn Broughton, *Men of Letters, Writing Lives: Masculinity and Literary Auto/Biography in the Late Victorian Period* (London: Routledge, 1999) pp.78–9.

15. Martin Danahay, *A Community of One: Masculine Autobiography and Autonomy in Nineteenth-Century Britain* (New York: State University of New York Press, 1993), p.7; p.9.

16. A.C. Benson, *The Trefoil*, p.170.

17. E.F. Benson, *Final Edition: Informal Autobiography*, 1940 (reprinted London: Hogarth Press, 1988), p.250.

18. E.F. Benson, *Our Family Affairs 1867–1896* (London: Cassell and Company, 1920), p.171.

19. Tosh, *A Man's Place*, p.162.

20. A.C. Benson, *The House of Quiet*, 1904 (reprinted London: John Murray, 1912), p.viii.

21. E.F. Benson, *Final Edition*, p.21.

22. A.C. Benson, *From a College Window*, 1906 (reprinted London: John Murray, 1919), p.11.

23. Tosh, *A Man's Place*, p.177.

24. Robert Hugh Benson, *Confessions of a Convert* (London: Longmans, Green & Co, 1913), p.6.

25. E.F. Benson, *Mother* (London: Hodder and Stoughton, 1925), p.71.

26. E.F. Benson, *Final Edition*, pp.11, 12, 19.

27. Ibid., p.129.

28. Ibid., pp.33, 194.

29. *Streets and Lanes of the City by Mary Eleanor Benson. With a Brief Memoir by her Father* (London and Bungay: Richard Clay & Sons, 1891), p.xviii.

30. *Life and Letters of Maggie Benson by her Brother Arthur Christopher Benson* (London: John Murray, 1917), p.418.

31. Virginia Woolf, 'A Sketch of the Past', in Jeanne Schulkind (ed.), *Moments of Being*, 2nd edn (London and New York: Harcourt Brace & Company, 1985), p.123. Woolf adds that the noise was actually caused by 'a cat's anguished love making'.

32. Arthur Christopher Benson, *The Leaves of the Tree: Studies in Biography* (London: Smith, Elder & Co, 1911), p.19.
33. E.F. Benson, *Final Edition*, p.186.
34. A.C. Benson, *The Leaves of the Tree*, p.9.
35. E.F. Benson, *Mother*, p.219.

Index